Worrier to Warrior

CHAIRMAN
Rabbi Moshe Kotlarsky

PRINCIPAL BENEFACTOR
Mr. George Rohr

EXECUTIVE DIRECTOR
Rabbi Efraim Mintz

AUTHOR
Rabbi Naftali Silberberg

CURRICULUM DEVELOPMENT
Rabbi Yisroel Altein
Rabbi Yakov Gershon
Rabbi Shmuel Gomes
Rabbi Lazer Gurkow
Rabbi Yaakov Paley
Casey Skvorc, PhD

EDITORIAL BOARD
Rabbi Yochonon Goldman
Rabbi Moshe Gourarie
Rabbi Mendy Mangel
Rabbi Avi Richler
Rabbi Aryeh Weinstein

COORDINATOR
Mrs. Rivki Mockin

ADMINISTRATOR
Mrs. Chana Dechter

Cover Art: *In the Magic Mirror* (detail), Paul Klee,
oil on canvas, 1934. (Art Institute of Chicago)

(888) YOUR-JLI/718-221-6900
WWW.MYJLI.COM

Worrier to Warrior:

**Jewish Secrets
to Feeling Good
However You Feel**

JLI

JEWISH LEARNING INSTITUTE

STUDENT TEXTBOOK

JLI acknowledges the generous support of the following individuals and foundations:

PARTNERING FOUNDATIONS

AVI CHAI FOUNDATION

COMMUNITY CEMETERY EDUCATION PROJECT BY JEWISH REACH

CRAIN-MALING FOUNDATION

ESTATE OF ELLIOT JAMES BELKIN

GOLDSTEIN FAMILY FOUNDATION

KOHELET FOUNDATION

KOSINS FAMILY FOUNDATION

LEE AND PATTI SCHEAR FAMILY FOUNDATION

MAYBERG FOUNDATION

MEROMIM FOUNDATION

MYRA REINHARD FAMILY FOUNDATION

OLAMI—WOLFSON FOUNDATION

RUDERMAN FAMILY FOUNDATION

WILLIAM DAVIDSON FOUNDATION

WORLD ZIONIST ORGANIZATION

YEHUDA AND ANNE NEUBERGER PHILANTHROPIC FUND

PRINCIPAL BENEFACTOR

GEORGE ROHR
New York, NY

ADVISORY BOARD OF GOVERNORS

YAAKOV AND KAREN COHEN
Potomac, MD

YITZCHOK AND JULIE GNIWISCH
Montreal, QC

BARBARA HINES
Aspen, CO

DANIEL B. MARKSON
S. Antonio, TX

DANIEL AND ROSIE MATTIO
Seattle, WA

DAVID MINTZ
Tenafly, NJ

DR. STEPHEN F. SERBIN
Columbia, SC

LEONARD A. WIEN, JR.
Miami Beach, FL

PILLARS OF JEWISH LITERACY

KEVIN BERMEISTER
Sydney, Australia

PABLO AND SARA BRIMAN
Mexico City, Mexico

ZALMAN AND MIMI FELLIG
Miami Beach, FL

YOSEF GOROWITZ
Redondo Beach, CA

DR. VERA KOCH GROSZMANN
S. Paulo, Brazil

HERSCHEL LAZAROFF
Monsey, NY

JENNY LJUNGBERG
New York, NY

DAVID MAGERMAN
Gladwyne, PA

DR. MICHAEL MALING
Deerfield, IL

YITZCHAK MIRILASHVILI
Herzliya, Israel

BEN NASH
New Jersey

YAIR SHAMIR
Savyon, Israel

LARRY SIFEN
Virginia Beach, VA

SPONSORS

MARK AND REBECCA BOLINSKY
Long Beach, NY

DANIEL AND ETA COTLAR
Houston, TX

GORDON DIAMOND
Vancouver, BC

AMIR AND DAFNA ELYASHAR
Ramat Aviv, Israel

SHMUEL AND SHARONE GOODMAN
Chicago, IL

JOE AND SHIRA LIPSEY
Aspen, CO

ELLEN MARKS
S. Diego, CA

RACHELLE NEDOW
El Paso, TX

PETER AND HAZEL PFLAUM
Newport Beach, CA

FRANK (A"H) AND FRUMETH POLASKY
Saginaw, MI

MOSHE AND YAFFA POPACK
Fisher Island, FL

HERCHEL AND JULIE PORTMAN
Denver, CO

EYAL AND AVIVA POSTELNIK
Marietta, GA

DR. ZE'EV RAV-NOY
Los Angeles, CA

CLIVE AND ZOE ROCK
Irvine, CA

ZVI RYZMAN
Los Angeles, CA

ALAN ZEKELMAN
Bloomfield Hills, MI

MYRNA ZISMAN
Cedarhurst, NY

The Rohr Jewish Learning Institute
gratefully acknowledges the pioneering
and ongoing support of

George and Pamela Rohr

Since its inception, the Rohr JLI has been
a beneficiary of the vision, generosity, care,
and concern of the Rohr family.

In the merit of the tens of thousands of hours
of Torah study by JLI students worldwide,
may they be blessed with health, *Yiddishe
nachas* from all their loved ones, and
extraordinary success in all their endeavors.

LOCAL COURSE SPONSORSHIPS

Mr. and Mrs. Paul
& Donna Sanderson
ALAMO, CA

Mr. and Mrs. David
Beesemer
AMSTERDAM, NL

Mr. and Mrs. Simon
& Audrey Wachsberg
BELLAIRE, TX

In memory of Mr. Gary
Arthur Singer
BLOOMFIELD HILLS, MI

Mr. and Mrs. Jim
& Renee Hon
BOISE, ID

Dr. Yura Stoly
BROOKLYN, NY

In memory of Rabbi
Daniel Moscowitz
CHICAGO, IL

Mr. and Mrs. Stuart
& Shelly Hanfling
ELGIN, IL

Mr. Louis Berkowitz
FAIRFIELD, CT

Dr. and Mrs. Gary
& Marlene Price
FORT MYERS, FL

Eugene and Marjorie Lipsky
LEAWOOD, KS

In memory of Rivka Sara bat
Efraim Fishel Gejerman
LOS ANGELES, CA

In memory of Mr. Isidor
Blumenthal
MADISON, NJ

Mr. and Mrs. Y. K. Cohen
MILWAUKEE, WI

In memory of Baila bat Chaim
NEWTON, MA

Mr. and Mrs. Reuven
& Inna Malts
NEWTOWN, PA

In honor of Mrs. Maxine Finkel
NORTHEAST PORTLAND, OR

In memory of Shelly Goldin
OLNEY, MD

In memory of Meyer Goldberg
ORINDA, CA

Mr. Peter Forman
PORT WASHINGTON, NY

Mr. and Mrs. Alan Zekelman
RANCHO S. FE, CA

In memory of David Sacks
SKOKIE, IL

In memory of those
who came before us
SOUTH LAKE TAHOE, CA

The Hellman Memorial Chapels
SPRING VALLEY, NY

Mr. Mark Eichner
VENICE, FL

In memory of Dr. Arthur Conn
VIENNA, VA

In memory of Rabbi Levi Deitsch
VIENNA, VA

Kosins Family Foundation
WEST BLOOMFIELD, MI

Jackson, Chasen & Ilan
WESTMINSTER, CO

In memory of
Mrs. Marlene Davis
WILMETTE, IL

Endorsements

"It is well-known that positive emotions rest at the heart of overall well-being and happiness. But how to effectively enhance positive emotion remains challenging. *Worrier to Warrior* approaches this challenge from an insightful perspective grounded in contemporary psychology and Jewish literature. It addresses a number of core underlying factors that keep us from achieving a more positive outlook, such as guilt, shame, and the feeling of being inauthentic. It then teaches us how to foster positive emotions through true authenticity, building resilience, harnessing guilt, finding meaning in adversity, loving others, and focusing on altruistic efforts and accomplishments. To me, this is an exciting and very impressive course that is unlike any that I have seen."

STEVEN M. SOUTHWICK, M.D.
Department of Psychiatry,
Yale University School of Medicine;
Author, *Resilience: The Science of Mastering
Life's Greatest Challenges*

"*Worrier to Warrior* is a great curriculum with much needed age-old wisdom backed up by modern social science that could not come at a more important time."

PROFESSOR CATHERINE PANZARELLA
Clinical Professor of Psychology and Director of the
Psychology Training Clinic,
University of Texas at Austin

"The JLI course *Worrier to Warrior* provides a nuts-and-bolts roadmap for an enriched personal quality of life. The fusion of Torah wisdom and scholarship with practical psychological insights provides solutions to the challenges of the stressors of modern everyday life. I highly recommend this course and its supporting materials."

CASEY SKVORC, PHD, JD
National Institutes of Health; Doctoral Faculty,
Strategic Intelligence Studies, American Military University

"In a time when many psychological approaches to worry and emotion regulation, however meritorious, struggle to reach a wide audience, JLI's efforts to disseminate this work is vital and timely. Integrating both contemplative and empirical wisdom on how we can approach greater authenticity, this course provides an accessible and validating platform for having these especially meaningful conversations."

PROFESSOR ZINDEL SEGAL
Director of Clinical Training,
Graduate Department of Clinical Psychological Science,
University of Toronto Scarborough;
Author, *The Mindful Way through Depression*

"*Worrier to Warrior* is a life-affirming exploration of the human condition that promotes speaking to life with a higher voice and with our finer attributes.

The content is precise and definitive, yet thorough and universal. I personally know a JLI education to be an enduring experience which echoes in one's conscience longitudinally and directs what I consider to be our greatest assets—time and health—to productive end."

PATRICIA SCHNEIDER, PHD
New York State Licensed Psychologist

"At this time of uncertainty and distress, anxiety is the number one health issue globally. I applaud JLI for offering this timely course. *Worrier to Warrior* incorporates accumulated wisdom of the ages and cutting-edge research from the behavioral sciences. Participants will benefit from learning how to gain freedom from fear and lead a more compassionate and meaningful life."

GRETA HIRSCH, PHD
Clinical Director, Ross Center for Anxiety

"Recently, the field of psychology has begun to make efforts to culturally adapt treatment interventions to be more relevant to diverse communities. In *Worrier to Warrior*, the effort to merge Jewish teachings with psychology constructs is an effort to harness these two traditions for health and well-being."

PROFESSOR SUZANN LAWRY
Department of Psychology, Georgia State University

Foreword

RABBI ADIN EVEN-ISRAEL (STEINSALTZ)

The *Tanya* is not only one of the fundamental works of Hasidism, but it is also one of the greatest books of moral teaching *(mussar)* of all time. Although the author modestly describes himself as a "compiler," this is a most original work, both in its basic premise and in the many ideas and insights it expresses parenthetically.

Most moral works address themselves to personal problems and to the ways that a person can attain specific goals in specific areas. The advantage in such an individualized approach is that it deals with the specific questions that a person might ask himself; the answers supplied are likewise specific and definitive. On the other hand, such a book is limited to the specific problems it raises and is thus of actual help only to specific individuals. Others might be impressed that the book is indeed a great and profound work, yet they will always feel that, as a book of moral teaching, it does not speak to them. It fails to answer their problems or to take into account their specific personalities and circumstances.

The *Tanya,* by contrast, does not, in the main, address specific problems but delves into their root causes, seeking to distill the predicaments of humankind down to their most elementary maxims and to solve them in the most comprehensive way. The crux of the book is an in-depth summation of the workings of the inner soul and an analysis of good and evil in general and as fundamental forces at play in the soul and the primary sources of its dissonance. The *Tanya* trains its students to see the many thousands of complexities, doubts, and drives within them as expressions of a single basic problem: the struggle between the good and evil in the human soul.

Although the book is written with great restraint, it energetically and dramatically depicts human life as an immense battle between good and evil that one endures throughout one's lifetime, a battle between the forces that drag the soul down and the forces that strive heavenward. Each chapter develops from the previous one, and all are interconnected, progressively leading their student to recognize the inner soul, its intrinsic duality, the array of conflicting forces within it and their respective strengths and weaknesses, and the battle's nature and vicissitudes.

In describing this battle, the author offers a completely new approach. The battle in a person's soul is actually not between good and evil (expressions he rarely uses, except when he needs to clarify a point by using the ordinary semantics of these terms) but between the two elements within the human soul: the G-dly soul and the animal soul. The G-dly soul is that part of the soul that aspires to the divine, in all its connotations. The animal soul is the part that relates to one's physical identity and one's involvement in the material world. These are not merely alternative terms for *good* and *evil* or for *body* and *soul*; they draw a far subtler distinction. The animal soul is not negative in essence, nor is it necessarily hedonistic. The animal soul can become refined and wise and achieve much in the life of the spirit yet remain animal. The animal soul is the soul of a human being as a biological creature, at a specific level of development in the zoological system. Even in this sense, humans are superior to other creatures in our ability to attain great heights in the realms of thought and feeling; still, we remain an animal among animals.

It is in the G-dly soul, in its aspiration to the divine, where man's uniqueness lies. The G-dly soul yearns to cleave to and be absorbed by the divine, and only by this aspiration, by the constant struggle of the G-dly soul to transcend its needs and its very self in order to attain identification with the divine light, does one achieve a true identity as a human being.

It is from this definition of the inner struggle of the soul that the appropriate solution emerges. This is not a war to the death, in which a person tries to destroy and obliterate a part of the self. As the animal soul is not fundamentally evil, the battle against it is essentially a battle of education. A person's task is to train the animal soul, to elevate it to a higher level of awareness and understanding, until it is unified, both in its objectives and in its aspirations, with the G-dly soul. Thus, one achieves full harmony of body and soul, of earthliness and transcendence.

The perpetual battle in the human soul, which stems from its dual nature, also has moral and pragmatic implications. The teachers of *mussar* have always recognized the almost vital need for a person to achieve total inner identification with his deeds and actions. The assumption is that a purely mechanical act has a low moral and spiritual value. However, few individuals are capable of truly attaining such an inner identification. This leaves to most the choice of either giving up the spiritual struggle or descending into hypocrisy and self-delusion. The *Tanya,* by delving into the nature of the relationship between a person's two souls, finds an approach that is very different, even revolutionary. It

readily acknowledges that not everyone is able to achieve complete victory for the G-dly soul over the animal soul but also that not everyone is required to do so. A state of war within the human soul, says the *Tanya,* is not a negative thing. A person might achieve perfection with respect not only to deeds but also to speech and even to inner thoughts—without achieving complete perfection within the soul. The *Tanya* requires a person to achieve perfection in the "garments" of the soul (thought, speech, and action) but not in the soul's essence.

Thus, the *Tanya* removes the veil of hypocrisy that has cloaked many a soul as a result of the demand to elevate us beyond our capacity. The recognition of the intrinsic duality of the soul enables a person to understand that his moral imperfection need in no way impede his aspiration and ability to fulfill his divinely ordained role. Once we know that our undesirable lusts and thoughts emanate from a fundamental source within ourselves that might not be within our power and duty to uproot, their presence within us is not tragic, nor will it necessarily bring about an unsolvable inner crisis. On the contrary, a person can achieve perfection precisely through this knowledge. One can be righteous in all particulars of one's life and at the same time be engaged in the constant struggle within one's soul. The *Tanya* assigns to this spiritual persona a new moral status— that of the *beinoni,* the "intermediate." The intermediate is the hero of this book: the book addresses, discusses, and carries the name of the *beinoni* (one of the titles the author gave the *Tanya* is the Book of *Beinonim).* The intermediate is the "one who serves G-d," whose entire life is a perpetual battle for the sake of the divine, whose inner struggle is a hymn of praise to his or her Creator. The concept of the *beinoni* as an ideal to which every person should aspire opens the door to everyone, regardless of spiritual status, to be counted among those who aspire for true greatness—those who serve G-d in truth.

But these points, despite their centrality to the work, do not summarize the *Tanya*. This is a book in which the incidental ideas, as well as the supporting chapters surrounding the central theme, are no less important than the main topics. The more one reads this book, the more one discovers an illuminating and comprehensive outlook on life, insight into the structure of Jewish history, and moral guidance on countless problems. This short book encapsulates an entire philosophy and guide to life. As Rabbi Zusha from Anipoli expressed it, "How did he put such a great and awesome G-d into such a small book?"

If it is at all possible to define a work such as the *Tanya*, its best description lies in the words of the previous Lubavitcher Rebbe, who said, "*Tanya* is the 'Written Torah' of Hasidism, and studying it is like studying *Chumash* [the Bible]: everyone studies it, from the greatest scholars to the most simple of folk; each, according to their level, understands what they understand, and no one understands it at all."

It is therefore gratifying to encounter the work of the Rohr Jewish Learning Institute (JLI) in creating classes and courses for a broad range of audiences, based on the fundamental concepts of the *Tanya*. Through their efforts, many thousands of Jews are provided access to the *Tanya*'s transformative ideas and are guided in applying its core wisdoms to their individual lives. I hope that with JLI's clarity and user-friendly approach, the *Tanya*'s solutions can be successfully extracted and applied to all areas, thereby improving lives, outlooks, personalities, and relationships.

There is no challenge for which the *Tanya* does not offer a resolution in the form of an internal perspective. Those who invest significant resources in researching and delivering such perspectives perform a sacred service for all of our people.

RABBI ADIN EVEN-ISRAEL (STEINSALTZ)
Jerusalem, Israel

Accreditation

FOR MENTAL HEALTH AND MEDICAL PRACTITIONERS

ACCREDITATION STATEMENT

This activity has been planned and implemented in accordance with the accreditation requirements and policies of the **Accreditation Council for Continuing Medical Education (ACCME)** through the joint providership of Albert Einstein College of Medicine and the Rohr Jewish Learning Institute. Albert Einstein College of Medicine is accredited by the ACCME to provide continuing medical education for physicians.

CREDITS DESIGNATION

Albert Einstein College of Medicine designates this live activity for a maximum of **15.0 AMA PRA Category I Credits™**. Physicians should claim only the credit commensurate with the extent of their participation in the activity.

Albert Einstein College of Medicine is approved by the **American Psychological Association** to sponsor continuing education for psychologists. Albert Einstein College of Medicine maintains responsibility for this program and its content. This activity offers a maximum of **15 CE credits**.

Note: Participants may earn up to fifteen (15) CE credits from the APA: nine (9) credits for participation in the live course, and up to six (6) additional credits for self-study of the Additional Readings.

TO CLAIM CREDIT for attending the course (9 credits), professionals should submit their name, profession, email, and mailing address to their instructor or online at: **myJLI.com/continuingeducation**. To obtain credit for self-study of the Additional Readings (6 credits), professionals should complete the brief online quiz at the above Web address.

Contents

Lesson

1

ACHIEVING AUTHENTICITY

ADDRESSING IMPOSTOR SYNDROME

Child and Mask, Kaoru Kawano, color woodcut print on heavy paper, Japan, 1955.

Positive emotions are paramount for successful living, but genuine happiness and contentment are highly elusive. A common challenge is discomfort with our own accomplishments simply because we feel hypocritical. This lesson explores why positivity is critical, charts a path to tackling impediments to happier living, and unveils the means of embracing and effectively expressing our innate authenticity.

Exercise 1.1

Positive and Negative Affect Schedule*

Indicate the extent to which you have experienced each of the following feelings during the past week.

Score Key:

1 = Very slightly or not at all

2 = A little

3 = Moderately

4 = Quite a bit

5 = Extremely

	FEELING	SCORE		FEELING	SCORE
1	Interested		11	Irritable	
2	Distressed		12	Alert	
3	Excited		13	Ashamed	
4	Upset		14	Inspired	
5	Strong		15	Nervous	
6	Guilty		16	Determined	
7	Scared		17	Attentive	
8	Hostile		18	Jittery	
9	Enthusiastic		19	Active	
10	Proud		20	Afraid	

SCORING

Add the scores on items 1, 3, 5, 9, 10, 12, 14, 16, 17, and 19.

Positive Affect Score: _____

Add the scores on items 2, 4, 6, 7, 8, 11, 13, 15, 18, and 20.

Negative Affect Score: _____

---

* David Watson, et al., "Development and Validation of Brief Measures of Positive and Negative Affect: The PANAS Scales," *Journal of Personality and Social Psychology*, 54:6 (1988), p. 1063.

TEXT 1

THE REBBE, RABBI MENACHEM MENDEL SCHNEERSON, *IGROT KODESH* 20, P. 41

בְּעוֹלָמֵנוּ זֶה הַכֹּל מְעוֹרָב טוֹב וָרַע, וְעַל הָאָדָם לִבְחוֹר מַה לְהַדְגִּיש וּבַמֶּה לְהִתְבּוֹנֵן, וּבַמֶּה לְהִתְעַנְיֵן, כִּי בְּחַיֵּי כָּל אֶחָד וְאֶחָד שְׁנֵי דְרָכִים יֶשְׁנָם, לִרְאוֹת אֶת הַטּוֹב הַסּוֹבֵב אוֹתוֹ אוֹ וכו' . . .

וַהֲרֵי מְאַלְפֵנוּ סִיפּוּר חֲכָמֵינוּ זִכְרוֹנָם לִבְרָכָה, אֲשֶׁר אָדָם הָרִאשׁוֹן, עוֹד קוֹדֶם הַגֵּירוּשׁ בִּהְיוֹתוֹ בְּגַן עֵדֶן, הִתְאוֹנֵן עַל עִנְיָנָיו, וּקְרָאוֹהוּ כְּפוּי טוֹבָה, וּבְנֵי וּבְנוֹת יִשְׂרָאֵל, שֶׁנִּמְצְאוּ בְּמַחֲנוֹת הַהֶסְגֵּר שֶׁל הָאַשְׁכְּנַזִים יִמַּח שְׁמָם וּבִתְקוּפָה הֲכִי אֲיוּמָה רַחֲמָנָא לִיצְלָן, בֵּרְכוּ בִּרְכַּת הַשַּׁחַר וכו' הוֹדָאָה וּבְרָכָה לְבוֹרֵא עוֹלָם וּמַנְהִיגוֹ, וַהֲרֵי סוֹף סוֹף כָּל אֶחָד וְאֶחָד הוּא בֵּין הַקְּצָווֹת הָאֲמוּרִים.

מוּבָן וְגַם פָּשׁוּט, שֶׁאֵין בְּהַנִּזְכָּר לְעֵיל חַס וְשָׁלוֹם עִנְיָן שֶׁל הַצְדָּקַת הַדִּין עַל מִי שֶׁהוּא, וּבִפְרָט וכו', כִּי אִם הַדְגָּשַׁת הַמְּצִיאוּת כְּמוֹ שֶׁהִיא. וְהַנְּקוּדָה - אֲשֶׁר אוֹפֶן וְסוּג חַיֵּי הָאָדָם, אִם חַיִּים מְלֵאִים שְׂבִיעַת רָצוֹן וְתוֹכֶן, אוֹ בְּקוּ הַהֶפְכִי, תָּלוּי בְּמִדָּה חֲשׁוּבָה וּגְדוֹלָה - בִּרְצוֹן הָאָדָם, הַמּוֹשֵׁל בִּרְאִיַּת עֵין שִׂכְלוֹ לְהִסְתַּכֵּל לְצַד יָמִין אוֹ לְצַד שְׂמֹאל.

RABBI MENACHEM MENDEL SCHNEERSON 1902–1994

The towering Jewish leader of the 20th century, known as "the Lubavitcher Rebbe," or simply as "the Rebbe." Born in southern Ukraine, the Rebbe escaped Nazi-occupied Europe, arriving in the U.S. in June 1941. The Rebbe inspired and guided the revival of traditional Judaism after the European devastation, impacting virtually every Jewish community the world over. The Rebbe often emphasized that the performance of just one additional good deed could usher in the era of Mashiach. The Rebbe's scholarly talks and writings have been printed in more than 200 volumes.

In our world, everything is a mixture of good and bad. Human beings must choose which aspects they will emphasize, contemplate, and pursue. For in each person's life there are two possible approaches: to see the good that surrounds us or [the opposite]. . . .

It is instructive that our sages tell us that Adam was an ingrate. Even before he was banished from the Garden of Eden [where he lived in a literal paradise], he complained about his circumstances. Conversely, there were Jewish men and women who thanked and blessed the Creator and recited the morning blessings while living through the most horrifying times in the German concentration camps. Ultimately, each individual's circumstances will lie somewhere between these two extremes.

Needless to say, my intention is not to imply that anyone deserves suffering, G-d** forbid. My point is simply to underscore the reality: the type of lives that we live, whether full of satisfaction and meaning or the opposite, depends, in large measure, on our choice, which dictates whether we will focus on the positive or on the negative.

** Throughout this book, "G-d" and "L-rd" are written with a hyphen instead of an "o" (both in our own translations and when quoting others). This is one way we accord reverence to the sacred divine name. This also reminds us that, even as we seek G-d, He transcends any human effort to describe His reality.

Le Violoniste (The Fiddler), Marc Chagall, oil on canvas, Paris, 1914. (Kunstsammlung Nordrhein-Westfalen, Düsseldorf)

TEXT 2

W. GERROD PARROTT, "THE FUNCTIONAL UTILITY OF NEGATIVE EMOTIONS," IN LISA FELDMAN BARRETT AND PETER SALOVEY, EDS., *THE WISDOM IN FEELING: PSYCHOLOGICAL PROCESSES IN EMOTIONAL INTELLIGENCE* (NEW YORK: THE GUILFORD PRESS, 2002), PP. 343–344

Negative emotions—such as fear, sadness, shame, anger, contempt, guilt, disgust, anxiety, disappointment, embarrassment, loneliness, envy, and hatred—share the property of involving an appraisal that something is wrong. One's well-being is threatened, one's goals have to be abandoned, one lacks what one desires, one views oneself as wrong or as not projecting the desired appearance to others, and so on.

In contrast, positive emotions—happiness, gratitude, pride, love, relief, hope, and so on—involve appraisals that one is meeting one's goals, that a bad event has not come to pass, that one is meeting or exceeding one's own standards, that one's relationship with another is secure, and so on.

W. GERROD PARROTT, PHD
Professor of psychology at Georgetown University. Dr. Parrott's central interest is the nature of human emotion. He has published numerous scholarly articles and books.

Why Are Negative Emotions So Toxic? Noted Tanya *scholar* **Rabbi Shais Taub** *explains:*

MYJLI.COM/WARRIOR

Exercise 1.2

Which of the following negative emotions do you hope
that this course will help you resolve or reduce?

☐	Anger	☐	Hypocrisy
☐	Anxiety	☐	Inauthenticity
☐	Despair	☐	Loneliness
☐	Disappointment	☐	Negative self-image
☐	Fear	☐	Sadness
☐	Grief	☐	Shame
☐	Guilt	☐	Worry
☐	Hate	☐	Other _____

Exercise 1.3

Which of the following positive emotions do you hope that this course will help you foster and strengthen?

☐ Alacrity		☐ Love	
☐ Enthusiasm		☐ Optimism	
☐ Excitement		☐ Positive self-image	
☐ Fulfillment		☐ Self-confidence	
☐ Gratitude		☐ Serenity	
☐ Hope		☐ Zeal	
☐ Joy		☐ Other _____	

TEXT 3a

RABBI SHNE'UR ZALMAN OF LIADI, *TANYA*, CH. 26

כְּמוֹ שֶׁנִּצָּחוֹן לְנַצֵּחַ דָּבָר גַּשְׁמִי, כְּגוֹן שְׁנֵי אֲנָשִׁים הַמִּתְאַבְּקִים זֶה עִם זֶה
לְהַפִּיל זֶה אֶת זֶה, הִנֵּה אִם הָאֶחָד הוּא בְּעַצְלוּת וּכְבֵדוּת, יְנֻצַּח בְּקַל וְיִפֹּל,
גַּם אִם הוּא גִּבּוֹר יוֹתֵר מֵחֲבֵרוֹ. כָּכָה מַמָּשׁ בְּנִצָּחוֹן הַיֵּצֶר ...

When attempting to be victorious over a physical opponent—such as in the case of two individuals who are wrestling with each other, each one striving to fell the other—one who is lazy and sluggish will be easily defeated and will fall, even if that individual is stronger than the other. It is exactly so in the struggle against one's negative impulses. . . .

RABBI SHNE'UR ZALMAN OF LIADI (ALTER REBBE) 1745–1812

Chasidic rebbe, halachic authority, and founder of the Chabad movement. The Alter Rebbe was born in Liozna, Belarus, and was among the principal students of the Magid of Mezeritch. His numerous works include the *Tanya*, an early classic containing the fundamentals of Chabad Chasidism, and *Shulchan Aruch HaRav,* an expanded and reworked code of Jewish law.

TEXT 3b

TANYA, IBID.

כָּכָה מַמָּשׁ בְּנִצָּחוֹן הַיֵּצֶר: אִי אֶפְשָׁר לְנַצְּחוֹ בְּעַצְלוּת וּכְבֵדוּת הַנִּמְשָׁכוֹת
מֵעַצְבוּת וְטִמְטוּם הַלֵּב כָּאֶבֶן ...

It is exactly so in the struggle against one's negative impulses: it is impossible to conquer them with laziness and sluggishness, which originate in negative emotion and in a heart that is numb like a stone. . . .

A 1-minute meditation on winning:

MYJLI.COM/WARRIOR

TEXT 3c

TANYA, IBID. ⊞

> כִּי אִם, בִּזְרִיזוּת הַנִּמְשֶׁכֶת מִשִּׂמְחָה וּפְתִיחַת הַלֵּב וְטָהֲרָתוֹ מִכָּל נִדְנוּד
> דְּאָגָה וְעֶצֶב בָּעוֹלָם.

Rather, [conquering one's negative impulses requires] alacrity, which derives from positive emotion and from a heart that is free and cleansed from any trace of worry and negative emotion whatsoever.

Handwritten correspondence by Rabbi Shne'ur Zalman of Liadi, dated 1811. (Library of Agudas Chassidei Chabad, Brooklyn)

TEXT 4

ADAGE ATTRIBUTED TO RABBI AHARON OF KARLIN

There is no biblical commandment mandating that we be joyful. Likewise, negative emotion is not proscribed by any biblical prohibition. But joy accomplishes what no mitzvah can accomplish, and negative emotion causes greater damage than any sin.

RABBI AHARON OF KARLIN
1736–1772

Chasidic rebbe. Rabbi Aharon was a disciple of Rabbi Dov Ber of Mezeritch. He was known as Rabbi Aharon the Great and was one of the pioneers of Chasidism in Lithuania. He is known for his ecstatic and unrestrained fervor during his prayers and for his caring for the needy. He is the composer of the Shabbat hymn *Kah Echsof*.

TEXT 5

TANYA, COMPILER'S FOREWORD

בִּיוֹדְעַיי וּמְכִירַיי קָאֲמֵינָא, הֵם כָּל אֶחָד וְאֶחָד מֵאַנְשֵׁי שְׁלוֹמֵינוּ שֶׁבִּמְדִינָתֵנוּ וּסְמוּכוֹת שֶׁלָּהּ, אֲשֶׁר הָיָה הַדִּבּוּר שֶׁל חִבָּה מָצוּי בֵּינֵינוּ, וְגִלּוּ לְפָנַי כָּל תַּעֲלוּמוֹת לִבָּם וּמוֹחָם בַּעֲבוֹדַת ה' הַתְּלוּיָה בַּלֵּב.

אֲלֵיהֶם תִּטּוֹף מִלָּתִי וְלִשׁוֹנִי עֵט סוֹפֵר בְּקוּנְטְרֵיסִים אֵלוּ הַנִּקְרָאִים בְּשֵׁם "לִקּוּטֵי אֲמָרִים"... וְכֻלָּם הֵן תְּשׁוּבוֹת עַל שְׁאֵלוֹת רַבּוֹת אֲשֶׁר שׁוֹאֲלִין בְּעֵצָה כָּל אַנְשֵׁי שְׁלוֹמֵינוּ דִמְדִינָתֵנוּ תָּמִיד, כָּל אֶחָד לְפִי עֶרְכּוֹ, לָשִׂית עֵצוֹת בְּנַפְשָׁם בַּעֲבוֹדַת ה'. לִהְיוֹת כִּי אֵין הַזְּמַן גְּרָמָא עוֹד לְהָשִׁיב לְכָל אֶחָד וְאֶחָד עַל שְׁאֵלָתוֹ בִּפְרָטוּת, וְגַם הַשִּׁכְחָה מְצוּיָה.

עַל כֵּן רָשַׁמְתִּי כָּל הַתְּשׁוּבוֹת עַל כָּל הַשְּׁאֵלוֹת לְמִשְׁמֶרֶת לְאוֹת, לִהְיוֹת לְכָל אֶחָד וְאֶחָד לְזִכָּרוֹן בֵּין עֵינָיו, וְלֹא יִדְחַק עוֹד לִיכָּנֵס לְדַבֵּר עִמִּי בִּיחִידוּת, כִּי בָּהֶן יִמְצָא מַרְגּוֹעַ לְנַפְשׁוֹ וְעֵצָה נְכוֹנָה לְכָל דָּבָר הַקָּשֶׁה עָלָיו בַּעֲבוֹדַת ה'.

I address those who know me well, each and every member of the Chasidic community who lives in our land and in adjacent lands, those with whom I have had frequent warm conversations and who revealed to

What is the most revolutionary idea in Tanya? *Scholars share their thoughts:*

MYJLI.COM/WARRIOR

me all the secrets of their hearts and minds in all that pertains to their heartfelt service of G-d.

To them I direct my words in this work, entitled *Likutei Amarim* (A Compilation of Discourses). . . . This work is comprised of responses to the many questions frequently posed by Chasidim in our land, seeking advice and moral guidance in the service of G-d, each according to their spiritual station. Time no longer permits me to reply to everyone individually and in detail. Furthermore, [I record these ideas because] people tend to forget [the responses I gave them].

I have, therefore, recorded all the replies to all the questions, to be preserved for perpetuity and to be readily available to all. There is no longer any need for people to press to be admitted to talk with me in private, for in this work everyone can find counsel to soothe their soul and proper guidance on any matter that one finds difficult in the service of G-d.

*What is Tanya's uniqueness in the field of Chasidic literature? Hear **Rabbi YY Jacobson**'s answer:*

MYJLI.COM/WARRIOR

Exercise 1.4

Complete the following sentence:

"For most people, the primary struggle in life is between _____ and _____."

TEXT 6a

TANYA, CH. 1

שֶׁכָּתַב הָרַב חַיִּים וִיטַל זִכְרוֹנוֹ לִבְרָכָה בְּשַׁעֲרֵי הַקְּדֻשָּׁה [וּבְעֵץ חַיִּים, שַׁעַר נ פֶּרֶק ב], דְּלְכָל אִישׁ יִשְׂרָאֵל, אֶחָד צַדִּיק וְאֶחָד רָשָׁע, יֵשׁ שְׁתֵּי נְשָׁמוֹת, וּכְדִכְתִיב: "וּנְשָׁמוֹת אֲנִי עָשִׂיתִי" (יְשַׁעְיָהוּ נז, טז), שֶׁהֵן שְׁתֵּי נְפָשׁוֹת. נֶפֶשׁ אַחַת מִצַּד הַקְּלִיפָּה וְסִטְרָא אַחֲרָא . . . וּמִמֶּנָּה בָּאוֹת כָּל הַמִּדּוֹת רָעוֹת.

Why is the two-soul doctrine personally relevant? **Rabbi Manis Friedman** *responds:*

MYJLI.COM/WARRIOR

Rabbi Chaim Vital writes in *Shaarei Hakedushah* (and in ETS CHAYIM 50:2) that each of us, whether righteous or wicked, has two souls, two distinct life forces, as it is written, "I have created souls" (ISAIAH 57:16).

One life force originates in unholiness. . . . All negative character traits stem from this life force.

TEXT 6b

TANYA, IBID.

וְגַם מִדּוֹת טוֹבוֹת . . . כְּמוֹ רַחֲמָנוּת וּגְמִילוּת חֲסָדִים, בָּאוֹת מִמֶּנָּה.

This life force is also the source of good character traits . . . such as mercy and benevolence.

TEXT **6**c

TANYA, CH. 2

וְנֶפֶשׁ הַשֵּׁנִית בְּיִשְׂרָאֵל הִיא חֵלֶק אֱלוֹ-הַּ מִמַּעַל מַמָּשׁ.

The second life force is a part of G-d above, literally.

Figure 1.1

Two Battlefronts

	CONVENTIONAL UNDERSTANDING	*TANYA* UNDERSTANDING
Conflict between	Right vs. wrong	Divine vs. natural soul
Nature of the conflict	Moral vs. immoral	G-d- and mission-oriented vs. self-oriented
Driving question	What I will do?	What will my identity be?
Time of conflict	At a moment when I am posed with a moral choice	Constant

TEXT 7

ISAIAH 29:19

וְיָסְפוּ עֲנָוִים בַּה׳ שִׂמְחָה.

Those who are humble shall continuously rejoice in G-d.

What is the most dangerous but common negative emotion? Five scholars respond:

MYJLI.COM/WARRIOR

TEXT 8

ABIGAIL ABRAMS, "YES, IMPOSTOR SYNDROME IS REAL. HERE'S HOW TO DEAL WITH IT," *TIME MAGAZINE*, JUNE 20, 2018

Have you ever felt like you don't belong? Like your friends or colleagues are going to discover you're a fraud, and you don't actually deserve your job and accomplishments?

If so, you're in good company. These feelings are known as impostor syndrome, or what psychologists often call impostor phenomenon. An estimated 70% of people experience these impostor feelings at some point in their lives, according to a review article published in the *International Journal of Behavioral Science*. Impostor syndrome affects all kinds of people from all parts of life: women, men, medical students, marketing managers, actors and executives. . . .

Impostor syndrome can apply to anyone "who isn't able to internalize and own their successes," says psychologist Audrey Ervin.

Impostor syndrome expert Valerie Young, who is the author of a book on the subject, *The Secret Thoughts of Successful Women*, has also found patterns in people who experience impostor feelings:

"Perfectionists" set extremely high expectations for themselves, and even if they meet 99% of their goals, they're going to feel like failures. Any small mistake will make them question their own competence.

QUESTION FOR DISCUSSION

How might living a divine-soul, purpose-oriented life preclude the feelings described in this text?

TEXT 9a

GENESIS 25:22

וַיִּתְרוֹצְצוּ הַבָּנִים בְּקִרְבָּהּ, וַתֹּאמֶר, "אִם כֵּן, לָמָה זֶה אָנֹכִי?" וַתֵּלֶךְ
לִדְרֹשׁ אֶת ה'.

The children struggled within her, and she said, "If so, why [did] I [desire to conceive]?" And she went to seek divine [counsel].

TEXT 9b

IBID., VERSE 23

וַיֹּאמֶר ה' לָהּ, "שְׁנֵי גוֹיִם בְּבִטְנֵךְ וּשְׁנֵי לְאֻמִּים מִמֵּעַיִךְ יִפָּרֵדוּ, וּלְאֹם מִלְאֹם
יֶאֱמָץ וְרַב יַעֲבֹד צָעִיר".

G-d said to her, "Two nations are in your belly; two kingdoms will separate from your womb. One kingdom will always be mightier than the other kingdom, and [eventually,] the elder will serve the younger."

TEXT 10

TANYA, CH. 28 ⓘ

אַל יִפֹּל לִבּוֹ בְּקִרְבּוֹ לִהְיוֹת מִזֶּה עָצֵב נִבְזֶה בִּשְׁעַת הָעֲבוֹדָה, שֶׁצָּרִיךְ לִהְיוֹת בְּשִׂמְחָה רַבָּה. אֶלָּא אַדְרַבָּה, יִתְחַזֵּק יוֹתֵר וְיוֹסִיף אוֹמֶץ בְּכָל כֹּחוֹ בְּכַוָּונַת הַתְּפִלָּה בְּחֶדְוָה וְשִׂמְחָה יְתֵרָה, בְּשׂוּמוֹ אֶל לִבּוֹ כִּי נְפִילַת הַמַּחֲשָׁבָה זָרָה הִיא מֵהַקְּלִיפָּה שֶׁבְּחָלָל הַשְּׂמָאלִי, הָעוֹשָׂה מִלְחָמָה בְּבֵינוֹנִי עִם נֶפֶשׁ אֱלֹקִית שֶׁבּוֹ . . .

וְלֹא כְּטָעוּת הָעוֹלָם, שֶׁטּוֹעִים לְהוֹכִיחַ מִנְּפִילַת הַמַּחֲשָׁבָה זָרָה, מִכְּלָל שֶׁאֵין תְּפִלָּתָם כְּלוּם, שֶׁאִילוּ הִתְפַּלֵּל כָּרָאוּי וְנָכוֹן, לֹא הָיוּ נוֹפְלִים לוֹ מַחֲשָׁבוֹת זָרוֹת. וֶהֱאֱמֶת הָיָה כְּדִבְרֵיהֶם, אִם הָיְתָה נֶפֶשׁ אַחַת לְבַדָּהּ הִיא הַמִּתְפַּלֶּלֶת, וְהִיא הַמְחַשֶּׁבֶת וּמְהַרְהֶרֶת הַמַּחֲשָׁבוֹת זָרוֹת. אֲבָל בֶּאֱמֶת לַאֲמִיתּוֹ, הֵן שְׁתֵּי נְפָשׁוֹת הַנִּלְחָמוֹת זוֹ עִם זוֹ.

Do not be upset or dejected while serving G-d [in prayer], for it ought to be a joyous experience. On the contrary, intensify your efforts and focus your energy to concentrate on your prayer with increased joy and gladness. Understand that the foreign thought that has entered [your mind] derives from the natural soul, which wages war against the divine soul within all strugglers. . . .

[Do not ascribe to] the commonly held error that a foreign thought is evidence that your prayer is worthless and that if your prayer was proper, no foreign thoughts would intrude. This would be true if you possessed only one soul—a single soul that both prays as well as experiences the foreign thoughts. The deepest truth, however, is that you have two souls that wage war against each other.

Figure 1.2

Benefits of the Divine-Soul Model

AREA	RATIONALE
Negative emotion that results from feeling inauthentic.	Every selfless deed is a 100 percent authentic expression of the divine soul.

Exercise 1.5

In what area of your life can you adopt a divine-soul perspective and thereby reduce feelings of inauthenticity?

KEY POINTS

1 Life is a constant struggle. We have the tools necessary to be victorious in our struggles, but we cannot win if we are lazy and lethargic.

2 Laziness and lethargy are not root issues; they are symptoms of negative emotions (uncomfortable emotions that make us feel bad). Conversely, positive emotions (pleasant emotions that make us feel good) allow us to be victorious in our struggles.

3 Because our life-struggles are constant, positive emotion is needed at *all* times.

4 The human being's ultimate battle is not only between good and evil but between the divine (selfless, purpose- and G-d-oriented) soul and the natural (self-centered) soul. This is a battle over who we *are*—how we define ourselves—and it is ever-present.

5 Throughout this course, we will demonstrate that living with a divine soul paradigm is the solution to negative emotions and the key to experiencing positive emotions.

6 Sometimes, we cannot capitalize on positive emotions available to us because we feel hypocritical, drawn in polar opposite directions ("impostor syndrome"). This is countered by the realization that we have two soul-identities and that any sacred, selfless act that we do is an authentic expression of our divine soul.

Appendix

TEXT **11**

STEPHEN R. COVEY, ET AL., *FIRST THINGS FIRST: TO LIVE, TO LOVE, TO LEARN, TO LEAVE A LEGACY* (NEW YORK: FREE PRESS, 2003), P. 59

Years ago, as I was wandering between the stacks of books at a university library, I chanced to open a book in which I encountered one of the most powerful, significant ideas I've ever come across. The essence of it was this:

Between stimulus and response, there is a space.

In that space is our power to choose our response.

In our response lies our growth and our freedom.

**STEPHEN RICHARDS COVEY
1932–2012**

Educator and author. Covey was an internationally respected leadership authority, family expert, teacher, and organizational consultant. He was named one of *TIME* magazine's 25 Most Influential Americans. His books have sold more than 25 million copies in 38 languages, and *The 7 Habits of Highly Effective People* is frequently named by business leaders as one of the most influential business books of the 20th century.

TEXT **12**

PAULINE ROSE CLANCE AND SUZANNE IMES, "THE IMPOSTOR PHENOMENON IN HIGH ACHIEVING WOMEN: DYNAMICS AND THERAPEUTIC INTERVENTIONS," *PSYCHOTHERAPY: THEORY, RESEARCH, AND PRACTICE*, 15:3 (1978), PP. 241–247

In the past five years we have worked in individual psychotherapy, theme-centered international groups, and college classes with over 150 highly successful women—women who have earned PhDs in various specialties, who are respected professionals in their fields, or who are students recognized for their academic excellence. However, despite their earned degrees, scholastic honors, high achievement on standardized tests, praise and professional recognition from colleagues and respected authorities, these women do not experience an internal sense of success. They consider themselves to be "impostors." Women who experience the impostor phenomenon maintain a strong belief that they are not intelligent; in fact, they are convinced that they have fooled anyone who thinks otherwise. For example, students often fantasize that they were mistakenly admitted to graduate school because of an error by the admissions committee. Numerous women graduate students state that their high examination scores are due to luck, to misgrading, or to the faulty judgment of professors. Women professionals in our sample feel overevaluated by colleagues and administrators. One women professor said, "I'm not good enough to be on the faculty here. Some mistake was made in the selection

PAULINE ROSE CLANCE, PHD

Psychologist and author. Dr. Clance has been in practice for over 30 years. She is best known as the author of *The Impostor Phenomenon: Overcoming the Fear that Haunts Your Success.*

SUZANNE IMES, PHD

Psychologist and author. Dr. Imes has a private practice in Atlanta, Georgia. She is the codeveloper of the impostor phenomenon theory.

process." Another, the chairperson of her department, said, "Obviously I'm in this position because my abilities have been overestimated." Another woman with two master's degrees, a PhD, and numerous publications to her credit considered herself unqualified to teach remedial college classes in her field. In other words, these women find innumerable means of negating any external evidence that contradicts their belief that they are, in reality, unintelligent.

Self-declared impostors fear that eventually some significant person will discover that they are indeed intellectual impostors. One woman stated, "I was convinced that I would be discovered as a phony when I took my comprehensive doctoral examination. I thought the final test had come. In one way, I was somewhat relieved at this prospect because the pretense would finally be over. I was shocked when my chairman told me that my answers were excellent and that my paper was one of the best he had seen in his entire career."

Women who exhibit the impostor phenomenon do not fall into any one diagnostic category. The clinical symptoms most frequently reported are generalized anxiety, lack of self-confidence, depression, and frustration related to inability to meet self-imposed standards of achievement.

TEXT 13

JARUWAN SAKULKU AND JAMES ALEXANDER, "THE IMPOSTOR PHENOMENON," *INTERNATIONAL JOURNAL OF BEHAVIORAL SCIENCE*, 6:1 (2011), PAGES 82 AND 86

In summary, studies suggested that family background could contribute to the emergence of Impostorism. However, from the review above, correlations between family background variables and Impostorism were not strong. The strongest relationship was a perceived lack of parental care in Sonnak and Towell's (2001) study. Want and Kleitman (2006) suggested this perception may be specific to perceived paternal care but this correlation was slightly weaker than the one reported in Sonnak and Towell's study (2001). A weak positive relationship was also found between Impostorism and perceived parental control/overprotection and this relationship may also be stronger for the perception of control/overprotection from the father. In addition, confusing messages about achievement from the family appeared more strongly related to Impostorism than family achievement values that emphasized achievement via competition. . . .

For personality factors, while one study has shown that Neuroticism was strongly related with Impostorism, others suggested it was a bit less related. Similarly, a strong negative correlation has been demonstrated for Conscientiousness and Impostorism in one study, though a few have found smaller correlations. As

JARUWAN SAKULKU, PSY.D

Clinical psychologist, member of the Thai Clinical Psychologist Association. Dr. Sakulku is currently a lecturer at the Department of Psychology at Thammasat University, Bangkok.

JAMES ALEXANDER, PHD

Psychologist. Dr. Alexander received his degree from the University of Tasmania.

perfectionism is considered one of the most important characteristics of Impostorism, aspects of perfectionism and Impostorism would be expected to correlate relatively highly. Perfectionistic cognitions and non-display of imperfection were relatively strongly correlated with Impostorism, more highly than the correlation between Impostorism and trait anxiety. However, non-disclosure of imperfection was not significantly related to Impostorism.

TEXT 14

GAIL MATTHEWS AND PAULINE ROSE CLANCE, "TREATMENT OF THE IMPOSTOR PHENOMENON IN PSYCHOTHERAPY CLIENTS," *PSYCHOTHERAPY IN PRIVATE PRACTICE*, 3:1 (1985), PP. 78–80

A very critical element in the therapeutic treatment of the impostor phenomenon is that the therapist must take the client's doubts and fears very seriously. Too often in their history, the clients have received quick reassurances when mentioning their fears. It is important that the therapist ask very concrete questions about the nature of the impostor feelings, thereby reinforcing serious responses. Such questions might be "How long have you (the client) experienced these feelings? When are these feelings likely to occur? How often do these doubts occur? What helps decrease the doubts and

GAIL MATTHEWS, PHD

Psychologist. Dr. Matthews is currently a private practitioner and psychology professor at Dominican University of California.

what increases them?" These questions let clients know they are being heard; and they also increase the clients' knowledge and awareness of how and when impostor experiences occur.

Clients with impostor feelings often experience themselves as being the only persons who have these feelings, and they feel isolated as a result. Knowing that they are not alone is very beneficial to clients, and ideally we recommend group psychotherapy or short term growth-oriented groups where the clients can discover that other persons who also are really bright can experience the same impostor ideas. In these therapy groups, the clients become aware of and begin to label their impostor feelings. . . . If a group treatment is not appropriate or available, then the therapist can teach the client to begin to label the experiences that fit with the impostor phenomenon. We have found that it is helpful to give clients some basic reading material on the phenomenon and will have them read the Clance and Imes (1978) article and discuss it in therapy. After this process, clients often recognize the impostor feelings as they occur and can begin to choose to deal with them differently. They are able to say, "I am having these feelings which probably are not based on the reality of what I actually can do. I'm distrusting my abilities but it doesn't mean I can't do this project. I'll own and deal with my fears but proceed on with the project." When they can label their own experience of doubt as an impostor experience, many clients who were considering not applying for a promotion, a grant, or an honor become more willing to accept these changes.

Another critical part of the therapy work is to deal with the client's terror of failure. Considerable work must be done to help the person realize that failing or even doing poorly at a task will not lead to disaster. The rational emotive techniques of Ellis (1977) or the desensitization work of Wolpe and Wolpe (1981) may be helpful for countering this fear. Clients need to stop imagining failure and quit telling themselves that they cannot cope with any degree of failure no matter how small.

Additional Readings

INTRODUCTION TO *TANYA*

BY RABBI NISSAN MINDEL, PHD

1. The Book

The author called his work by three distinct names. Each of these names characterizes the book in its own way. These names are:

Likkutei Amarim—"Collected Discourses." By this name, the author describes his work in his "Compiler's Foreword," thereby humbly disclaiming any originality of this work. In fact, the author explicitly states that his treatise constitutes a collection of discourses "which have been selected from books and teachers, heavenly saints, who are renowned among us." Under this title, the book was first published (Slavita, 1796).[1]

Tanya—after the initial word of the book, quoting a Baraitic source.[2] The quotation from Tannaitic lore serves the author more than a homiletic introduction to his system. Dealing, as it does, with the mystic descent of the soul and its destiny, it provides the author with a starting point, based in the Talmud, from which to unfold his whole system. Under this title, the book appeared for the second time (Zolkiev, 1798), with *Likkutei Amarim* as the subtitle.[3]

Sefer shel Benonim—"Book of the Intermediates," so called after the type of personality on which the book centers attention, that is, the intermediate type whose moral position is between the *tzaddik* ("righteous man") and *rasha* ("wicked man"). Thus, the author pointedly indicates that his primary concern

RABBI NISSAN MINDEL, PHD, 1912–1999

Secretary to the Lubavitcher Rebbe. Born in Latvia, Rabbi Mindel immigrated to the U.S., where he received a doctorate in Semitic languages from Columbia University. He translated many works into English, including the *Tanya*, the seminal text of Chabad philosophy, and was a prolific writer who authored numerous works including *Philosophy of Chabad* and *My Prayer*.

is not with the *tzaddik,* upon whose veneration general Chasidut had placed so much emphasis, nor with the *rasha,* upon whose condemnation much has been said in other Jewish ethical works, but with the *benoni,* the "intermediate" man, whose rank is within reach of every person.[4] The name *Sefer shel Benonim* appeared as a subtitle in the first edition (*Likkutei Amarim,* Part One, called *Sefer shel Benonim).* Actually, however, the author often refers to the whole book, and not merely its first part, when using the title *Sefer shel Benonim.*[5]

The standard complete editions of this work include the following five parts, each of which is an independent treatise:

Part I: *Likkutei Amarim,* or *Tanya,* or *Sefer shel Benonim,* proper, comprising a Foreword and fifty-three chapters (148 pp.).

Part II: *Shaar Hayichud VehaEmunah* ("Portal of Unity and Belief"), with a Foreword and twelve chapters (30 pp.).

Part III: *Iggeret Hateshuvah* ("Epistle of Repentance"), with twelve chapters (22 pp.).

Part IV: *Iggeret Hakodesh* ("Sacred Epistle"), with thirty-two sections (102 pp.).[6]

Part V: *Kuntres Acharon* ("Latest Treatise"), (20 pp.).

Altogether, over 6,000 printings of the *Likkutei Amarim,* or *Tanya,* complete or in part, have appeared to date,[7] with both names alternating as title and subtitle, respectively. Yet this work, as the other Chabad classics, has never been translated into any European language.[8] Even in its Hebrew original, it is not an easy book because of its construction, almost complete lack of punctuation, and also because some of its basic doctrines are not treated fully therein and must be sought in the author's other works. There seems, therefore, ample reason for presenting to the

English-speaking Jewish world a translation of this fundamental work of Chabad, with an introduction and notes, which, it is hoped, will facilitate the comprehension of this book and its doctrine. Our present study will confine itself to Part I, to which we shall refer, for the sake of convenience, by its shorter name—*Tanya.*

The author worked on the *Tanya* for twenty years,[9] elaborating its style and form so punctiliously that it came to be regarded by his followers as the "Written Torah" of Chabad, where every word and letter was meaningful. Indeed, the author divided it into fifty-three chapters to correspond to the number of *Sidrot* (weekly portions) in the Pentateuch. It soon became the custom of many Chabad Chasidim to study a chapter of the *Tanya* each week, with the same regularity with which the weekly portions of the Pentateuch were recited.[10]

In his attempt to design the *Tanya* so that it would meet the widest possible need, both of the analytical and searching mind as well as of the less scholarly, the author has succeeded to a high degree. The former find in it an inexhaustible profundity, and several commentaries have been authored to explain its depth. This translator has been fortunate in having access to some of the manuscripts in question.[11]

The less scholarly, too, each according to his intellectual capacity, find in it edifying instruction at varying levels. This quality, together with the authority it enjoys, accounts for the widespread recognition which the *Tanya* has commanded from the time of its appearance to the present day.

The *Tanya* was written, as the author indicates in his Foreword, for the "seekers" and the "perplexed." One is tempted to draw a parallel between this author and his book and Maimonides and his *Guide.* Indeed, both men present some striking points in common. Each of them first established his reputation as a Talmudist and Codifier before publishing a work of philosophy; both had written Codes of Jewish Law, which are still authoritative and popular. Each of them created a new lasting school of thought in Jewish philosophy, and the one, like the other, set out to write a work which aimed at helping those who needed guidance in their religious beliefs. Yet both of

them evoked sharp opposition from the direction of a part of orthodox Jewry; both were misunderstood and their philosophical treatises were banned.

However, this is as far as the parallel goes. The *Guide* and the *Tanya* represent two widely divergent systems, in essence as well as in form. The two authors were separated by some six centuries in time and far apart also geographically and in respect of the whole cultural milieu in which they flourished. Maimonides is the rational Jewish philosopher *par excellence;* Rabbi Schneur Zalman is basically a mystic. The "perplexed" for whom they wrote were two entirely different types of people. Maimonides wrote for the man whose perplexity derived from the fact that he desired to retain his traditional beliefs, but was puzzled by the apparent contradiction between tradition and philosophy, yet loath to give up either.[12] The object of the *Guide,* therefore, was to effect a reconciliation between the two.

No such problem confronted Rabbi Schneur Zalman. Philosophy and science hardly had a place among the masses of Eastern European Jewry at that time. The *Haskalah* movement had not yet made any serious inroads upon the minds of the masses. Rabbi Schneur Zalman addressed himself to those "who are in pursuit of righteousness and seek the L-rd . . . whose intelligence and mind are confused and they wander about in darkness in G-d's service, unable to perceive the beneficial light that is concealed in the books." In other words, he writes for those whose beliefs have not been troubled by doubts, but who merely seek the right path to G-d.

We will, therefore, not find in the *Tanya* the type of scholastic philosophy with which the *Guide* is replete, or any polemics, nor even an attempt to treat systematically many of the philosophical problems which engaged Maimonides' attention. Such basic beliefs as the existence of G-d, *creatio ex nihilo,* Revelation, and others, are taken for granted by the author. Others, such as the Divine attributes, Providence, Unity, Messianism, etc., are treated as integral parts of his ethical system and illuminated by the light of Kabbalah.

The *Tanya* is essentially a work on Jewish religious ethics. The author is primarily concerned with the forces of good and evil in human nature and in the surrounding world, and his objective, as already pointed out, is to pave a new way to achieving the ultimate purpose of creation. He is aware, of course, of the existence of Hebrew literature dealing with the same subject. If he is impelled to write a new book, it is not, as he is careful to note, because of the shortcomings of the available works *per se*, but because the human mind is not equally receptive, nor equally responsive to, the same stimuli. The implication is that many works on Jewish philosophy and ethics were useful for their time and age, or for the specific groups for whom they were written. Now there was a need for a new approach (in the light of the Chasidic doctrine), and for a "guide" that would command a universal appeal. However, the author realizes that even this book, in parts at least, cannot be so simple as to be understood by all. Consequently, he urges the more learned not to be misled by a sense of misplaced modesty and not to withhold their knowledge from those who would seek it from them in the understanding of these "discourses."[13]

R. Schneur Zalman knew his "perplexed" intimately. They flocked to him in great numbers, and they flooded him with written inquiries. Most of them, undoubtedly, were simple folk and laymen. But there were also many students of the Talmud, and philosophically inclined young men, who, like himself in his teens, sought a new way of life and new outlets for their intellectual as well as spiritual drive. The consideration of such a variegated audience largely determined the form and style of the book.

Speaking of form and style, it should also be remembered that long before he committed his teachings and doctrines to writing, he preached them orally.[14] His sermons and discourses, delivered mostly on Shabbat and on Festivals (which accounts for their homiletic style), were subsequently recorded from memory by his disciples. These manuscripts had a wide circulation among his followers. Not infrequently, Rabbi Schneur Zalman expounded his doctrines in the form of epistles which, being of general interest, were regarded by his followers as pastoral letters and also copied and recopied for the widest possible circulation. In the course of time, as his community of devotees had greatly increased, R. Schneur Zalman

felt, as he explains in his Foreword, that the time was ripe to present an outline of his teachings, in the form of a book, which was to supersede the circulating pamphlets, many of which were replete with errors as a result of repeated copying and transcription or by the malicious mischief of opponents.[15] This is how the *Likkutei Amarim,* or *Tanya,* in its present composition, was born.

2. The Sources

We have already noted that the author of the *Tanya* made no claim to originality for his work. On the contrary, he emphasized his dependence on his predecessors. Among the "books and sages" which influenced his thinking, the Scriptures, Talmud, and Lurianic Kabbalah must be given foremost place. This is indicated already in the first chapter, which opens the book with Talmudic quotations, references to the Zoharitic literature and R. Chaim Vital, the great exponent of Lurianic Kabbalah, and with interspersed quotations from Scripture. Here we already have an indication of the author's cast of mind and his aim to build his system on the combined foundations of scriptural, Rabbinic, and Kabbalistic sources.

Rabbi Schneur Zalman's interpretations and doctrines are based upon the teachings of the Baal Shem Tov, the founder of general Chasidut, and his own "masters," Rabbi DovBer of Miezricz, the Baal Shem Tov's successor, and Rabbi DovBer's son Rabbi Avraham, the "Angel."

The author draws abundantly from the *Zohar* and the *Tikkunei Zohar.* He mentions by name Maimonides (the *Code*), and Rabbi Moshe Cordovo (*Pardes*). Of other "books and scribes" which influenced him, though he does not mention them by name in the *Tanya,* are R. Yeshaya Hurwitz's *Shnei Luchot Habrit,* the works of the Maharal (Rabbi Yehudah Loew) of Prague, and Rabbenu Bachya ben Asher's *Commentary* on the Bible.[16]

Halevi's *Kuzari* was held in high esteem by Rabbi Schneur Zalman and his successors. He is known to have studied it ardently with his son and grandson who succeeded him. Similarly, Bachya ibn Pakuda's *Duties of the Heart,* which enjoyed great popularity among Talmudic scholars of the day, as it still does.[17] Albo's *Ikkarim* was another popular source for the philosophically inclined. It is safe to assume that Rabbi Schneur Zalman was intimately familiar with these, and no doubt also with the whole range of Medieval Jewish philosophy, but there is no evidence of influence by these sources on the composition of the *Tanya*.

It has been wisely said that the proper approach to a problem is in itself half a solution. Quite often it is the approach to the problem, and the method of treating it, that displays the greatest degree of ingenuity and originality, and in themselves constitute the main contribution of the thinker. This is true of R. Schneur Zalman and of the Chabad system which he created. For, while his basic concepts have been gleaned from various sources, his doctrines nevertheless present a complete and unified system, and there is much refreshing originality in its presentation and consistency.

But R. Schneur Zalman did more than that. Very often he has so modified, reinterpreted, or remodeled the ideas which he had assimilated as to give them an originality of their own.

To Rabbi Schneur Zalman, as to Kabbalists in general, the Torah, the Jewish Written and Oral Law embodied in the Bible and Talmud (the latter including both the Halachah and Aggadah), was more than a Divinely inspired guide to achieving the ultimate purpose of creation. It constituted the essential law and order of the created universe.[18] The Kabbalah, in its interpretation, was nothing but the inner, esoteric dimension of the Torah, its very "soul." Without this dimension the Torah could not be fully understood. Consequently, when he looked for the "inner," or esoteric, meaning of Biblical and Talmudic texts it was not for the purpose of adding homiletic poignancy to his exposition, but rather to reveal their inner dimension. In his system, the esoteric and exoteric, the Kabbalah and the Talmud, are thoroughly blended and unified, just as the physical and metaphysical, the body and soul, emerge under his treatment as two aspects of the same thing. The polarity of things is but external; the underlying reality of everything is unity, reflecting the unity of the Creator. To bring out this unity of the microcosm and macrocosm, as they merge within the mystic unity of the *En Sof* (The Infinite)—that is the ultimate aim of his system.

3. The Composition of the *Tanya*

Structurally, the *Tanya* may be divided into a number of sections, each dealing with a major subject and comprising a number of composite topics.

The first section of the work (chapters 1–8) is devoted to an analysis of the psychological structure of the Jewish personality.[19] Here the author discusses the two levels of consciousness (to use modern terminology) on which a person operates. These two levels of consciousness are derived from two sources, which the author terms the "divine soul" and the "animal soul." He examines the essential attributes and practical faculties of each. In dealing with the "animal soul," the author discusses also the nature of evil, both metaphysical and moral. Evil is basically conceived in terms of disunity, good in terms of unity.

Next (chapters 9–17), the author goes on to examine the inevitable conflict ensuing from the two divergent sources of consciousness. He evaluates the relative strength of the two souls and their respective functions, whereby the essential unity of the human personality is strongly upheld. Experientially, however, the conflict produces a variety of personalities, from one extreme to the other, which the author proceeds to define. His attention is focused on the personality of the *benoni,* which falls midway between the extremes. However, in Rabbi Schneur Zalman's definition, the *benoni* is not one whose sins and virtues balance, while the *tzaddik* is a person whose good deeds outweigh his sins, as sometimes defined in the Talmud.[20] The *benoni* of the *Tanya* is a person who exercises complete self-control and never commits a sin knowingly in any of the three areas of human activity: thought, speech, and deed. The *benoni* of the *Tanya* is thus superior to the *tzaddik* of the Talmud. Nevertheless, our author insists that this ideal personality is within grasp of the average individual, although not without constant effort and vigilance. The underlying doctrine here is that man is essentially and inherently a moral being.

The following chapters (18–25) are designed to support the author's basic theory, namely, that the ideal personality of the *benoni* is not a mere concept, but one that can actually be realized. To this end, he re-examines the functions of the soul, both on the conscious and subconscious level. With regard to the former, the author insists on the supremacy of the intellect. As for the subconscious level, the author draws upon the *Zohar* for certain mystical categories, such as the innate or "hidden" love and fear (awe) of G-d. The "hidden" love provides a subconscious urge for oneness with G-d; the sense of awe for the Divine Being provides a dread of separateness. Love and awe are therefore not conflicting, but rather complementary categories. The author emphasizes the special, and to a considerable extent also hereditary, nature of the Jew and his attachment to the idea of the unity of G-d, originating with the Patriarchs. This thought is, in some respects, strongly reminiscent of Halevi's concept of the "Divine Influence" (*al'amar al'ilahi*), which Halevi considers germane to the Jewish people.[21]

In this connection, the doctrine of Divine Unity comes under discussion.

However, never losing sight of the practical, the author discusses certain states of mind which have a direct bearing on the quest for personal unity as a prelude to unity in the cosmic order, which in turn is *sine qua non* for the realization of the Divine Unity. He offers a series of practical suggestions to attain mental and emotional stability and inner harmony. The emphasis is on joy, stemming from an intellectually achieved faith, while sadness and dejection are severely censured. All this forms the subject matter of chapters 26–31.

Chapter 32 stands out by itself, as an interpolation not immediately related to the specific discussion. The careful student will note that chapter 31 is more directly continued in chapter 33. It would appear that the author chose to include this particular chapter parenthetically, as it were, in order to give emphasis at this point to one of the cardinal teachings of the Baal Shem Tov, which is a cornerstone of Chasidut, and which receives special attention in Chabad.[22] We refer to the subject of *ahavat yisrael,* love for a fellow Jew (Leviticus 18:19). In his familiar way, our author gives this precept a mystic-ethical exposition, based on the close soul-relationship within the community of Israel, to which he alluded in his Foreword and chapter 2, and which now receives fuller treatment in this chapter. Hence, some leading Chasidim note the significance of the number of this chapter—32—corresponding to the Hebrew word לב, "heart."[23]

The drama of the inner personal conflict leads the author to an examination of man's destiny, the meaning and purpose of life, and man's place in the cosmic order. These problems are dealt with in chapters 33–37. In the last of these, the author outlines his concept of the Messianic Era and the Resurrection, when the cosmic order will have attained the acme of perfection and fulfillment as a direct result of man's conscious effort to work toward that goal.

At this point, the author might have concluded his treatise. However, he is not content with leaving us with the impression that life is merely a prelude to afterlife. There must be more to life, and to religious experience than serving merely as a means to an end. In the next, and last, fifteen chapters of his work, the author evolves his concept of the Kingdom of Heaven on earth in the *here and now.* In his daily life, man is offered a foretaste of the afterlife, and, in some respects, it is of a quality surpassing even the spiritual bliss of the hereafter. The author, therefore, takes up again those categories of man's spiritual phenomena which enable him to transcend his physical limitations and to partake of the supernatural in this life. Here again the mystic is very much in evidence. The author provides new insights into the concept of *kavanah* (the "intention" which must accompany every human act), which is the vehicle of transcendence (chapters 38–40). He discusses the various qualities of fear *(awe)* and love, and introduces also the quality of *mercy,* as the basic elements of this transcendency, and as innate qualities in human nature to leap over the gulf that separates the created from the Creator, and to come in direct contact with the *En Sof* the Limitless (chapters 41–47).

The next two chapters (48–49) are devoted to the all-important Lurianic doctrine of *tzimtzum* which, in the author's system, holds the key to both the mystery of creation and the destiny of man. Both man and the world in which he lives are two-dimensional creatures of matter and spirit. The tension that inheres in such an order can be relieved only by spiritualizing the material. Man has it in his power to achieve personal harmony and unity by realizing his inner nature. In so doing, he becomes the instrument through which the world in which he lives also achieves fulfillment. To be a true master of the world which the Creator had entrusted in his hands, man must first be master of himself. Creation is seen as a process leading from G-d to man; fulfillment is seen as a process leading from man to G-d. The process leading from G-d to man is one of materializing the spiritual, that leading from man to G-d—one of spiritualizing the material. There is a community of interests, as it were, between the Creator and His "counterpart" on earth, a community of interests which is realizable because of a community of "nature," since man partakes in the Divine nature (by reason of the fact that his soul is a "part" of G-dliness), as G-d concerns Himself with human affairs.

Man's moral acts must be holy acts.[24] The good and the holy are identical; man's duty and purpose in life is to identify himself with his Creator, through identifying his will with that of his Creator. Man is the Divine instrument "to make this world a fitting abode for the *Shechinah* (Divine Presence)," in which both man and G-d can share intimately and fully, in complete harmony and union. On this mystical note, the final chapters (50–53) of the treatise conclude.

Endnotes

[1] See *List of Tanya Editions and Printings, Tanya,* Bilingual Edition (Brooklyn, N.Y., 2014), p. 803 ff.

[2] *Niddah* 30b.

[3] See *List,* ibid.

[4] *Likkutei Amarim*, Part I, beg. ch. 14.

[5] See *Notes, Tanya,* Bilingual Edition (Brooklyn, N.Y., 2014), p. 907.

[6] Parts IV and V, comprising epistles written by the author at different times and on various occasions, are incorporated by the author's sons.

[7] See *List,* ibid.

[8] About other translations, see *List of Tanya Translations, Tanya,* Bilingual Edition (Brooklyn, N.Y., 2014), p. 904.

[9] *Kitzurim Vehe'arot L'Sefer Likkutei Amarim* (Kehot, 1948; 1989), p. 121.

[10] Ibid., pp. 123, 124.

[11] Two are by Rabbi Shmuel Gronem Esterman, first dean of the Yeshiva Tomchei Tmimim, founded in Lubavitch in 1897—currently being prepared for publication. A third, extant only in part, is believed to have been written by Rabbi Yaakov Kadaner, a disciple of Rabbi Schneur Zalman's son and successor—published in 2012.

[12] *The Guide for the Perplexed,* tr. M. Friedlander (London, 1942), Introduction, p. 2.

[13] Ibid., below, p. 28.

[14] Rabbi Schneur Zalman is said to have preached his doctrines orally for twelve years before committing them to writing. See *Kitzurim Vehe'arot*, p. 136.

[15] Ibid., pp. 137, 139.

[16] The *Zohar* is mentioned in the *Tanya* (Part I) forty-nine times; the Arizal—ten times; R. Chaim Vital and his works—twenty-nine times; Maimonides (*Code*)—five times; Nachmanides—once. See *Index of Books and Persons in Tanya, Tanya,* Bilingual Edition (Brooklyn, N.Y., 2014), p. 776 ff.

[17] Even where philosophical speculation was frowned upon, Rabbenu Bachya's *Duties of the Heart* enjoyed a unique position. The influential R. Yeshaya Hurwitz, for example, severely criticized in his work R. Avraham ibn Ezra, Maimonides (*Guide*), and Gersonides, but held the *Duties of the Heart* in high esteem. See *Shnei Luchot Habrit*, pp. 2b; 8a; 20b; 47b; 183a; 193b.

[18] Comp. "He looked into the Torah and created the world," *Zohar* II:161a; III:35b; etc. See also *Tanchuma*, beg., on Proverbs 8:30, to the effect that the Torah was the Divine "tool" in creating the universe.

[19] With R. Yeshaya Hurwitz and all Kabbalists, Rabbi Schneur Zalman considered the Jewish psychological composition in a category of its own. R. Yehudah Halevi made the special destiny of the Jewish people one of the basic doctrines of his *Kuzari*. In the *Tanya*, the emphasis is on the individual Jew rather than on the Jewish people as a whole.

[20] *Berachot* 7a; *Rosh Hashanah* 16b. See discussion of this subject in *Likkutei Amarim*, Part I, beg. ch. 1.

[21] *Kuzari* 1:25, 27 ff.

[22] See e.g., *Likkutei Torah, Matot* 85d ff.: *Derech Mitzvotecha* 28a ff., et al.

[23] I am indebted to the Lubavitcher Rebbe for calling my attention to the subject of this chapter.

[24] Comp. *Shnei Luchot Habrit*, pp. 326b; 380b.

Rabbi Shne'ur Zalman of Liadi, *Likutei Amarim: Tanya,* Bi-Lingual Edition (Brooklyn, N.Y.: Kehot Publication Society, 1998), Introduction by Rabbi Nissan Mindel, pp. 832–842

THE MEANING OF SADNESS, PART I

BY RABBI ADIN EVEN-ISRAEL (STEINSALTZ)

Sadness is a great obstacle to the worship of G-d, and man must struggle against it as much as he can. Even though there is a passage in the Bible that states: "In all sadness, there would be profit. . . ." (Proverbs 14:23), which may appear to be a contradiction. Of course, the meaning is not that sadness in itself can ever be profitable, but that there is a joy that often follows on sadness, which, thus, may be good. For there is also the matter of catharsis or purification, as well as the fact that there is a time for everything.

Sadness can, therefore, be a vehicle for attaining something else, a bitter remedy for a worse ailment. On the other hand, life furnishes enough genuine reasons for being downcast. Thus in order to prevent sadness from being a dominant factor in life, we appoint special times for it—such as fast days or days of penitential prayer—and banish it from the rest of our lives.

Nevertheless, there is sometimes a real need for a contrite heart, because the greatest hindrance to spiritual awakening is a certain smugness, a dullness of the heart and mind. In this case, all the books and all the messages of spiritual love will not avail. Indeed, self-complacency is a more serious obstacle than depression or stupidity.

To overcome it, to smash through the barrier of "fatness" of soul, it is often necessary to pass through some sort of crisis or tragic experience. And this is often brought about by heavenly intervention, against one's own wishes and designs.

RABBI ADIN EVEN-ISRAEL (STEINSALTZ), 1937–

Talmudist, author, and philosopher. Rabbi Even-Israel (Steinsaltz) is considered one of the foremost Jewish thinkers of the 20th century. Praised by *Time* magazine as a "once-in-a-millennium scholar," he has been awarded the Israel Prize for his contributions to Jewish study. He lives in Jerusalem and is the founder of the Israel Institute for Talmudic Publications, a society dedicated to the translation and elucidation of the Talmud.

Indeed, it is a disquieting fact that it is more difficult to gain knowledge of the Divine through ordinary, positive living, than through negative or tragic experience. The negative seems to have much more power to break down one's resistance; the positive tends to reinforce one's smugness. Of course, sadness can also drag a person into depths beyond sensitivity; but, here too, the direction is important. And when one is aware of one's degradation, the sense of shame or of self-pity can function to restore the balance. Because it is sometimes necessary for a person to come to the conclusion that his life is not worth anything. Only when a person is burned so badly that his skin begins to peel, will he begin to feel himself.

A Kabbalistic insight claims: "It is Jacob who redeems Abraham." Abraham is Chesed, or Love, and Jacob is Tiferet (Mercy and Beauty). One may discover in life that grace is absent and that one cannot awaken love in one's heart. Upon such discovery, one falls back on pity; and this stimulates the love and the grace which had been absent. This stirring of compassion in the heart awakens great love, even the love of G-d. Here too, the essential confrontation is with Truth, the truth of oneself, and the need to break down the partition or veil that separates one from the Divine.

The Psalmist expressed it: "A broken and contrite heart, O G-d, thou wilt not despise" (Psalms 51:19). Just as a ladder cannot be useful unless it has something to lean against, so too, is there nothing more whole than a broken heart; even though, to be sure, G-d prefers vessels that are without blemishes or cracks, and it is written in the *Zohar* that the Shechinah does not lodge itself anywhere except in a whole vessel. Nevertheless, this does not include a broken heart. As Rabbi Schneur Zalman of Liadi mentions elsewhere: If one does not have a broken and contrite heart, one cannot be said to have a heart at all.

The central factor here is the demolition of sadness, the explosion which releases the joy. And many men do not really know true happiness, because they have never experienced the release from sadness. It is not a matter of contrasts, of course; it is a matter of getting to the truth of experience, of breaking out of the self-delusion, entertained by many, that they are alive, something that only a genuine shock can bring about. A great number of civilized human beings live comfortably with the notion that they would like to know G-d; and this is as much of a search for meaning they can indulge in. They do not get beyond the daily obligations of ethics and religion. Their search is, at best, the search for an earthly fortune, a matter of putting effort into something and getting a more or less just compensation. However, using the same logic, the story of the rich man who asked the rabbi: "What will I get out of the next life?" The rabbi answered: "At least as much as you invest in it." If you put a lot of money and effort into an earthly endeavor, you are likely to earn even more; if you put a lot of thought and energy into your spiritual endeavors, you're liable to gain more in the heavenly hereafter. The trouble is that men are much more troubled about the loss of a ten-pound note on earth than about losing a spiritual opportunity to perform a kindness.

For the heart is dull and heavy, and it is difficult to reach true joy. Thus, we have had to set fixed times for sadness and times for joy. The Ari used to teach his group in Safed to practice Tikun Chatzot, the nightly midnight sessions. These were mainly devoted to the recitation of Lamentations and the confession of sin, followed by hymns of praise and hours of joyful study of Torah and Kabbalah. The rationale is that when one thinks of the Exile of the Shechinah, we invoke a feeling of loss and abandonment. When this does not have the desired effect because it is too abstract, then one must think about the exile of the Shechinah in oneself. Then a person can experience the sorrow and the heartbreak of his life. And afterwards, he can more easily come around to the joy of prayer and study, so that sadness at fixed times can be a way of release from routine dullness and an opening for light and inner happiness.

The light that comes from the darkness has a certain excellence, like the wisdom that results from folly. To feel true happiness, it is perhaps necessary to go through the darkness of pain and the pit of anguish;

in order to truly know happiness, one must make a place for it in oneself, and this can best be done by great pain which thrusts all else aside.

For example, the greatest happiness of all, the pleasure of being alive, is hardly ever experienced in ordinary circumstances; and only when life is threatened, in passing through the danger of death, does one know it fully. In other words, only when a person realizes the full pain and terror of his life, can he make a place for G-d in himself. But of course, this applies to the times in history or in personal life when a person can allow himself the luxury of experiencing sadness at fixed times, when one is not the victim or the object of suffering. Sadness is well and good if it can be taken out and put away at will. As the instructions in certain old prayer books directed: "Here one is to weep. . . ." The fact is that life was perhaps harder in the old days, and in order to overcome the immense sadness of it, Jews had to put aside certain times for grief and weeping. It used to be a wry joke among Jews to say to someone full of complaints against fate, "Save it for the proper occasion in the course of prayer."

This preponderance of suffering in the world naturally caused wonderment in previous generations. Largely, it was attributed to the Exile of the Shechinah, the general scheme of incompleteness in the world. All of an individual's personal pain was part of this universal impairment of the world, like the defective moon prayed over by Israel until it becomes full. The incomplete moon was a sign of the crippled world, an omen of what was missing. And the praying Jew had only to recollect that his own and the world's suffering betokened the incompleteness and pain of the Shechinah, and that he could help bring about the restoration of the wholeness by prayer. One's own anguish was a part of the greater anguish of the Shechinah in exile.

Sadness is, thus, only a stage on the way, a passage to joy. Essentially, a person must worship G-d with a "glad and joyful heart." It is even said that much of the suffering of Israel has come because Jews did not worship with gladness. Because when a person worships with gladness, it shows a certain connection, a oneness with G-d. And what is sin, if not separation from G-d? Can any man be judged whether he keeps the mitzvot properly or acts in righteousness for its own sake? This brings to mind a story about a king who had to decide whether the commander of his army, who had just lost an important battle, was a traitor or whether he was inept, a victim of his own error. To help make the decision, he sent another general to do battle with the same foe, and when he returned victorious, the king observed the reactions of the commander who had failed. If he was happy at the victory of his rival, it proved his loyalty to the king; if he showed any sign of unhappiness, he was a traitor at heart and deserved to be dealt with accordingly.

Indeed, if one worships G-d with "gladness and a joyful heart," then, in spite of sin and misfortune, one remains strong in the attachment to the Divine, and it is simple to return to Him. But if one does not worship G-d in this heartfelt, joyful manner, if it is a matter of some agreement or pact with G-d, then to transgress invites endless trouble and tragedy for the soul. It is all the difference between being a son of the house or working for the house as a day laborer.

Sadness then is something to be used with restraint and caution, like those little bottles of medicine labeled "poison." It may become necessary to imbibe a little for the sake of overcoming sickness, but great care has to be exercised in doing so. Only at certain times, and only to restore life, can sadness be useful. There is a sadness, however, that comes when a person feels his inferiority and impotence, which happens often enough with those who are of the category of the Benoni, the intermediate personality between the saint and the sinner. Even then, melancholy has to be controlled, allowed to surface only at specified times, and at other times kept submerged. As the Rabbi of Kotzk is purported to have said: "Everything has its own time. For eating, when one is young. For sleeping, only when a person is in the grave. For sadness—never!"

Thus, it is impossible to conquer one's nature with a sluggish heart. Alacrity, which is derived from joy, is needed.

Rabbi Adin Even-Israel (Steinsaltz), *The Long Shorter Way* (Jerusalem: Koren Publishers, Inc., 1988), pp. 173–177

GREAT PRETENDERS

BY BIRGIT SPINATH, PHD

"That was a really impressive exam. Why don't you write your dissertation on that subject? Let's set up an appointment for you to come by, and we'll talk about it," said the professor to Nina after she completed a test. Unfortunately, the up-and-coming mathematician was unable to take in and enjoy the compliment. Rather her head was full of thoughts such as "What a nice man, and he asked me such easy test questions. That was a close call! Now I've got to make sure not to talk shop with him because then he'll realize that I faked it. He'll see right through me." By the time Nina had finished going through her well-worn mental routine, she realized that there was no way she was going to accept her professor's offer.

In spite of her brilliance on the examination, which required real mastery of the subject, she sees herself as a fraud. Psychologists call this the impostor phenomenon. Those who are afflicted believe that their successes cannot be attributed to their own abilities. Instead they are convinced that other people's praise and recognition of their accomplishments are the result of charm, deception or simple good luck. Interestingly, such thoughts tend to surface in people—such as Nina—whose lives have been an apparently uninterrupted string of successes.

Many people have a tendency to blame external circumstances for their own accomplishments or failures. But those plagued with impostor thinking go well beyond this. They actually view themselves as swindlers who cheat their way into success without in any way having earned it. They live in constant terror of being exposed. Recently researchers have been taking a closer look at the emotional characteristics of people plagued by such ideas. By better understanding how the impostor phenomenon differs from

BIRGIT SPINATH, PHD

Psychologist. Dr. Spinath is a professor at the University of Heidelberg in Germany. Her research interests include teacher education and psychology in educational contexts.

related mental states such as social anxiety, depression and low self-esteem, psychologists are learning how to help people recognize and dispel the troubling thought that they are nothing but phonies.

Feeling like a Phony
The term "impostor phenomenon" was coined in the 1970s by psychologists Pauline Clance and Suzanne Imes, both then at Georgia State University. Clance and Imes noticed that many of their students with excellent test scores and good grades admitted during counseling that they felt they did not belong at the school. Although these students were successful and accomplished, they expressed the idea that they had somehow conned their way into their current positions. They were astutely aware of their weaknesses and tended to overestimate the strengths and abilities of others. In their minds, they always failed to measure up—and they dreaded the day they would make a mistake and reveal to the world the grand illusion.

Clance and Imes described this impostor phenomenon in a 1978 paper, taking care not to call it a "syndrome" or a "disorder," because it is not a debilitating medical condition. Still, such thinking can be persistently troubling for those who suffer from it, and it may even keep some people from fulfilling their potential or finding contentment.

In 1985, after further studying the associated feelings and ideas, Clance developed a questionnaire to help individuals determine if they show an impostor-like pattern of thinking. The test, widely used today by counselors and psychotherapists, covers the three main components of such thinking: feeling like a fake, discounting praise and achievements, and attributing successes to luck. The first component, feeling fake, is the core of impostordom. People feel that they have pulled the wool over everyone's eyes—that they are not really as smart, talented or hardworking as they have convinced everyone they are. The second facet is the inability to acknowledge praise or good performance, which means that even after working hard and achieving a goal, these so-called impostors will ignore the fact of their success and continue to focus on their perceived weaknesses. And finally, when faced with their own conspicuous achievements, sufferers will attribute their good fortune to chance or some other external factor rather than taking credit for it.

This last point deserves further elaboration. Whenever people think about who or what is responsible when something good or bad happens to them, they are practicing attribution—they ascribe the cause to a particular thing. According to psychologist Martin Seligman of the University of Pennsylvania, we all have a certain style of attribution that we tend to use to explain life events. This style of attribution consists of three dimensions: the reasons can lie either within or outside our own person (internal versus external); they may be lasting or transient (stable versus unstable); and they may apply to many situations or uniquely to a single situation (global versus specific).

Attribution style has frequently been associated with emotional health. Emotionally robust people tend to attribute positive events to internal, stable and global factors ("I'm just smart!"); in contrast, with negative occurrences they tend to cite unstable and specific factors ("bad luck this time!"). Depressive people, on the other hand, tend to exhibit the reverse pattern: they make themselves responsible for their failures but attribute their successes to luck.

People who fit the impostor phenomenon profile use this latter style of attribution, which raises an obvious question: Are they simply depressed? In 2002 psychologist Naijean S. Bernard, then at Southern Illinois University, and her co-workers gave Clance's questionnaire to almost 200 students. The researchers found an association between impostor thinking and depression—a finding that has since been confirmed by numerous other studies.

But depression cannot entirely account for the impostor phenomenon—and neither can other related mental states. In 2001 psychologist Scott Ross of De-Pauw University found that people afflicted with the impostor phenomenon are in general more apt than others to feel ashamed for one reason or another. This tendency is coupled with a general increase in fearfulness, as psychologists Shamala Kumar and Carolyn Jagacinski found in 2006 after interviewing more than 130 students at Purdue University.

Fear and shame go hand in hand with disorders and traits such as social anxiety, neuroticism and low self-esteem, and many research groups have explored the relations between these feelings and impostordom. By administering Clance's questionnaire to various groups of people alongside rigorous tests for social anxiety, neuroticism, low self-esteem and other related mental states, these researchers have determined that the impostor phenomenon seems to be a truly distinct experience. As expected, high scores on Clance's test correlate with higher-than-normal scores on the surveys for social anxiety and low self-esteem—but no combination of these other psychological states can accurately identify people who report feeling like frauds or adequately describe their specific fear of having fooled the world.

A Female Affliction?

When Clance and Imes first described the impostor phenomenon, they suggested that women might be particularly susceptible to this type of thinking. But the data on gender differences remain inconclusive. Some studies have borne out the idea that women are especially vulnerable to ideas about being a sham, including research currently being conducted by psychologist Christine Roth of the University of Heidelberg in Germany. Roth has been looking at the distribution of the phenomenon among psychology students. Because psychology is a very competitive subject at the university, most of the students had already been quite successful in their studies—in other words, they met an important criterion for the impostor phenomenon. And in fact, the number of women in the group who reported impostor-related thinking was far larger than the number of women in the group without such feelings.

Some psychologists suggest that the phenomenon could be a possible contributing factor to the low number of women who achieve top positions in their fields. Although girls on average get better grades in school than boys, they may have a greater tendency to feel that those grades are undeserved. A *Journal of General Internal Medicine* study in 2008 of medical residents found that female residents scored higher, on average, on Clance's questionnaire than did male residents. Other studies, however, have shown no gender difference in terms of the frequency or intensity of feeling like a counterfeit. For instance, a different study in 2008, from the *Journal of Physician Assistant Education*, found no gender difference in practicing physicians' assistants' likelihood of experiencing impostor thoughts and feelings.

A possible explanation for these murky results may be that people are more likely to experience impostor feelings at certain points in their lives—and rather than being a stable trait, such thinking waxes and wanes as an individual's situation changes. According to Clance, now professor emerita at Georgia State University, the feeling of having conned everyone seems to appear for the first time at the end of high school or early in a person's college career or professional life—a time at which even those who have become accustomed to success have to meet increased challenges. Those who seemed to sail through school and get good grades without really trying may, according to Clance, have failed to learn how to prepare appropriately for performance situations or to ascribe their success to their own ability.

Self-Sabotage

It may seem impossible that people who have always performed at a high level can fail to believe in their own abilities, but that perspective may get stabilized within a closed thought loop. To ensure that their "failure" is not uncovered in a performance situation, such people may avail themselves of two seemingly opposite strategies: overdoing and underdoing. Overdoing involves disproportionate efforts such as studying and restudying material they have already mastered or obsessively preparing and practicing every detail of a short, routine presentation. This strategy certainly increases the likelihood of success. But it also springs a nasty trap: achievement seems to result not from their intrinsic abilities but from their Herculean preparations. And because they know that they will not always be able to match that effort, it strengthens the fear that their accomplishment may never be duplicated—and that eventually their "true" nature will be found out.

Underdoing looks somewhat different. Given a particular performance situation, a person will, for example, fail to prepare or prepare much too late, doing other, extraneous things instead. In the 1970s social psychologist Edward E. Jones dubbed this behavior "self-handicapping." (For more on self-handicapping as it relates to perfectionism, see "Can You Be Too Perfect?," by Emily Laber-Warren; *Scientific American Mind*, July/August 2009.) When these underdoers perform well, despite putting obstacles in their own way by not studying or preparing, they ascribe their success to luck rather than their own ability. It was just a fluke. Thus, people who have an impostor mind-set who fall into the underdoing trap end up viewing the future as just as uncertain as those who overprepare.

Breaking the Pattern

How can this vicious cycle of impostor thinking be interrupted? Clance, who continues to work with sufferers as a psychotherapist, makes several recommendations. One central approach is to practice appropriate attribution: self-defined impostors must learn to ascribe their successes to their own abilities, to the extent justifiable. Although it is generally appropriate to say "I was successful because I worked hard," the actual hard labor must itself be commensurate with the task at hand. Labor is not commensurate in overdoers, and therefore it is not useful for them to attribute success to the sweat of their efforts. Instead they should acknowledge the intelligence or skill that contributed to their success. And when things go wrong, people should cite factors that can be changed such as too little effort or an incorrect learning strategy.

There are other ways to disrupt impostor thinking and even to keep it from cropping up in the first place. One potential approach is to increase feelings of self-esteem, which simultaneously decreases fear and depression. For example, ponder the various facets of your personality, especially reflecting on your strengths, positive relationships with other people, and competence. Such introspective exercises have been shown to boost self-esteem, confidence and performance.

Research on the impostor phenomenon indicates that our conflicted student Nina is not alone. Some very successful people suffer from the feeling that they are frauds and that their successes are not a result of their own abilities. But as soon as they learn to recognize and appreciate their accomplishments, they will better be able to fulfill their potential, and they will likely find themselves enjoying a greatly renewed sense of personal worth.

Do You Feel like a Fraud?

Everyone occasionally feels self-doubt. But for people who suffer from the impostor phenomenon, the feeling of being a fake is persistent and painful—despite a lifetime of success. To measure levels of impostor thinking, Georgia State University psychologist Pauline Clance developed a questionnaire in 1985 that is still the most widely used tool for impostor evaluation today. Here are some of the items on the 20-question test (available in full at www.paulineroseclance.com):

- I can give the impression that I'm more competent than I really am.
- I sometimes think I obtained my present position or gained my present success because I happened to be in the right place at the right time or knew the right people.
- I'm afraid people important to me may find out that I am not as capable as they think I am.
- I often compare my ability to those around me and think they may be more intelligent than I am.
- At times, I feel my success has been due to some kind of luck.
- I avoid evaluations if possible and have a dread of others evaluating me.
- When people praise me for something I've accomplished, I'm afraid I won't be able to live up to their expectations of me in the future.

Real Cheats

The impostor phenomenon is defined as the mistaken feeling that one's successes are unearned and that at any moment the charade could end. The emphasis is on "mistaken"—these people are not really frauds.

Or are they? Psychologist Joseph R. Ferrari of DePaul University asked this question in 2005. He studied how often self-defined impostors engaged in plagiarism and other types of dishonest behavior. His results supported the original idea that the fraudulence is all in their head: the supposed impostors reported on a survey that they cheated less often than control subjects who did not have impostor feelings.

Some people who score high on tests of impostor thinking may be engaged in a different kind of deception, however—albeit a more benign one. According to a 2007 study by Rory O. McElwee and Tricia Yurak of Rowan University in Glassboro, N.J., some people may adopt an impostorlike stance as a way of appearing humble or of lowering others' expectations so that their accomplishments seem more noteworthy. The psychologists built on a 2000 study from Wake Forest University in which self-styled impostors told researchers they expected to do poorly on a test, but those low expectations disappeared when they were in private. McElwee and Yurak gave 253 students a battery of tests and found that impostor thinking looked a lot like a self-presentation strategy, rather than a character trait. Under scrutiny, the researchers conclude, we all tend to doubt our abilities and discount our strengths.

Scientific American Mind, March/April 2011, pp. 33–37

Lesson

2

EMBRACING FLAWS
ADDRESSING SHAME, FRUSTRATION, AND FEELINGS OF INADEQUACY

States of Mind: Those Who Go, Umberto Boccioni, ink on paper, Italy, 1912. (Metropolitan Museum of Art, New York)

Self-disappointment can be debilitating; we long to view ourselves as ethical individuals, but are frustrated at perpetual wrestling with character flaws such as pettiness, greed, thoughtlessness, anger, lack of integrity, or spiritual insensitivity. Reflecting on our flaws produces a destructive sense of shame and inadequacy. This lesson explains the intended role of character flaws in the human condition, and explores methods of maintaining genuine optimism and positivity despite their lingering presence.

TEXT 1

MARTIN V. DAY, "GUILT," IN TIMOTHY R. LEVINE, ED., *ENCYCLOPEDIA OF DECEPTION*
(THOUSAND OAKS, CA: SAGE PUBLICATIONS, 2014), PP. 426–427

The emotion of guilt is a negative feeling that people can experience for a wrongdoing, such as being untruthful or deceptive to others. . . .

Guilt is often confused with shame. People may refer to these emotions incorrectly or interchangeably; however, much evidence suggests that they are distinct. Similar to guilt, shame is an unpleasant feeling, but shame tends to be a more painful experience and is characterized by feeling worthless, exposed, and small. There are not reliable distinctions between the types of situations that can separately evoke guilt or shame, and it is possible to feel a certain level of both emotions after a misdeed or failure. . . .

Guilt and shame can be distinguished by the negative evaluations that individuals make after lying or following some other harmful action. Negatively judging the self by focusing on what "I" did wrong can elicit shame, whereas negatively judging the wrongful behavior by focusing on what I "did" wrong can evoke guilt. Thus, it is perhaps easier to understand why guilt may feel less painful than shame, because guilt stems from a greater focus on a temporary act as "terrible" rather than a global evaluation of the self as a "terrible person."

MARTIN V. DAY, PHD

Assistant professor of psychology at Memorial University (Newfoundland, Canada). Dr. Day was previously a postdoctoral college fellow in the psychology department at Harvard University. His primary research interests include social psychology and societal cognition.

*If we are good people, why do we have unkind thoughts? What is the cause of inner conflict? A lecture by **Mrs. Menucha Schochet**:*

MYJLI.COM/WARRIOR

Figure 2.1

Shame vs. Guilt

SHAME	GUILT
"I can't believe I binged again. What a weak idiot I am."	"I binged again. That is so harmful to my well-being."
"I'm such a bad parent. I can't control my kids."	"I'm having difficulty controlling my kids. I need to do a better job."
"I should really visit my mother more often. I'm really a bad daughter."	"I have not been visiting my mother as often as I should. That's not okay; she deserves better."
"I promised not to get angry anymore. But I did. I must be crazy."	"I promised not to get angry anymore. But I did. I feel terrible about the damage that my outbursts are causing."
"There is no excuse for coming home drunk again. I'm just a rotten person."	"I feel awful. Once again I came home drunk. This behavior is unacceptable."

QUESTION FOR DISCUSSION

Everything has purpose and meaning; so, what is the point of character struggles?

TEXT 2

TALMUD, YOMA 38B

> רָאָה הַקָּדוֹשׁ בָּרוּךְ הוּא שֶׁצַּדִּיקִים מוּעָטִין, עָמַד וּשְׁתָלָן בְּכָל דּוֹר וָדוֹר . . .
> שֶׁנֶּאֱמַר, "וְצַדִּיק יְסוֹד עוֹלָם" (מִשְׁלֵי י, כה).

G-d saw that the righteous are few in number, so He planted them in every generation . . . as it is written, "The *tsadik* is the foundation of the world" (PROVERBS 10:25).

BABYLONIAN TALMUD

A literary work of monumental proportions that draws upon the legal, spiritual, intellectual, ethical, and historical traditions of Judaism. The 37 tractates of the Babylonian Talmud contain the teachings of the Jewish sages from the period after the destruction of the 2nd Temple through the 5th century CE. It has served as the primary vehicle for the transmission of the Oral Law and the education of Jews over the centuries; it is the entry point for all subsequent legal, ethical, and theological Jewish scholarship.

TEXT 3

RABBI SHNE'UR ZALMAN OF LIADI, *TANYA*, CH. 14

וְהִנֵּה, מִדַּת הַבֵּינוֹנִי הִיא מִדַּת כָּל אָדָם, וְאַחֲרֶיהָ כָּל אָדָם יִמְשֹׁךְ. שֶׁכָּל אָדָם יָכוֹל לִהְיוֹת בֵּינוֹנִי בְּכָל עֵת וּבְכָל שָׁעָה. כִּי הַבֵּינוֹנִי אֵינוֹ מוֹאֵס בָּרַע, שֶׁזֶּהוּ דָּבָר הַמָּסוּר לַלֵּב, וְלֹא כָּל הָעִתִּים שָׁווֹת. אֶלָּא "סוּר מֵרַע וַעֲשֵׂה טוֹב" (תְּהִלִּים לד, טו), דְּהַיְינוּ בְּפוֹעֵל מַמָּשׁ בְּמַעֲשֶׂה דִּבּוּר וּמַחֲשָׁבָה, שֶׁבָּהֶם הַבְּחִירָה וְהַיְכֹלֶת וְהָרְשׁוּת נְתוּנָה לְכָל אָדָם לַעֲשׂוֹת וּלְדַבֵּר וְלַחְשׁוֹב גַּם מַה שֶׁהוּא נֶגֶד תַּאֲוַת לִבּוֹ וְהֶפְכָּהּ מַמָּשׁ . . .

מַה שֶׁאֵין כֵּן בְּדָבָר הַמָּסוּר לַלֵּב, דְּהַיְינוּ שֶׁיְּהֵא הָרַע מָאוּס מַמָּשׁ בַּלֵּב וְשָׂנאוּי בְּתַכְלִית שִׂנְאָה, אוֹ אֲפִילוּ שֶׁלֹּא בְּתַכְלִית שִׂנְאָה, הִנֵּה זֶה אִי אֶפְשָׁר שֶׁיִּהְיֶה בֶּאֱמֶת לַאֲמִיתוֹ אֶלָּא עַל יְדֵי גֹדֶל וְתֹקֶף הָאַהֲבָה לַה' בִּבְחִינַת אַהֲבָה בְּתַעֲנוּגִים לְהִתְעַנֵּג עַל ה' מֵעֵין עוֹלָם הַבָּא. וְעַל זֶה אָמְרוּ רַבּוֹתֵינוּ זִכְרוֹנָם לִבְרָכָה: "עוֹלָמְךָ תִּרְאֶה בְּחַיֶּיךָ" (בְּרָכוֹת יז, א) כו'. וְאֵין כָּל אָדָם זוֹכֶה לָזֶה.

RABBI SHNE'UR ZALMAN OF LIADI (ALTER REBBE) 1745–1812

Chasidic rebbe, halachic authority, and founder of the Chabad movement. The Alter Rebbe was born in Liozna, Belarus, and was among the principal students of the Magid of Mezeritch. His numerous works include the *Tanya*, an early classic containing the fundamentals of Chabad Chasidism, and *Shulchan Aruch HaRav*, an expanded and reworked code of Jewish law.

The status of *beinoni* is [attainable] for all people; achieving this status ought to be every person's goal. At any time, any person can be a *beinoni* because the *beinoni* does not have an aversion for the unholy. [To have an aversion for the unholy is not practical for all people because] that is a feeling [that we cannot necessarily control], and not all times are alike. [The *beinoni's* task is] only to "turn away from evil and do good" (PSALMS 34:15) in actual practice—in deed, speech, and thought. In these areas, the choice, ability, and freedom are given to every person to act, speak, and think in ways that are contrary to the desire of the heart and even diametrically opposed to it. . . .

Rabbi Yitzchok Schochet on the significance of the fact that Tanya is addressed to the beinoni:

MYJLI.COM/WARRIOR

To change one's feelings, on the other hand, namely, to truly detest the unholy—absolutely or even less than that—this is only possible when one has a great and intense love of G-d, the kind of ecstatic love and divine bliss that is similar to the pleasure experienced in the World to Come. Of this experience the sages said, "You will experience your World [to Come] in your lifetime. . . ." (TALMUD, BERACHOT 17A), but not every person merits this.

What is the function of the "perfect person," the one who doesn't struggle? Rabbi Simon Jacobson replies:

MYJLI.COM/WARRIOR

The Praying Jew,
Marc Chagall,
oil on canvas, 1914.
(Art Institute of Chicago,)

Figure 2.2

Two Soul Types

TYPE A	TYPE B
Tsadik	*Beinoni*
Perfect, flawless	Struggler, internally flawed
A gift from G-d to select individuals	The lot of the overwhelming majority of us

Exercise 2.1

Realistically, to which degree are the following scenarios likely to frustrate you?

SCALE KEY
1 = very frustrated
2 = somewhat frustrated
3 = not at all frustrated

TRANSPORTATION	SCALE
Your car breaks down and you need to get around via Uber.	1 2 3
You can't afford the car of your choice.	1 2 3
You can't afford the luxury car of your choice.	1 2 3
You can't afford a private jet.	1 2 3
You haven't yet sprouted wings.	1 2 3

HOUSING	SCALE
You are homeless.	1 2 3
You can't afford an apartment or home that meets your needs.	1 2 3
You can't afford to buy, only to rent.	1 2 3
You can't afford to buy the luxurious home you wish.	1 2 3
You can't afford to purchase Buckingham Palace.	1 2 3

LEISURE	SCALE
You're an avid amateur golfer. The local golf club shut down. There's nowhere local for you to play.	1 2 3
The only local golf course is not as nice as you'd like.	1 2 3
You can't beat your buddies in golf.	1 2 3
You can't shoot a five under par.	1 2 3
You did not win a PGA tournament.	1 2 3

QUESTION FOR DISCUSSION

Looking at your responses to the exercise, can you infer any conclusions about the root of frustration?

TEXT 4

RABBI AVRAHAM IBN EZRA, EXODUS 20:14

"לֹא תַחְמֹד" (שְׁמוֹת כ, יד).

אֲנָשִׁים רַבִּים יִתְמְהוּ עַל זֹאת הַמִּצְוָה: אֵיךְ יִהְיֶה אָדָם שֶׁלֹּא יַחְמֹד דָּבָר
יָפֶה בְּלִבּוֹ כָּל מַה שֶּׁהוּא נֶחְמָד לְמַרְאֶה עֵינָיו? וְעַתָּה אֶתֵּן לְךָ מָשָׁל: דַּע, כִּי
אִישׁ כַּפְרִי שֶׁיֵּשׁ לוֹ דַעַת נְכוֹנָה וְהוּא רָאָה בַּת מֶלֶךְ שֶׁהִיא יָפָה, לֹא יַחְמֹד
אוֹתָהּ בְּלִבּוֹ שֶׁיִּשְׁכַּב עִמָּהּ, כִּי יֵדַע כִּי זֶה לֹא יִתָּכֵן. וְאַל תַּחְשׁוֹב זֶה הַכַּפְרִי
שֶׁהוּא כְּאֶחָד מִן הַמְשֻׁגָּעִים שֶׁיִּתְאַוֶּה שֶׁיִּהְיוּ לוֹ כְּנָפַיִם לָעוּף הַשָּׁמַיִם...
וְאַחַר שֶׁיֵּדַע שֶׁאֵשֶׁת רֵעֵהוּ אָסְרָה הַשֵּׁם לוֹ, יוֹתֵר הִיא נִשְׂגָּבָה בְּעֵינָיו מִבַּת
מֶלֶךְ בְּלֵב הַכַּפְרִי. עַל כֵּן הוּא יִשְׂמַח בְּחֶלְקוֹ וְלֹא יָשִׂים אֶל לִבּוֹ לַחְמוֹד
וּלְהִתְאַוּוֹת דָּבָר שֶׁאֵינוֹ שֶׁלּוֹ.

RABBI AVRAHAM IBN EZRA
1092–1167

Biblical commentator, linguist, and poet. Ibn Ezra was born in Toledo, Spain, and fled the Almohad regime to other parts of Europe. It is believed that he was living in London at the time of his death. Ibn Ezra is best known for his literalistic commentary on the Pentateuch. He also wrote works of poetry, philosophy, medicine, astronomy, and other topics.

"You shall not covet [your neighbor's house. You shall not covet your neighbor's wife, servant . . . or whatever belongs to your neighbor]" (EXODUS 20:14).

Many people wonder about this commandment: How is a man not to covet in his heart that which is beautiful and that which he finds desirable? I will give you a parable [to explain this]. If a common villager of sane mind sees the king's daughter, he will not covet her although she is beautiful. Because he knows that this is impossible. This villager will not think like a lunatic who desires to have wings to fly in the sky. . . .

This verse tells us that we need to understand that the wife of a neighbor, whom G-d has forbidden us, is more removed from us than is the princess from the villager. If we have this frame of mind, we will be happy with our lot, and it will not enter our mind to covet and desire something that is not ours.

Woman with a Mirror, Fernand Leger, oil on canvas, 1920. (Paris Museum of Modern Art)

TEXT 5

TANYA, CH. 27 ⊕

וְאַדְּרַבָּה, הָעַצְבוּת הִיא מִגַּסוּת הָרוּחַ, שֶׁאֵינוֹ מַכִּיר מְקוֹמוֹ, וְעַל כֵּן יֵרַע
לִבָבוֹ עַל שֶׁאֵינוֹ בְּמַדְרֵגַת צַדִּיק, שֶׁלְּצַדִּיקִים בְּוַדַּאי אֵין נוֹפְלִים לָהֶם
הִרְהוּרֵי שְׁטוּת כָּאֵלּוּ.

כִּי אִילוּ הָיָה מַכִּיר מְקוֹמוֹ, שֶׁהוּא רָחוֹק מְאֹד מִמַּדְרֵגַת צַדִּיק, וְהַלְוַאי הָיָה
בֵּינוֹנִי וְלֹא רָשָׁע כָּל יָמָיו אֲפִלּוּ שָׁעָה אַחַת, הֲרֵי זֹאת הִיא מִדַּת הַבֵּינוֹנִים
וַעֲבוֹדָתָם, לִכְבּוֹשׁ הַיֵּצֶר.

To the contrary! Despondency [over your spiritual struggles] stems from an inflated self-assessment, from not recognizing your place. This delusion leads you to feel badly that you are not on the level of the perfect person, who is certainly not bothered by such foolish thoughts.

Know your place. You are very far from the level of the perfect person [and perfection ought not to be your goal]. Rather, you should aspire to always be a *beinoni* and never for a moment to fail [in thought, speech, and action]. And this, after all, is the lot of the *beinoni* and their task in life: to [struggle against and] subdue their negative impulses.

QUESTION FOR DISCUSSION

Is the conclusion we reached sufficient to resolve the frustration that results from internal struggles?

TEXT 6

TANYA, IBID.

וְלָכֵן אַל יִפֹּל לֵב אָדָם עָלָיו, וְלֹא יֵרַע לְבָבוֹ מְאֹד גַּם אִם יִהְיֶה כֵּן כָּל יָמָיו בְּמִלְחָמָה זוֹ, כִּי אוּלַי לְכָךְ נִבְרָא וְזֹאת עֲבוֹדָתוֹ, לְאַכְפְיָא לְסִטְרָא אַחֲרָא תָּמִיד . . .

וּשְׁנֵי מִינֵי נַחַת רוּחַ לְפָנָיו יִתְבָּרֵךְ לְמַעְלָה: אֶחָד, מִבִּיטּוּל הַסִּטְרָא אַחֲרָא לְגַמְרֵי וְאִתְהַפְּכָא מִמְּרִירוּ לְמִתְקָא וּמֵחֲשׁוֹכָא לִנְהוֹרָא עַל יְדֵי הַצַּדִּיקִים. וְהַשֵּׁנִית, כַּד אִתְכַּפְיָא הַסִּטְרָא אַחֲרָא בְּעוֹדָהּ בְּתָקְפָּהּ וּגְבוּרָתָהּ . . . עַל יְדֵי הַבֵּינוֹנִים.

וְזֶהוּ שֶׁאָמַר הַכָּתוּב, "וַעֲשֵׂה לִי מַטְעַמִּים כַּאֲשֶׁר אָהַבְתִּי" (בְּרֵאשִׁית כז, ד). מַטְעַמִּים לָשׁוֹן רַבִּים, שְׁנֵי מִינֵי נַחַת רוּחַ. וְהוּא מַאֲמַר הַשְּׁכִינָה לְבָנֶיהָ כְּלָלוּת יִשְׂרָאֵל, כְּדְפֵּרְשׁוּ בְּתִקּוּנִים.

וּכְמוֹ שֶׁבְּמַטְעַמִּים גַּשְׁמִיִּים, דֶּרֶךְ מָשָׁל, יֵשׁ שְׁנֵי מִינֵי מַעֲדַנִּים: אֶחָד מִמַּאֲכָלִים עֲרֵבִים וּמְתוּקִים, וְהַשֵּׁנִי מִדְּבָרִים חֲרִיפִים אוֹ חֲמוּצִים, רַק שֶׁהֵם מְתוּבָּלִים וּמְתוּקָּנִים הֵיטֵב, עַד שֶׁנַּעֲשׂוּ מַעֲדַנִּים לְהָשִׁיב הַנֶּפֶשׁ.

Do not feel distressed or exceedingly troubled even if you are engaged in this conflict all your life, for perhaps this is the reason why you were created and this is your calling—to constantly subdue the [thoughts and feelings that emanate from] unholiness. . . .

There are two kinds of enjoyment for G-d. One is from the complete annihilation of unholiness. This is accomplished by perfect people, who transform [their internal] bitterness to sweetness and darkness to light. The second is from the subduing of unholiness while it is at the apex of its strength . . . through the effort of strugglers.

This is alluded to in the verse, "Make me delicacies as I enjoy" (GENESIS 27:4). [Although this verse, in its simple sense, describes Isaac's instruction to Esau,] the *Zohar* explains that [this conversation reflects a deeper reality, and] these are words spoken by the Divine Presence to her children, the community of Israel. The word *delicacies*, in plural form, indicates the [aforementioned] two types of enjoyment.

In physical food, there are two varieties of delicacies: pleasant and sweet foods, and savory or tart foods that have been well seasoned and prepared so that they have become delicacies that refresh the soul.

TEXT 7

THE REBBE, RABBI MENACHEM MENDEL SCHNEERSON,
TORAT MENACHEM 5715:1 (13), PP. 9–10 🕎

"וְלֵב מְלָכִים אֵין חֵקֶר" (מִשְׁלֵי כה, ג), וְכַאֲשֶׁר רוֹצִים לְבַקְּשׁוֹ דָּבָר, הֲרֵי
כָּל הָעִנְיָנִים הֵם בְּאֵין עֲרֹךְ אֵלָיו. אָמְנָם עַל יְדֵי שֶׁמְּבִיאִים לְפָנָיו דְּבַר
חִידּוּשׁ, וּכְמוֹ צִפּוֹר הַמְדַבֶּרֶת, הִנֵּה בָּזֶה דַּוְקָא מְעוֹרְרִים אֶת הַמֶּלֶךְ.
וְהַיְינוּ, דְּעִם הֱיוֹת שֶׁדִּיבּוּר הַצִּפּוֹר אֵינוֹ בְּעֶרֶךְ כְּלָל לְדִיבּוּר הָאָדָם, דְּדִיבּוּר
הָאָדָם שֶׁמְּדַבֵּר בְּדֵיעָה וְהַשְׂכֵּל, מַה שֶּׁאֵין כֵּן הַצִּפּוֹר גַּם כְּשֶׁתְּדַבֵּר הֲרֵי זֶה
רַק מַה שֶּׁלִּמְּדוּהָ לְדַבֵּר (אַ אוֹיסְגֶעלֶערְנְטֶער), וְגַם חִיתּוּךְ הַדִּיבּוּר אֵינוֹ
כְּמוֹ בְּהָאָדָם, מִכָּל מָקוֹם, לִהְיוֹתוֹ דְּבַר חִידּוּשׁ, הֲרֵי בָּזֶה דַּוְקָא מְעוֹרְרִים
אֶת הַמֶּלֶךְ.

וּכְמוֹ כֵן יוּבַן בְּעִנְיַן הַמְּלוּכָה לְמַעֲלָה... הַכַּוָּונָה הִיא בַּנְּשָׁמוֹת שֶׁנִּמְצָאִים
לְמַטָּה וְלֹא בְּמַלְאָכִים. דְּאַף שֶׁגַּם בְּמַלְאָכִים יֵשׁ אַהֲבָה וְיִרְאָה וִידִיעָה
בֶּאֱלֹקוּת, וְלֹא עוֹד אֶלָּא שֶׁעֲבוֹדַת הַנְּשָׁמוֹת לְמַטָּה אֵינָה בְּעֶרֶךְ כְּלָל
לַעֲבוֹדַת הַמַּלְאָכִים, דִּלְבַד זֹאת שֶׁעֲבוֹדַת הַנְּשָׁמוֹת בָּאָה בִּיגִיעָה גְדוֹלָה,
הִנֵּה גַם לְאַחֲרֵי הַיְגִיעָה אֵין זֶה בְּעֶרֶךְ לַעֲבוֹדַת הַמַּלְאָכִים. מִכָּל מָקוֹם
עֲבוֹדַת הַמַּלְאָכִים אֵינָה דְּבַר חִידּוּשׁ, לְפִי שֶׁאֵינָם נִמְצָאִים בְּמָקוֹם
הָרָע... וְרַק עֲבוֹדַת הַנְּשָׁמוֹת לְמַטָּה דַּוְקָא, שֶׁנִּמְצָאִים בְּמָקוֹם הָרָע וְעוֹד
זֹאת שֶׁיֵּשׁ לָהֶם יֵצֶר הָרָע הַמֵּסִית וּמֵדִיחַ, הִנֵּה עֲבוֹדָתָם הִיא דְּבַר חִידּוּשׁ.

RABBI MENACHEM MENDEL SCHNEERSON
1902–1994

The towering Jewish leader of
the 20th century, known as "the
Lubavitcher Rebbe," or simply as "the
Rebbe." Born in southern Ukraine,
the Rebbe escaped Nazi-occupied
Europe, arriving in the U.S. in June
1941. The Rebbe inspired and guided
the revival of traditional Judaism
after the European devastation,
impacting virtually every Jewish
community the world over. The
Rebbe often emphasized that the
performance of just one additional
good deed could usher in the era
of Mashiach. The Rebbe's scholarly
talks and writings have been printed
in more than 200 volumes.

"The hearts of kings are unfathomable" (PROVERBS 25:3). [This poses a difficulty] when one wishes to [capture a king's attention with an impressive gift in order to then] request something from him. After all, [even valuable] gifts are of no consequence to the king. However, when we bring him something surprisingly original, such as a talking bird—this is precisely the kind of gift that impresses the king. Granted, a bird's speech is infinitely inferior to human speech, for a person speaks with intelligence and wisdom, whereas a talking bird merely repeats the sound of words as it has been trained [without true comprehension], and even then, its enunciation is inferior to that of a human. Nevertheless, because it is [a delightfully] original [phenomenon], it impresses the king favorably.

A similar dynamic plays out before the King of the universe . . . whereby G-d's ultimate purpose [for creation] involves souls in this material world, not angels: It is true that angels have love and awe for G-d, and a profound understanding of the Divine, whereas the service performed by souls in this world cannot compare to the angels' service. [Unlike the angels,] our service requires tremendous effort and exertion, and after all that effort, our work still cannot compare to that of angels. Nevertheless, the angels' service offers nothing surprising, for they do not inhabit a world of unholiness. . . . By contrast, the service performed by souls down here emerges from a background of unholiness and, even then, only after overcoming an evil inclination that entices and tempts a person. G-d views such service as a [delightful] novelty.

TEXT 8

TANYA, CH. 27 ⚏

זֹאת הִיא מִדַּת הַבֵּינוֹנִים וַעֲבוֹדָתָם: לִכְבּוֹשׁ הַיֵּצֶר וְהַהִרְהוּר הָעוֹלֶה מֵהַלֵּב לַמּוֹחַ, וּלְהָסִיחַ דַּעְתּוֹ לְגַמְרֵי מִמֶּנּוּ וְלִדְחוֹתוֹ בִּשְׁתֵּי יָדַיִם, כַּנִּזְכָּר לְעֵיל.

וּבְכָל דְּחִיָּה וּדְחִיָּה שֶׁמַּדְחֵהוּ מִמַּחֲשַׁבְתּוֹ, אִתְכַּפְיָא סִטְרָא אַחֲרָא לְתַתָּא, וּבְאִתְעֲרוּתָא דְלְתַתָּא אִתְעֲרוּתָא דִלְעֵילָא, וְאִתְכַּפְיָא סִטְרָא אַחֲרָא דִלְעֵילָא . . .

וּכְמוֹ שֶׁהִפְלִיג בְּזֹהַר פָּרָשַׁת תְּרוּמָה [דַּף קכח] בְּגוֹדֶל נַחַת רוּחַ לְפָנָיו יִתְבָּרֵךְ כַּד אִתְכַּפְיָא סִטְרָא אַחֲרָא לְתַתָּא, דְּאִסְתַּלֵּק יְקָרָא דְקֻדְשָׁא בְּרִיךְ הוּא לְעֵילָא עַל כּוֹלָא, יַתִּיר מִשְּׁבָחָא אַחֲרָא, וְאִסְתַּלְּקוּתָא דָא יַתִּיר מִכּוֹלָּא.

The lot of strugglers and their task in life is to subdue their negative impulses and the thoughts that these impulses spawn—to completely divert their minds from such thoughts and utterly reject them, as has been explained earlier.

Every time strugglers expel a negative thought from the mind, the force of unholiness below is suppressed. Because a "stimulus from below causes a stimulus from above," the cosmic forces of unholiness are also suppressed. . . .

The *Zohar* (PARSHAT TERUMAH, P. 128) marvels at the tremendous pleasure that G-d derives from the suppression of unholiness below. This causes "G-d's glory to rise above all, an unparalleled ascent, a feat not accomplishable through any other praise."

TEXT **9a**

TALMUD, SHABBAT 88B

בְּשָׁעָה שֶׁעָלָה מֹשֶׁה לַמָּרוֹם, אָמְרוּ מַלְאֲכֵי הַשָּׁרֵת לִפְנֵי הַקָּדוֹשׁ בָּרוּךְ הוּא: "רִבּוֹנוֹ שֶׁל עוֹלָם! מַה לִּילוּד אִשָּׁה בֵּינֵינוּ?"

אָמַר לָהֶן, "לְקַבֵּל תּוֹרָה בָּא".

אָמְרוּ לְפָנָיו, "חֲמוּדָה גְּנוּזָה שֶׁגְּנוּזָה לְךָ . . . אַתָּה מְבַקֵּשׁ לִיתְּנָהּ לְבָשָׂר וָדָם? 'מָה אֱנוֹשׁ כִּי תִזְכְּרֶנּוּ וּבֶן אָדָם כִּי תִפְקְדֶנּוּ' (תְּהִלִּים ח, ה). 'ה' אֲדֹנֵינוּ מָה אַדִּיר שִׁמְךָ בְּכָל הָאָרֶץ אֲשֶׁר תְּנָה הוֹדְךָ עַל הַשָּׁמָיִם' (שָׁם, ב)".

אָמַר לוֹ הַקָּדוֹשׁ בָּרוּךְ הוּא לְמֹשֶׁה: "הַחֲזֵיר לָהֶן תְּשׁוּבָה".

When Moses ascended on high [to receive the Torah], the ministering angels spoke before G-d: "Master of the Universe! What business does a mortal being have among us?"

"He has come to receive the Torah," G-d answered.

The angels said to G-d, "The hidden treasure that has been hidden with You . . . You wish to give to flesh and blood? 'What is man that You should consider him?' (PSALMS 8:10). 'O G-d, our Master! How exalted is Your name throughout the Earth! Your glory should remain upon the Heavens!' (IBID. 8:5)"

"Answer them," G-d said to Moses.

TEXT **9b**

TALMUD, SHABBAT, 88B–89A

אָמַר לְפָנָיו: "רִבּוֹנוֹ שֶׁל עוֹלָם, תּוֹרָה שֶׁאַתָּה נוֹתֵן לִי מַה כְּתִיב בָּהּ . . . 'לֹא תִרְצַח, לֹא תִנְאָף, לֹא תִגְנֹב' (שְׁמוֹת כ, יג). קִנְאָה יֵשׁ בֵּינֵיכֶם, יֵצֶר הָרָע יֵשׁ בֵּינֵיכֶם?"

מִיָּד הוֹדוּ לוֹ לְהַקָּדוֹשׁ בָּרוּךְ הוּא.

Moses said, "Master of the Universe! What is written in the Torah that You wish to give to me? . . . 'You shall not murder. You shall not commit adultery. You shall not steal' (EXODUS 20:13)."

[Turning to the angels, Moses said,] "Is there jealousy among you? Is the evil inclination among you?"

The angels immediately conceded.

Am Felde (In the Fields), Emil Orlik, etching on paper, 1897. (The Jewish Museum, New York)

TEXT 10

SIFRA, LEVITICUS 20:26

לֹא יֹאמַר אָדָם: "אִי אֶפְשִׁי לִלְבּוֹשׁ שַׁעַטְנֵז. אִי אֶפְשִׁי לֶאֱכוֹל בְּשַׂר חֲזִיר. אִי אֶפְשִׁי לָבוֹא עַל הָעֶרְוָה".

אֲבָל: "אֶפְשִׁי. וּמָה אֶעֱשֶׂה וְאָבִי שֶׁבַּשָּׁמַיִם גָּזַר עָלַי כָּךְ?"

SIFRA
(TORAT KOHANIM)

An ancient rabbinic exegesis on the Book of Leviticus. The subject matter of this work is predominately Temple-era-related laws inasmuch as much of the Book of Leviticus focuses on the Temple service. According to Maimonides, the compiler and editor of this work was the Talmudic sage Rav (175–247 CE). Others attribute it to an earlier redactor. The work is quoted often in the Talmud.

Do not say: "I cannot tolerate wearing a garment made of *shaatnez* [a biblically forbidden mixture of wool and linen]. I find the meat of the swine repulsive. I have no desire for illicit sexual relations."

Instead, say: "I can and would. What shall I do, however? My Father in Heaven has instructed me not to!"

Figure 2.3

Benefits of Divine-Soul Model

AREA	RATIONALE
Negative emotion that results from feeling inauthentic	Every selfless deed is a 100 percent authentic expression of the divine soul.
Shame, feelings of inadequacy, and frustration that result from our internal struggles	These negative emotions are negated by understanding that character flaws are a gift and our struggles are our purpose in life.

Exercise 2.2

In what area of your life can you adopt a divine-soul perspective and thereby reduce feelings of shame, inadequacy, and frustration?

TEXT 11

TANYA, CH. 27 🗣

דְּאִתְכַּפְיָא סִטְרָא אַחֲרָא לְתַתָּא, אִסְתַּלֵּק יְקָרָא דְּקֻדְשָׁא בְּרִיךְ הוּא וּקְדוּשָׁתוֹ לְעֵילָא הַרְבֵּה. וּמִקְּדוּשָׁה זוֹ נִמְשֶׁכֶת קְדוּשָׁה עֶלְיוֹנָה עַל הָאָדָם לְמַטָּה, לְסַיְּיעוֹ סִיּוּעַ רַב וְעָצוּם לַעֲבוֹדָתוֹ יִתְבָּרַךְ.

וְזֶהוּ שֶׁאָמְרוּ רַבּוֹתֵינוּ זִכְרוֹנָם לִבְרָכָה: "אָדָם מְקַדֵּשׁ עַצְמוֹ מְעַט לְמַטָּה, מְקַדְּשִׁין אוֹתוֹ הַרְבֵּה מִלְמַעְלָה" (יוֹמָא לט, א) . . . אַף שֶׁבֶּאֱמֶת אֵינוֹ קָדוֹשׁ וּמוּבְדָּל מִסִּטְרָא אַחֲרָא, כִּי הִיא בְּתָקְפָּהּ וּגְבוּרָתָהּ כְּתוֹלַדְתָּהּ בֶּחָלָל הַשְּׂמָאלִי, רַק שֶׁכּוֹבֵשׁ יִצְרוֹ וּמְקַדֵּשׁ עַצְמוֹ . . . סוֹפוֹ לִהְיוֹת קָדוֹשׁ וּמוּבְדָּל בֶּאֱמֶת מֵהַסִּטְרָא אַחֲרָא, עַל יְדֵי שֶׁמְּקַדְּשִׁים אוֹתוֹ הַרְבֵּה מִלְמַעְלָה וּמְסַיְּיעִים אוֹתוֹ לְגָרְשָׁהּ מִלִּבּוֹ מְעַט מְעַט.

When we subdue unholiness below, we cause a great revelation of G-d's glory and holiness in the higher worlds. From this holiness issues a sublime holiness on us below to assist and empower us in our service of G-d.

This is what the sages had in mind when they said, "When we sanctify ourselves a little below, we are sanctified much more from above" (TALMUD, YOMA 39A). . . . In truth, we are not holy nor are we removed from the unholiness that is at its full strength in our hearts. Yet, if we subdue our unholiness and act in a holy manner . . . ultimately we will be truly holy and separated from all unholiness. This is due to the holiness we receive from Above, which helps us to gradually expel the unholiness from our hearts.

KEY POINTS

1 Perfect people do exist. Endowed with lofty souls, such people are extremely rare. They are holy, selfless, flawless, and have vanquished their negative impulses and character flaws. The majority of people, however, struggle their entire lives against their character flaws and unhealthy impulses. For most, inner perfection is unattainable.

2 It is typical to feel frustrated by our internal struggles. This frustration is a result of an unreasonable expectation of perfection. We need to come to terms with who we are and always will be and understand that struggling is our mission in life.

3 Common wisdom attributes value to struggle because it is part of a process that leads to a beneficial result. From the Jewish perspective, the struggle *is* the goal!

4 When we struggle against and suppress our internal unholy instincts, we create a cosmic impact: we trigger the suppression of the cosmic forces of unholiness, unleashing a tremendous amount of divine light.

5 G-d enjoys the sweet and pleasant service of the perfect person, but G-d enjoys as much, if not more, the savory, spicy service of the struggler. In fact, G-d derives exquisite *nachas* from the extraordinary work of the struggler. Our flaws are not impediments. They are gifts; they make us valuable and cosmically relevant.

6 This perspective also resolves feelings of shame and inadequacy, which result from seeing character flaws as *liabilities*, instead of *gifts*.

7 Adopting this perspective requires divine-soul-focused and mission-focused living and thinking.

Appendix

TEXT **12**

HELEN B. LEWIS, "SHAME AND GUILT IN NEUROSIS,"
PSYCHOANALYTIC REVIEW, 58:3 (1971), PP. 424–432

The self is an important construct in the psychological dissection of [guilt and shame]. Shame, for instance, involves more self-consciousness and more self-imaging than guilt. In guilt, the self is negatively evaluated in connection with something, but is not itself the focus of the experience. Since the self is the focus of awareness in shame, "identity" imagery may be evoked. . . . In general, then, guilt involves less experience of the self than shame. Shame is about the self; guilt involves activity *of* the self." . . .

In shame, hostility against the self is experienced in the passive mode. The self feels not "in control" but overwhelmed and paralyzed by the hostility directed against it. One could "crawl through a hole," or "sink through the floor" or "die" with shame. The self feels small, helpless and childish. . . .

The objective character of guilt and the affinity between it and rational assignment of responsibility can result in the person's becoming very busy in making amends for his guilt or in an insoluble dilemma of thought about his guilt. The self is active in this pursuit. It is intact and self-propelled, in contrast to the self's divided functioning in shame.

HELEN B. LEWIS, PHD
Psychoanalyst and professor emeritus of psychology at Yale University. Dr. Lewis was the founding editor of the *Psychoanalytic Psychology* journal published by the American Psychological Association. She was the author of *Shame and Guilt in Neurosis*, now a standard text.

Figure 2.4a

Key Similarities between Shame and Guilt[*]

FEATURES SHARED BY SHAME AND GUILT

Both fall into the class of "moral" emotions.

Both are "self-conscious," self-referential emotions.

Both are negatively valenced emotions.

Both are typically experienced in interpersonal contexts.

The negative events that give rise to shame and guilt are highly similar (frequently involving moral failures or transgressions).

---

[*] Tangney, J. P. and Dearing, R. L., *Shame and Guilt* (New York: Guilford Press, 2002), p. 25.

Figure 2.4b

Key Dimensions on Which Shame and Guilt Differ**

	SHAME	GUILT
Focus of evaluation	Global self: "*I* did that horrible thing."	Specific behavior: "I *did* that horrible *thing.*"
Degrees of distress	Generally more painful than guilt	Generally less painful than shame
Phenomenological experience	Shrinking, feeling small, feeling worthless, powerless	Tension, remorse, regret
Operation of "self"	Self "split" into observing and observed "selves"	Unified self intact
Impact on "self"	Self impaired by global devaluation	Self unimpaired by global devaluation
Concern vis-á-vis the "other"	Concern with others' evaluation of self	Concern with one's effect on others
Counterfactual processes	Mentally undoing some aspect of the self	Mentally undoing some aspect of behavior
Motivational features	Desire to hide, escape, or strike back	Desire to confess, apologize, or repair

** Tangney, J. P. and Dearing, R. L., Ibid.

TEXT 13

JUNE PRICE TANGNEY, "SELF-CONSCIOUS EMOTIONS," IN MARK R. LEARY AND JUNE PRICE TANGENY, EDS., *HANDBOOK OF SELF AND IDENTITY* (2ND ED.) (NEW YORK: GUILFORD PRESS, 2012), PP. 449–453

Research shows that shame and guilt lead to contrasting motivations or "action tendencies" (DE HOOGE, ZEELENBERG, & BREUGELMANS, 2007; FERGUSON, ET AL., 1991; KETELAAR & AU, 2003; LEWIS, 1971; LINDSAY-HARTZ, 1984; SHEIKH & JANOFF-BULMAN, 2010; TANGNEY, 1993; TANGNEY, ET AL., 1996; WALLBOTT & SCHERER, 1995; WICKER, ET AL., 1983). In the face of failure or transgression, shame typically leads to attempts to deny, hide or escape the shame-inducing situation; guilt typically leads to reparative action—confessing, apologizing, undoing. For example, when people anonymously describe and rate personal shame and guilt experiences along a number of phenomenological dimensions (TANGNEY, 1993; TANGNEY, MILLER, ET AL., 1996), their ratings indicate that they feel more compelled to hide from others and less inclined to admit what they had done when feeling shame as opposed to guilt. Feelings of guilt motivate people to restore wealth-based equity when resources are distributed unevenly in their favor (GINO & PIERCE, 2009). Even when unconsciously primed, guilt leads people to avoid over-indulgence and to help less fortunate others, especially among those dispositionally prone to guilt (ZEMACK-RUGAR, BETTMAN & FITZSIMMONS, 2007).

JUNE PRICE TANGNEY, PHD

Professor of psychology at George Mason University. A fellow of the Society for Personality and Social Psychology and of the Association for Psychological Science, she is an associate editor of *American Psychologist*. Dr. Tangney's primary research interest is the development and implications of moral emotions.

Taken together, findings across studies suggest that guilt motivates people in a constructive, proactive, future-oriented direction, whereas shame motivates people toward separation, distance, and defense. . . .

But there is a widely held assumption that because shame is so painful, at least it motivates people to avoid "doing wrong," decreasing the likelihood of transgression and impropriety (BARRETT, 1995; FERGUSON & STEGGE, 1995; KAHAN, 1997; ZAHN-WAXLER & ROBINSON, 1995). As it turns out, virtually no direct evidence supports this presumed adaptive function of shame. To the contrary, research suggests that shame may even make things worse.

In a study of college undergraduates, Tibbetts (2003) found that criminal offending was negatively related to guilt-proneness. Results involving shame-proneness were mixed. An overall shame-proneness index, comprising three dispositional measures of shame, was unrelated to illegal behavior, raising questions about the presumed inhibitory function of shame. Similar results were obtained in two prospective studies examining the degree to which shame- and guilt-proneness predict criminal behavior in samples of adolescents. In one study, guilt-proneness assessed in the fifth grade negatively predicted arrests and convictions reported by the participant at age 18. In contrast, shame-proneness predicted neither (TANGNEY & DEARING, 2002). In another community sample of adolescents (STUEWIG & MCCLOSKEY, 2005), proneness to "shame-free" guilt again emerged as a protective factor, negatively predicting delinquency assessed both by juvenile court records and by self-report; proneness to "guilt-free" shame did not.

Additional Readings

MAN AS VERB
THE TRUTH ABOUT THE *TANYA*

BY RABBI TZVI FREEMAN

Once upon a time, every book was about being perfect. Every book told you, "This is how you are supposed to be; now go and be that."

Then Rabbi Schneur Zalman of Liadi (the "*Alter Rebbe*," 1745–1813) wrote a book for "the rest of us." He even called it *Sefer Shel Benonim*—meaning, the book for the average guy. The first Book of Kabalistic Enlightenment for the Everyguy. (We call it *Tanya* because that's the first word in the book.)

As it turns out, for the average guy who wants to get life right there's really only one question. That's the question Rabbi Schneur Zalman poses at the beginning of his book—and then repeats in different forms at frequent intervals. Not surprisingly, that question lies at the core of all the typical maladies of "the rest of us": Guilt, depression, apathy and feelings of inadequacy.

Here's how Rabbi Schneur Zalman presents the question:

Before you were born, the sages taught us, they made you take an oath: "Be righteous. Don't be wicked. Yet, even if the entire world tells you that you are righteous, think of yourself as though you were wicked."

This requires clarification. Didn't we learn in *The Ethics of the Fathers*, "Never consider yourself wicked"?

RABBI TZVI FREEMAN, 1955–

Rabbi, computer scientist, and writer. A published expert, consultant, and lecturer in the field of educational technology, Rabbi Freeman held posts at the University of British Columbia and the Digipen School of Computer Gaming. Rabbi Freeman is the author of *Bringing Heaven Down to Earth* and *Men, Women and Kabbalah*. He is a senior editor at Chabad.org.

Furthermore, if a person considers himself wicked, he will be disheartened and depressed and won't be able to serve G-d with joy. On the other hand, if he does not become at all depressed from this, he could come to treat life as a joke, G-d forbid.

Let's put this in modern language. Instead of righteous and wicked, let's use something that communicates the same ideas, but something closer to our modern psyche:

Here's a wild teaching from the ancient sages: They taught that before you were born, the Heavenly Court made you swear you would be a spiritually enlightened being and never be a failure. Then they told you that "even if the entire world guru-tizes you as the ultimate enlightened being, consider yourself a failure."

They couldn't possibly have meant this. After all, these are the same sages that taught us, "Never consider yourself a failure."

Furthermore, everyone knows that if you go around thinking, "I'm a failure, I'm a failure" you're bound to feel like a worm and it's going to be pretty hard to get up and go to work in the morning. But the Torah tells us you have to serve G-d with joy! How are you going to serve G-d with joy if you think of yourself as a perpetual failure?

Well, you could just decide not to take failure so seriously. You could say, "So I'm a loser. Big deal. I still have to be happy." G-d forbid to live such a life. A person living like that could end up doing anything.

Get the question? I didn't. Until, after some thirty years of studying the book, an old friend of mine who made good as a psychologist, Rabbi Dr. Y. Y. Shagalov, pointed it out to me:

The book addresses the big question: "Why shouldn't I be depressed?"

It's a question endemic to life on earth. It's a tension none of us can escape: knowing what we should be and knowing we will never reach it.

We see our failures every day—and even when we succeed, we still know inside that this is not the real thing. The real thing is in some Garden of Eden where we lived before we were born, but definitely not here. Yet we keep on expecting ourselves to be that perfect being that precedes life on this planet.

So we get tied up in knots over failure. And those knots just make it even harder to get anywhere—so we fail even more. And then they tell us to rejoice in our lot.

What's the answer? The answer is strewn across 53 short but pithy chapters that challenge every common intuition of normal human beings, using standard received wisdom to turn wisdom on its head. But that's okay, because my buddy psychologist turned me on to that, as well. If I were to sum it up in one line, it would have to be as follows:

Stop thinking about who you are and who you are supposed to be and start thinking of what you are supposed to be doing. Not *what am I* but *where am I*. "What am I" is: How do I feel about this? Have I achieved enlightenment yet? Are we there yet? "Where am I" is: What am I doing, speaking and thinking *right now*?

Actually, not to be insulting or anything, but the more you get yourself out of the picture, the better off you're going to be.

Take Rabbi Yochanan ben Zakkai, one of the great teachers of the Talmud. On his deathbed, before his students, he broke into tears. "Why are you crying, our teacher?" they asked.

He replied, "Know my children, that I see before me two paths upon which they take those who leave this world. One is to eternal reward and one is not so good. And I do not know on which path they will take me!"

Come on, Rabbi Yochanan! Until now you never thought about this?

No, he didn't. He never had time. All his life, Rabbi Yochanan was only thinking, "What is the best thing for me to invest myself into right now?" Only at his final moments did he take time to think into, "So where am I? What will be with me?"

That's something Rabbi Schneur Zalman once advised someone. It was a businessman—who was also a scholar and a chassid. He was bemoaning his financial losses, which did not allow him to pay his debts or fulfill his commitments to his family. "All I ask is that G-d provide me with the means to be upright and discharge my obligations to others!" he cried.

To which was responded, "I'm hearing a lot about what you need. Can we hear something about why you are needed?"

Who needs you? The world needs you. Otherwise you wouldn't have been put here. That's what all these challenges of life are about—they are the world beckoning you, "Take me on! Change me! Transform me!" You're here on a mission—not to be Superman or Wonderwoman—or even Super Soul—you're here on a mission impossible to wrestle in the dirt with the real world, from inside a very limiting body, with a frail human personality—in order to transform all those things into something Divine.

Sure you're going to fall flat on your face once in a while. The ultimate goal is something we can never reach on our own. Most of us end up with a pound of failures for every ounce of success. But what makes that your business? Your business is to keep the ship afloat and on course over the turbulent seas. Collateral damage? Seasickness? You try to avoid it, you fix it when it happens—but it goes with the territory.

Now you're going to say, "But what about finding myself? What about discovering the essence within?"

So I'll let you in on a little surprise: Who says that yourself is the real you? Maybe the real you is not a subject, not an object, but a verb? In other words, maybe the real you is to be found not in who you are but in those things you need to do. Because when G-d conceived of you, that's what He had in mind: a little creature, with a piece of His consciousness inside, doing these neat things. In that Divine Image He created you and in that you will find your true self—and Him, as well.

That's why Rabbi Schneur Zalman goes to great lengths to demonstrate that as lofty and divine our inner soul may be, it can never touch its essence until it is "dressed within the clothes of Torah and mitzvahs." "Clothes make the man," they say (I don't know why they never say that about women) and so it is with that G-dly essence within you.

Want to find your essential self? Do something that will bring some light into the world. There you are—your very essence. Not in the light, not in the something, but in the "do."

Rabbi Tzvi Freeman, "Man as Verb: The Truth about the *Tanya*," Chabad.org

Reprinted with permission of Chabad.org

"MY NAME IS . . . AND I AM A HUMAN BEING"
THE JEWISH IDEA OF PERFECTION

BY RABBI SHAIS TAUB

A one-liner from comedian Steven Wright: "They told me in school that 'practice makes perfect.' Then they told me, 'Nobody's perfect.' So I stopped practicing."

A droll observation. But it raises a serious issue. Between these two truisms, which one is really true? Or is the truth somewhere in between? Is perfection attainable or is it not?

If we're talking about proficiency and skill—like a major-league hitter batting a thousand—then perfection may be pie in the sky. But if we're talking about matters of integrity and decency, then perfection is actually our bottom line. Indeed, perfection doesn't seem like such an unreasonable expectation, if we are to think of the alternative as an employee who doesn't steal 99% of the profits, or a spouse who is faithful 99% of the time.

I Am, I Do

The first Rebbe of Chabad, Rabbi Schneur Zalman of Liadi (1745–1812; known as the "Alter Rebbe"), wrote a whole book as a step-by-step guide to actualizing one's complete personal potential. The book is called *Tanya*, and its premise is that anyone who earnestly applies the methods clearly outlined in the book will be able to attain personal perfection and, with continued effort, consistently maintain that state for the rest of his or her life.

In *Tanya*, R. Schneur Zalman points out an interesting dichotomy in the human condition. On one hand, man is fallible by nature, prone to selfishness

RABBI SHAIS TAUB

Chabad rabbi and author. Rabbi Taub is a teacher of Chabad philosophy and Jewish mysticism and wrote the JLI course *Soul Maps,* based on the teachings of the *Tanya,* the foundational text of Chabad philosophy. He is also an expert in addiction recovery and wrote the best-selling book, *G-d of Our Understanding: Jewish Spirituality and Recovery from Addiction.*

and self-justification. On the other hand, man is in control over his impulses. He is not an animal, and has free will to act as he wills at any given time.

In other words, we might not be perfect, but we have the choice to do perfect. Or to put it in psychological terms, not everything that is wrong with us on the inside do we necessarily have to bring into expression on the outside.

This is the perfection which, R. Schneur Zalman tells us, we can achieve—to become a person who, despite being rife with imperfections on the inside, chooses to behave perfectly on the outside.

The Lie of Being Genuine

There is a common knee-jerk reaction—at least from some people—to brand this advice as a prescription for hypocrisy. "If you're flawed on the inside, how dare you project perfection on the outside?"

But is impulse control hypocrisy? If you cover your mouth before you cough, are you a hypocrite? Do you have to say every random thought that pops into your head in order to be "real"?

The correct definition of a hypocrite is one who preaches one set of standards to others while personally adhering to another. But that's not at all what we're talking about here. Feeling like doing something selfish and rotten but forcing yourself to do something altruistic and noble isn't called hypocrisy; it's called being a healthy, normal, decent human being.

Whenever we overcome our impulses to behave in a particular way, we aren't pretending not to be something we're not; we are making the decision to do what ought to be done.

In 12-step programs like Alcoholics Anonymous, members introduce themselves at every meeting, "My name is so-and-so; I am an alcoholic."

Essential to his survival is the alcoholic's recognition of the difference between being and doing. On the one hand, he is an alcoholic. He says so at every meeting. And since that's who he is, it's obviously not his fault. On the other hand, he can't drink. He must maintain total abstinence. Because drinking or not drinking is something he does, and it is entirely up to him what to choose.

It is axiomatic that if we are human, then we suffer from the human condition. That's just who we are and we're not responsible for it. At the same time, the human condition is a poor excuse for misconduct. Whatever our foibles and flaws, behavior is a choice, and if we choose to do the wrong thing, we have no one to blame but ourselves.

Jimmy Carter's Heart

When Jimmy Carter first ran for president, a journalist asked the candidate if he had ever been unfaithful in his marriage. Carter's solemn response was, "I've lusted in my heart," to which he added, "But G-d knows I will do this and forgives me."

What is that supposed to mean? Was Carter admitting to having natural urges and desires? And, indeed, if that was the case, should we care? What kind of news is that?

Imagine asking a Jew, "Did you ever eat on Yom Kippur?" and he answers, "I felt hungry in my stomach."

You felt hungry. That's not a moral issue. It's a physiological issue. You were hungry. And even if you say that you felt hungry when it was only an hour into the fast and your stomach was still full from the pre-fast meals, then it is still just an emotional or psychological issue. The bottom line is that you did not eat! You didn't do it. You didn't talk about doing it. You didn't even entertain it as an actual thought. You felt it.

That's why Carter's statement that he "lusted in his heart" makes no sense in the Jewish idea of morality. If he was trying to convey that he had felt urges, then what substance is there to his "confession"? It seems rather like admitting to having driven 50 mph in a school zone . . . "in your heart."

If, on the other hand, what he was saying is that he hadn't just felt impulses but actually calculated and made plans to act them out, but never actually gone through with them, then that might be worthy of mention. But then the tag-on, "G-d knows I will do this and forgives me," makes no sense. Why

should G-d give out a free pass for a person's scheming, just because the All-Knowing is aware of it before it happens?

Either way you read the statement, both its logic and its belief system seem weak. At the very least, we can say that it's not a very Jewish answer.

1) The very notion that I am condemnable for impulses and feelings is consummately un-Jewish. Humanity is not damned for being human.

2) The idea that I am entitled to forgiveness for wrongdoing because my human frailty and fallibility excuses me is equally un-Jewish.

On the one hand, a Jew doesn't need to "come clean" about the fact that he is human; but neither does he assume absolution for misdeeds on those same grounds. Judaism teaches us that we are innately imperfect, but at the same time, G-d has high enough expectations of us to judge our actions against a standard of perfection.

When Benjamin Franklin wrote about self-perfection in the late 1700s, his ideas were thought to be very un-Christian by many of his coreligionists. After all, the chief tenet of that religion, the need for salvation, is predicated upon the assumption that we are all hopelessly imperfect. Self-perfection has no place in such a belief system. It throws a wrench into the theological gears.

But we Jews don't look to G-d for salvation from our imperfections, but for direction how to heal the world from its imperfection. Our job—the job we were chosen for—is to put our own imperfection aside and take actions that help make a perfect world.

A Jew thus has not only the license but the obligation to pursue perfection in his or her deeds. After all, there is really nothing stopping us. Or as the saying goes, "Everyone is just as much of a mentch as he wants to be."

Rabbi Shais Taub, "'My Name Is . . . And I Am a Human Being': The Jewish Idea of Perfection," Chabad.org

Reprinted with permission of the author

WHAT IS THE DIFFERENCE BETWEEN SHAME AND GUILT?

BY JUNE PRICE TANGNEY, PHD, AND RONDA L. DEARING, PHD

"Shame is regret. Guilt is sin-regret."

"Shame is when you know you did something wrong and you're sorry you did it. Guilt is when you did something that was wrong and you can't admit it."

"Shame is a feeling that you have when you're not happy with your individual outcome on a certain matter. Guilt is when you've done something you felt you shouldn't have."

"Shame is the feeling that everyone else thinks you have done wrong and all know what you have done. Guilt is the feeling that you know what you have done and by your standards it is wrong."

"Shame is when one has done something which contradicts their own morals or beliefs. Guilt is when one has gone against their true nature."

"Shame is feeling guilty. Guilt is feeling ashamed about something."

These are some of the answers we received from a group of college undergraduates when we asked them to define the words "shame" and "guilt" and describe the difference between the two emotions. Obviously, they did not do very well. For the most part, these bright, well-educated young adults could not provide consistent, meaningful definitions of these common human emotions. The big surprise was that when we asked college students to describe and rate *specific, personal* shame and guilt experiences, their ratings of these emotion experiences differed in consistent, theoretically meaningful ways. In other words, it appeared that these college students "knew more than they could say" about shame and guilt. As we describe in greater detail later in this chapter, their ratings of personal shame and guilt events strongly indicate that they, in fact, experience these as quite distinct emotions. But when asked to define these emotions in the abstract, the students really couldn't articulate any consistent clear differences between shame and guilt.

College students aren't unique in this regard. A quick review of the psychological literature shows that the "experts," too, often use the terms shame and guilt inconsistently or interchangeably. For example, psychologists frequently mention shame and guilt in the same breath, as moral emotions that help people choose the high moral road (e.g., Damon, 1988; Eisenberg, 1986; Harris, 1989; Schulman & Mekler, 1985), or as potentially problematic emotions that can cause any one of a number of psychological problems (Fossum & Mason, 1986; Potter-Efron, 1989; Rodin, Silberstein, & Streigel-Moore, 1985). In the clinical literature, especially, it is not uncommon to see psychologists refer to "feelings of shame and guilt" or to discuss the "effects of shame and guilt" without making any distinction between the two emotions.

In everyday conversations, people typically avoid the term "shame." In fact, one could easily argue that today's U.S. society is rather "shame-phobic." The average person rarely speaks of his or her own "shame."

JUNE PRICE TANGNEY, PHD

Professor of psychology at George Mason University. A fellow of the Society for Personality and Social Psychology and of the Association for Psychological Science, she is an associate editor of *American Psychologist*. Dr. Tangney's primary research interest is the development and implications of moral emotions.

RONDA L. DEARING, PHD

Psychologist. Dr. Dearing is a postdoctoral associate at the Research Institute on Addictions in Buffalo, New York. She became involved in the study of shame and guilt during her graduate training in clinical psychology at George Mason University, while working as a research assistant with Dr. June Tangney.

Instead, people refer to "guilt" (e.g., "I felt so *guilty* when I realized what an inconsiderate person I've been") when they mean they felt shame, guilt, or some combination of the two.

Recent theory and research, however, has identified important differences between these two closely related emotions—differences that appear to have rather profound implications both for psychological adjustment and for social behavior. In this chapter, we describe several theoretical distinctions between shame and guilt that have been suggested by social scientists over the years. We begin with a review of early attempts to differentiate shame and guilt, including those based on psychoanalytic and anthropological theories. For example, a common basis for distinguishing between shame and guilt focuses on presumed differences in the types of *situations* that elicit these emotions. We then summarize recent empirical results that seriously challenge this assumption and we describe the empirical support for H. B. Lewis's (1971) reconceptualization, which emphasizes shame's focus on the self versus guilt's focus on specific behaviors.

Early Distinctions between Shame and Guilt

Attempts to distinguish between shame and guilt are not new. Some of the most influential distinctions between the two emotions date back many decades, from psychoanalytic circles and from anthropology. Although recent empirical research has not provided much support for these earlier views, it is useful to be aware of these perspectives because they can be found, in one form or another, in both the psychological and popular literatures. In fact, in our research we saw evidence of these earlier notions of how shame and guilt differ in the definitions provided by some of our more articulate college students.

The Psychoanalytic Perspective

Over the years, psychoanalytically oriented theories have probably paid the most attention to shame and guilt. But the father of psychoanalysis, Sigmund Freud, too, largely neglected the distinction between these two emotions. In his earlier work, Freud (1905/1953b) briefly discussed shame as a reaction

formation against sexually exhibitionistic impulses. From this early perspective, feelings of shame were invoked to defend against desires to publically call attention to oneself sexually. But in his later writings (Freud, 1914/1957, 1923/1961d, 1924/1961c, 1925/1961b) he essentially ignored the construct of shame, focusing instead on a rather cognitive concept of guilt in relation to superego conflicts. According to Freud, feelings of guilt arise when id or ego impulses or behaviors clash with the moral standards of the superego (see H. B. Lewis, 1971, N. K. Morrison, 1987, and Tangney, 1994, for more detailed analyses of Freud's approach to shame and guilt). Lewis (1971) has argued that in developing a theory that focused almost exclusively on guilt, Freud (like many contemporary psychoanalysts) may have mislabeled his patients' shame experiences as guilt experiences.

A number of post-Freudian theorists made explicit attempts to distinguish between shame and guilt within a neo-Freudian framework (e.g., Hartmann & Loewenstein, 1962; Jacobson, 1954; Piers & Singer, 1953). Fairly early in his writing, Freud (1914/1957) introduces the notion of an "ego-ideal." Although Freud largely abandoned this construct in his later work, subsequent ego psychologists picked up on this theme and elaborated on the distinction between ego-ideal (roughly, an idealized moral self) and superego (or conscience) proper. A number of theorists applied this distinction to their conceptualization of shame and guilt. For example, Piers and Singer (1953) viewed guilt as a reaction to clashes between the ego and the superego (with its roots in fears of castration, similar to Freud's own notions). In contrast, shame was conceptualized as a reaction to clashes between the ego and the ego-ideal (with its roots in feelings of inferiority, and consequent fears of loss of love and abandonment). This neo-Freudian distinction between shame and guilt can be seen as a precursor of H. B. Lewis's (1971) later distinction between self-concerns and behavior concerns, and it is consistent with Erikson's (1950) descriptions of shame as a global exposed self-doubt versus guilt over misguided behavior (initiative). But the neo-Freudian structural distinction is not without its problems. For example, Hartmann and Loewenstein (1962) questioned the practical utility of such a structural distinction. And, more recently, Lindsay-Hartz (1984) provided evidence apparently contradicting Piers and Singer (1953), showing that shame typically results from a *negative* ideal (e.g., the recognition that "We are who we do not want to be"), rather than from a recognition that we have failed to live up to some *positive* ego-ideal.

With the emergence of self-psychology, shame gained an even more prominent place in psychodynamic theory. Quite a number of psychoanalytically oriented theorists have cited shame as a major factor in a range of psychological disorders (Kohut, 1971; A. P. Morrison, 1989; N. K. Morrison, 1987; Nathanson, 1987a, 1987b, 1987c). But in their new focus on shame, these theories tend to give short shrift to guilt. Ironically, in many cases, the construct of guilt (distinct from shame) is largely neglected and, as in traditional Freudian theory, the distinction between these two emotions has been lost.

The Anthropological Perspective

Outside of psychoanalytical circles, when people make a distinction between shame and guilt, they often refer to differences in the content and/or structure of events eliciting these emotions. The assumption here, popularized by mid-20th-century anthropologists (e.g., Benedict, 1946), is that certain *kinds of situations* lead to shame whereas other *kinds of situations* lead to guilt. For example, there is a long-standing notion that shame is a more "public" emotion than guilt. Shame is seen as arising from public exposure and disapproval of some shortcoming or transgression, whereas guilt is seen as a more "private" experience arising from self-generated pangs of conscience.

This public-private distinction remains a frequently cited basis for distinguishing between shame and guilt. Gehm and Scherer (1988), for example, speculated that "shame is usually dependent on the public exposure of one's frailty or failing, whereas guilt may be something that remains a secret with us, no one else knowing of our breach of social norms or of our responsibility for an immoral act" (p. 74).

As it turns out, there isn't much empirical support for this public—private distinction. In fact, results from several recent studies call into question this long-standing notion (Tangney, Marschall, Rosenberg, Barlow, & Wagner, 1994: Tangney, Miller, Flicker, & Barlow, 1996). For example, we conducted what appears to be the first systematic analysis of "audiences" to shame—and guilt—eliciting events (Tangney et al., 1994). In this study, we asked several hundred children and adults to describe recent events in which they had experienced shame, guilt, and pride. We then analyzed these narrative accounts of real-life emotion episodes to evaluate, among other things, just how public or private these events really were.

Our results clearly challenge the anthropologists' public—private distinction. Although shame and guilt were *both* most often experienced in the presence of others (among both children and adults), a substantial number of respondents reported shame experiences occurring alone—when *not* in the presence of others. More important, "solitary" shame was about as prevalent as "solitary" guilt. Among children, 17.2% of shame narratives versus 14.9% of guilt narratives involved situations in which no other person was present. Among adults, 16.5% of shame episodes versus 22.5% of guilt episodes were experienced alone. (Pride was most likely to be experienced alone; 33.8% of the children and 25.5% of the adults reported solitary pride experiences.)

Even more to the point, we assessed whether or not anyone was explicitly aware of the respondent's behavior. This audience awareness variable represents the strongest test of Benedict's (1946) notion that shame is differentially related to public exposure or scrutiny, because it is possible that others may have been present in the situation but not aware of the respondent's behavior (e.g., a respondent telling a lie). The only appreciable difference was between pride versus shame and guilt among adults. Adults perceived that others were more likely to be aware of their behavior in pride situations and somewhat less likely to be aware of their behavior in shame and guilt situations. Importantly, there was no difference in "audience awareness" when shame and guilt events were compared. In the accounts provided by both children and adults, others were no more likely to be aware of shame-inducing behaviors than they were guilt-inducing behaviors, in contrast to the anthropologists' public-private distinction (e.g., Benedict, 1946).

Helen Block Lewis's (1971) Reconceptualization: Shame and Guilt Differ in Focus on Self Versus Behavior

How do shame and guilt differ, then, if not in terms of the types of situations that elicit them? In 1971, Helen Block Lewis, a clinical psychologist at Yale University, presented a radically different and now highly influential distinction between these two emotions. In her landmark book *Shame and Guilt in Neurosis*, Lewis (1971) merged her extensive clinical background in psychoanalytic theory and ego psychology with ideas drawn from her experimental work with Herman A. Witkin on field-dependent versus field-independent cognitive styles. According to Lewis (1971), a key difference between shame and guilt centers on the role of the self in these experiences. She wrote: "The experience of shame is directly about the *self*, which is the focus of evaluation. In guilt, the self is not the central object of negative evaluation, but rather the *thing* done or undone is the focus. In guilt, the self is negatively evaluated in connection with something but is not itself the focus of the experience" (p. 30; emphasis in original).

Lewis (1971) proposed that this differential emphasis on self ("I did that horrible thing") versus behavior ("*I did* that horrible *thing*") leads to very different phenomenological experiences. She described shame as an acutely painful emotion that is typically accompanied by a sense of shrinking or of "being small" and by a sense of worthlessness and powerlessness. Shamed people also feel exposed. Although shame doesn't necessarily involve an actual observing audience that is present to witness one's shortcomings, there is often the imagery of how one's defective self would appear to others. Lewis (1971) described a split in self-functioning in which the self is both agent and object of observation and disapproval. An observing self witnesses and denigrates the focal self as unworthy and reprehensible. Finally, shame often leads to a desire to escape or to hide—to sink into the floor and disappear.

In contrast, Lewis (1971) viewed guilt as typically a less painful and devastating experience than shame because, in guilt, our primary concern is with a particular behavior, somewhat apart from the self. So guilt doesn't affect one's core identity or self-concept. Feelings of guilt can be painful nonetheless. Guilt involves a sense of tension, remorse, and regret over the "bad thing" done. People in the midst of a guilt experience often report a nagging focus or preoccupation with the transgression—thinking of it over and over, wishing they had behaved differently or could somehow undo the deed.

For example, 18-year-old Tyrone described this recent guilt experience:

> *"Last fall I got really sick at the beginning of the school semester. I missed the first month of classes and could not catch up. I had to withdraw from all but one class. When you withdraw, you don't get your money back. My mom and dad pay tuition, and they weren't real happy about losing $975. I felt guilty, so I got two jobs, worked 70 hours a week, and paid them back in 3 weeks."*

In contrast, feelings of shame are more likely to motivate a desire to hide or escape the shame-inducing situation, as illustrated by 47-year-old Maria's description of an early shame experience:

> *"When I was 6 years old, at the end of the kindergarten school year, I experienced shame. On the last day of school, only the older children were expected to go to school, but my mother didn't know this and she sent me to school anyway. I knew the kindergartners were not expected that day. Since my mother insisted that I go, I thought, 'Well, maybe I am to get some kind of special prize for being such a good student. Maybe they are going to announce that I can skip the first grade.' When I got to school, one of the teachers saw me and said, 'Oh, you are not supposed to be here today!' I turned around and ran all the way home, so ashamed that I had had these thoughts." [emphasis added]*

Similarly, 20-year-old Janice described this shame experience:

"It was a piano recital that I really had no desire to take part in, since I get extremely nervous on such occasions. . . . I performed and messed up the whole thing in a serious way, in front of people I knew and who had high expectations of me. What an embarrassment. I wanted to crawl into a hole and never come out!!" [emphasis added]

Feelings of shame involve an acute awareness of one's flawed and unworthy self, a response that often seems out of proportion with the actual severity of the event. For example, Mia, an 18-year-old college student, recalled this shame experience from childhood:

"It is, for some reason, extremely hard to remember. . . . When I was 10, I slept over at a friend's house. His mother came home in the middle of the night and asked if I was cold. I was freezing, but said 'no' to her offer of more blankets. The next day I complained to the friend about how cold I'd been. His mother found out and confronted me with it, and I felt awful—shamefully confused and unjustified in my existence." [emphasis added]

References

Andrews, Louis M. *I Deserve Respect.* Minnesota: Hazelden, 1993.

Bernie, Patricia, and Louis Savary. *Building Self-Esteem in Children.* New York: Continuum, 1981.

Branden, Nathaniel. *Breaking Free.* New York: Bantam Books, 1989.

--------. *The Disowned Self.* New York: Bantam Books, 1976.

--------. *The Psychology of Self-Esteem.* New York: Bantam Books, 1973.

Bryant, Roberta J. *Stop Improving Yourself and Start Living.* San Rafael, Calif.: New World Library, 1991.

Buxbaum, Edith. *Your Child Makes Sense.* New York: International Universities Press, 1949.

Chess, Stella, Alexander Thomas, and Herbert G. Birch. *Your Child Is a Person.* New York: Viking, 1965.

Cudney, Milton R., and Robert E. Hardy. *Self-Defeating Behaviors.* New York: Harper, 1991.

Dunbar, Flanders. *Your Preteenager's Mind and Body.* New York: Hawthorne Books, 1962.

Elkins, Dov P., ed. *Glad to Be Me.* Englewood Cliffs, N.J.: Prentice Hall, 1976.

English, O. Spurgeon. *Fathers Are Parents Too.* New York: Putnam, 1951.

Fraiberg, Selma H. *The Magic Years.* New York: Scribner, 1959.

Ginott, Haim G. *Between Parent and Child.* New York: Macmillian, 1965.

--------. *Between Parent and Teenager.* New York: Macmillian, 1969.

--------. *Between Teacher and Child.* New York: Macmillian, 1972.

Harris, Sydney. *The Authentic Person.* Allen, Tex.: Argus Communications, 1972.

Hegarty, Carol, and Earnie Larsen. *Believing in Myself.* New York: Prentice Hall/ Parkside, 1991.

Hendricks, Gay. *Learning to Love Yourself.* New York: Simon & Schuster, 1982.

Hillman, Caroline. *Recovery of Your Self-Esteem.* New York: Simon & Schuster, 1992.

Josselyn, Irene M. *The Happy Child.* New York: Random House, 1995.

Jourard, Sidney. *The Transparent Self.* New York: Van Nostrand, 1964.

Kalellis, Peter M. *A New Self-Image.* Allen, Tex.: Argus Communications, 1982.

Larsen, Tony. *Trust Yourself.* San Luis Obispo, Calif.: Impact Publishers, 1979.

Rapoport, Rhona, Robert Rapoport, and Ziona Stelitz. *Father, Mother, and Society.* New York: Basic Books, 1977.

Robinson, Brian. *Heal Your Self-Esteem.* Delray Beach, Fla.: Health Communications, 1991.

Rogers, Carl R. *On Becoming a Person.* Boston: Houghton Mifflin, 1961.

Steinem, Gloria. *Revolution From Within.* Boston: Little, Brown, 1992.

Wheelis, Allen. *How People Change.* New York: Harper Perennial, 1976.

June Price Tangney and Ronda L. Dearing, *Shame and Guilt* (New York: The Guilford Press, 2003), ch. 2

Reprinted with permission of the publisher

Lesson

3

RETHINKING
REGRET

ADDRESSING UNHEALTHY GUILT

Old Man in Sorrow (On the Threshold of Eternity), Vincent
van Gogh, oil on canvas, Saint-Rémy de Provence, France,
1890. (Kröller-Müller Museum, Otterlo)

*We all slip up at times, sometimes
drastically, and it is natural and
healthy to experience regret or
guilt. However, if such emotions
become paralyzing and distressful,
they seriously impede our efforts
to maintain positive and successful
living. This lesson explores the inner
workings of guilt and regret, and
delivers a transformative method
of tackling guilt and spinning it
into a catalyst for positive change.*

Exercise 3.1

Mentally identify a past choice that has left you with significant lingering feelings of guilt.

QUESTIONS FOR DISCUSSION

1 How do we differentiate between healthy and unhealthy remorse and guilt?

2 At what point can you forgive yourself and move on?

Jews Praying in the Synagogue on Yom Kippur, Maurycy Gottlieb, glazed, semitransparent oil on canvas, Poland, 1878. (Tel Aviv Museum of Art, Tel Aviv)

TEXT 1

RABBI SHNE'UR ZALMAN OF LIADI, *TANYA*, CH. 1

תַּנְיָא [בְּסוֹף פֶּרֶק ג' דְּנִדָּה]: "מַשְׁבִּיעִים אוֹתוֹ: 'תְּהִי צַדִּיק, וְאַל תְּהִי רָשָׁע. וַאֲפִילוּ כָּל הָעוֹלָם כּוּלּוֹ אוֹמְרִים לְךָ צַדִּיק אַתָּה, הֱיֵה בְּעֵינֶיךָ כְּרָשָׁע'".

וְצָרִיךְ לְהָבִין, דְּהָא תְּנַן [אָבוֹת, פֶּרֶק ב']: "וְאַל תְּהִי רָשָׁע בִּפְנֵי עַצְמֶךָ".

וְגַם, אִם יִהְיֶה בְּעֵינָיו כְּרָשָׁע יֵרַע לְבָבוֹ וְיִהְיֶה עָצֵב וְלֹא יוּכַל לַעֲבוֹד ה' בְּשִׂמְחָה וּבְטוּב לֵבָב. וְאִם לֹא יֵרַע לְבָבוֹ כְּלָל מִזֶּה, יָכוֹל לָבוֹא לִידֵי קַלּוּת חַס וְשָׁלוֹם.

RABBI SHNE'UR ZALMAN OF LIADI (ALTER REBBE) 1745–1812

Chasidic rebbe, halachic authority, and founder of the Chabad movement. The Alter Rebbe was born in Liozna, Belarus, and was among the principal students of the Magid of Mezeritch. His numerous works include the Tanya, an early classic containing the fundamentals of Chabad Chasidism, and *Shulchan Aruch HaRav*, an expanded and reworked code of Jewish law.

It has been taught (TALMUD, NIDAH, END OF CH. 3): "[Before birth, each soul] is administered an oath: 'Be righteous and do not be wicked. And even if the entire world tells you that you are righteous, regard yourself as a wicked person.'"

This requires clarification, for [it seemingly contradicts] the dictum: "Do not regard yourself as a wicked person" (ETHICS OF THE FATHERS 2:13).

Furthermore, if you consider yourself wicked, you will be troubled and despondent. That will prevent you from serving G-d with joy and positive emotion. On the other hand, if you are not at all perturbed by [your flaws], you may end up not taking [yourself or your actions] seriously, G-d forbid.

Why is guilt stereotypically considered a Jewish feeling?
***Rabbi Yitzchok Schochet** shares his thoughts:*

MYJLI.COM/WARRIOR

TEXT 2

PROVERBS 14:23

בְּכָל עֶצֶב יִהְיֶה מוֹתָר.

In every sadness there is a benefit.

TEXT 3

TANYA, CH. 26

וּמַה שֶּׁכָּתוּב, "בְּכָל עֶצֶב יִהְיֶה מוֹתָר", פֵּירוּשׁ, שֶׁיִּהְיֶה אֵיזֶה יִתְרוֹן וּמַעֲלָה
מְזֶה, הִנֵּה אַדְרַבָּה: מִלָּשׁוֹן זֶה מַשְׁמַע שֶׁהָעֶצֶב מִצַּד עַצְמוֹ אֵין בּוֹ מַעֲלָה,
רַק שֶׁיַּגִּיעַ וְיָבֹא מִמֶּנּוּ אֵיזֶה יִתְרוֹן.

"In every sadness there is a benefit" implies that there is benefit and gain to be derived from negative emotions. But the phraseology actually suggests that negative emotions per se have no virtue, and it is only that a benefit is *derived* from them.

TEXT 4

PSALMS 126:5

▮ הַזֹּרְעִים בְּדִמְעָה בְּרִנָּה יִקְצֹרוּ. ▮

Those who sow with tears will reap with songs of joy.

QUESTION FOR DISCUSSION

What benefit might be gained from negative emotions?

Illustration of Miriam and the Israelite women dancing, from the *Sister Haggadah*. Artist unknown, Spain, c. 2nd or 3rd quarter of the 14th century. (The British Library, London)

TEXT 5

MAIMONIDES, *MISHNEH TORAH*, LAWS OF *TESHUVAH* 5:1–2

רְשׁוּת לְכָל אָדָם נְתוּנָה: אִם רָצָה לְהַטּוֹת עַצְמוֹ לְדֶרֶךְ טוֹבָה וְלִהְיוֹת צַדִּיק, הָרְשׁוּת בְּיָדוֹ. וְאִם רָצָה לְהַטּוֹת עַצְמוֹ לְדֶרֶךְ רָעָה וְלִהְיוֹת רָשָׁע, הָרְשׁוּת בְּיָדוֹ . . .

אַל יַעֲבֹר בְּמַחֲשַׁבְתְּךָ דָּבָר זֶה שֶׁאוֹמְרִים טִפְּשֵׁי אוּמּוֹת הָעוֹלָם וְרוֹב גָּלְמֵי בְּנֵי יִשְׂרָאֵל שֶׁהַקָּדוֹשׁ בָּרוּךְ הוּא גוֹזֵר עַל הָאָדָם מִתְּחִלַּת בְּרִיָּתוֹ לִהְיוֹת צַדִּיק אוֹ רָשָׁע. אֵין הַדָּבָר כֵּן. אֶלָּא כָּל אָדָם רָאוּי לוֹ לִהְיוֹת צַדִּיק כְּמשֶׁה רַבֵּינוּ אוֹ רָשָׁע כְּיָרָבְעָם, אוֹ חָכָם אוֹ סָכָל אוֹ רַחֲמָן אוֹ אַכְזָרִי אוֹ כִּילַי אוֹ שׁוּעַ, וְכֵן שְׁאָר כָּל הַדֵּעוֹת. וְאֵין לוֹ מִי שֶׁיִּכְפֵּהוּ וְלֹא גוֹזֵר עָלָיו וְלֹא מִי שֶׁמּוֹשְׁכוֹ לְאֶחָד מִשְּׁנֵי הַדְּרָכִים, אֶלָּא הוּא מֵעַצְמוֹ וּמִדַּעְתּוֹ נוֹטֶה לְאֵי זוֹ דֶּרֶךְ שֶׁיִּרְצֶה. הוּא שֶׁיִּרְמְיָהוּ אָמַר, "מִפִּי עֶלְיוֹן לֹא תֵצֵא הָרָעוֹת וְהַטּוֹב" (אֵיכָה ג, לח). כְּלוֹמַר, אֵין הַבּוֹרֵא גּוֹזֵר עַל הָאָדָם לִהְיוֹת טוֹב וְלֹא לִהְיוֹת רַע.

וְכֵיוָן שֶׁכֵּן הוּא, נִמְצָא זֶה הַחוֹטֵא הוּא הִפְסִיד אֶת עַצְמוֹ. וּלְפִיכָךְ רָאוּי לוֹ לִבְכּוֹת וּלְקוֹנֵן עַל חֲטָאָיו וְעַל מַה שֶּׁעָשָׂה לְנַפְשׁוֹ וּגְמָלָהּ רָעָה. הוּא שֶׁכָּתוּב אַחֲרָיו, "מַה יִּתְאוֹנֵן אָדָם חָי וְגוֹמֵר" (שָׁם, לט).

RABBI MOSHE BEN MAIMON (MAIMONIDES, RAMBAM) 1135–1204

Halachist, philosopher, author, and physician. Maimonides was born in Córdoba, Spain. After the conquest of Córdoba by the Almohads, he fled Spain and eventually settled in Cairo, Egypt. There, he became the leader of the Jewish community and served as court physician to the vizier of Egypt. He is most noted for authoring the *Mishneh Torah,* an encyclopedic arrangement of Jewish law, and for his philosophical work, *Guide for the Perplexed*. His rulings on Jewish law are integral to the formation of halachic consensus.

Free will is granted to all humans. Should we desire to tread the path of goodness and be righteous, the choice is ours. Should we desire to turn to the path of evil and be wicked, the choice is ours. . . .

Do not entertain the view held by the fools of the nations and the majority of simpleminded Jews that from the moment of a human's conception, G-d decrees whether that person will be righteous or wicked. This is untrue. Rather, each individual can become righteous like our teacher Moses or wicked like Jeroboam. We can embrace wisdom or foolishness, be merciful or cruel, miserly or generous. The same is true of all character traits. No one compels, dictates, or leads us toward any of these paths. Rather, we, of our own initiative and decision, veer to the path of our choosing. This is [implied by the prophet] Jeremiah, who stated, "Neither evil nor good emerge from the mouth of the One Above" (LAMENTATIONS 3:38)—meaning that the Creator does not decree on a person whether they will be righteous or evil.

Consequently, those who do wrong have no one but themselves to blame. It is therefore proper to cry and mourn over our moral failings and the damage we have inflicted upon our souls. This is implied by the following verse: "What should [rightfully] aggrieve a person? His sins" (IBID., VERSE 39).

The halachic process of teshuvah, *explained by **Rabbi Mordechai Dinerman**:*

MYJLI.COM/WARRIOR

Exercise 3.2

How appropriate is guilt as a response to the following scenarios?

Key
1 = Very appropriate
2 = Somewhat appropriate
3 = Not at all appropriate
4 = It is complicated

	SCALE
Forgetting a spouse's birthday	1 2 3 4
Texting while driving and rear-ending another vehicle	1 2 3 4
Missing a child's graduation due to a medical emergency	1 2 3 4
Wasting years of life as a result of choosing a dead-end career	1 2 3 4
Eating unhealthily	1 2 3 4
Befriending a person who eventually causes harm to one's family	1 2 3 4

Figure 3.1a

Appropriate Remorse . . .

1	is only over a morally faulty *choice*.

TEXT **6**

TANYA, CH. 26

וּמַה שֶּׁכָּתוּב, "בְּכָל עֶצֶב יִהְיֶה מוֹתָר" (מִשְׁלֵי יד, כג), פֵּירוּשׁ, שֶׁיִּהְיֶה
אֵיזֶה יִתְרוֹן וּמַעֲלָה מִזֶּה, הִנֵּה אַדְרַבָּה: מִלָּשׁוֹן זֶה מַשְׁמַע שֶׁהָעֶצֶב מִצַּד
עַצְמוֹ אֵין בּוֹ מַעֲלָה, רַק שֶׁיַּגִּיעַ וְיָבֹא מִמֶּנּוּ אֵיזֶה יִתְרוֹן. וְהַיְינוּ, הַשִּׂמְחָה
הָאֲמִיתִּית בַּה' אֱלֹקָיו, הַבָּאָה אַחַר הָעֶצֶב הָאֲמִיתִּי.

"In every sadness there is a benefit" implies that there is
benefit and gain to be derived from negative emotions.
But the phraseology actually suggests that negative
emotions per se have no virtue, and it is only that a
benefit is *derived* from them. That benefit is the true joy
in G-d that follows genuine anguish.

Figure 3.1b

Appropriate Remorse . . .

1	is only over a morally faulty *choice*.
2	is productive:

	a	It leads to heightened joy.
	b	It leads to change.

TEXT 7

TANYA, CH. 26

אַךְ, הָעַצְבוּת מִמִּילֵי דִשְׁמַיָּא צָרִיךְ לַעֲשִׂית עֵצוֹת בְּנַפְשׁוֹ לִיפָּטֵר מִמֶּנָּה.

אֵין צָרִיךְ לוֹמַר בִּשְׁעַת עֲבוֹדָה, שֶׁצָּרִיךְ לַעֲבוֹד ה' בְּשִׂמְחָה וּבְטוּב לֵבָב. אֶלָּא אֲפִילוּ מִי שֶׁהוּא בַּעַל עֲסָקִים וְדֶרֶךְ אֶרֶץ, אִם נוֹפֵל לוֹ עֶצֶב וּדְאָגָה מִמִּילֵי דִשְׁמַיָּא בִּשְׁעַת עֲסָקָיו, בְּיָדוּעַ שֶׁהוּא תַּחְבּוּלַת הַיֵּצֶר כְּדֵי לְהַפִּילוֹ אַחַר כָּךְ בְּתַאֲווֹת חַס וְשָׁלוֹם, כַּנּוֹדָע. שֶׁאִם לֹא כֵן, מֵאַיִן בָּאָה לוֹ עַצְבוּת אֲמִיתִּית מֵחֲמַת אַהֲבַת ה' אוֹ יִרְאָתוֹ בְּאֶמְצַע עֲסָקָיו?

וְהִנֵּה, בֵּין שֶׁנָּפְלָה לוֹ הָעַצְבוּת בִּשְׁעַת עֲבוֹדָה בְּתַלְמוּד תּוֹרָה אוֹ בִּתְפִלָּה, וּבֵין שֶׁנָּפְלָה לוֹ שֶׁלֹּא בִּשְׁעַת עֲבוֹדָה, זֹאת יָשִׂים אֶל לִבּוֹ, כִּי אֵין הַזְּמַן גְּרָמָא כָּעֵת לְעַצְבוּת אֲמִיתִּית, אֲפִילוּ לְדַאֲגַת עֲוֹנוֹת חֲמוּרִים חַס וְשָׁלוֹם. רַק לָזֹאת צָרִיךְ קְבִיעוּת עִתִּים וּשְׁעַת הַכּוֹשֶׁר בְּיִשּׁוּב הַדַּעַת, לְהִתְבּוֹנֵן בִּגְדֻלַּת ה' אֲשֶׁר חָטָא לוֹ, כְּדֵי שֶׁעַל יְדֵי זֶה יִהְיֶה לִבּוֹ נִשְׁבָּר בֶּאֱמֶת בִּמְרִירוּת אֲמִיתִּית.

וְכִמְבוֹאָר עֵת זוֹ בְּמָקוֹם אַחֵר. וְשָׁם נִתְבָּאֵר גַּם כֵּן, כִּי מִיָּד אַחַר שֶׁנִּשְׁבַּר לִבּוֹ בָּעִתִּים קְבוּעִים הָהֵם, אֲזַי יָסִיר הָעֶצֶב מִלִּבּוֹ לְגַמְרֵי, וְיַאֲמִין אֱמוּנָה שְׁלֵמָה כִּי ה' הֶעֱבִיר חַטָּאתוֹ וְרַב לִסְלוֹחַ. וְזוֹ הִיא הַשִּׂמְחָה הָאֲמִיתִּית בַּה' הַבָּאָה אַחַר הָעֶצֶב כַּנִּזְכָּר לְעֵיל.

Do we ever really and totally move on from past mistakes? **Rabbi Mendel Kalmenson** *answers:*

MYJLI.COM/WARRIOR

Freeing ourselves of negative emotions that result from [remorse over] spiritual matters [is not a simple task. Nevertheless,] we must seek ways and means to do so.

Clearly, while serving G-d, [such as praying or studying Torah, we must rid ourselves of all negative emotion because] we must serve Him with gladness and a joyous heart. But even while involved in commerce or other mundane matters, if we experience negative emotions or worry regarding spiritual matters, we must know that this is a ploy of the evil inclination. Its goal is well known: to subsequently lure us into following its lustful desires, G-d forbid. Were it not so, how does genuine remorse, which is derived from love or fear of G-d, come to us in the midst of our mundane activities?

Now, regardless of whether the negative emotion happens upon us while we are involved in the service of G-d—studying or praying—we must realize that now is an inappropriate time for genuine remorse, even over egregious misdeeds, G-d forbid. For genuine remorse, we need designated times, appropriate times when we have calmness of mind. During those times, we should reflect upon the greatness of G-d against Whom we have sinned and thereby cause our hearts to be truly broken and genuinely embittered.

Elsewhere it is clarified precisely when this time should be, and there it is also explained that as soon as our hearts have been broken during these designated times, we should completely remove the sorrow from our hearts and believe with a perfect faith that G-d, in His abundant forgiveness, has removed our sin. [We are then free to experience] the true joy in G-d that comes after the remorse, as mentioned above.

Exercise 3.3

What relevant takeaways and fresh ideas pertaining to productive remorse can you glean from this reading?

1	
2	
3	
4	
5	
6	

TEXT **8**

ISAIAH 5:20

הוֹי הָאֹמְרִים לָרַע טוֹב, וְלַטּוֹב רָע. שָׂמִים חֹשֶׁךְ לְאוֹר וְאוֹר לְחֹשֶׁךְ, שָׂמִים מַר לְמָתוֹק וּמָתוֹק לְמָר.

Woe to those who call evil good, and good evil; who present darkness as light and light as darkness; who regard bitter as sweet and sweet as bitter.

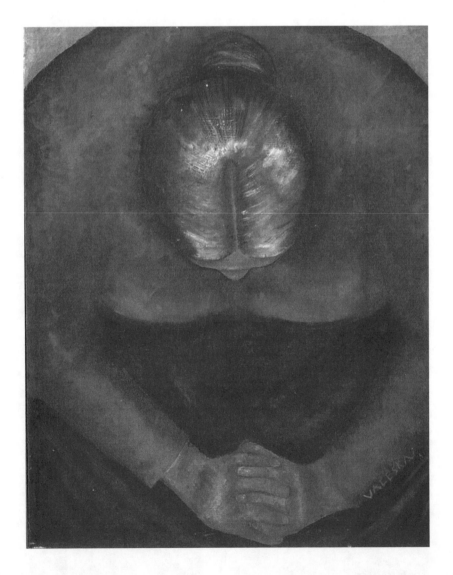

Despair, Lette Valeska, painting, 1954. (Lette Valeska Collection)

TEXT 9

RABBI YAAKOV YITSCHAK HALEVI HOROWITZ, CITED IN *IMREI NO'AM* (DZIKOV),
PARSHAT METSORA 👥

יוֹתֵר חָשׁוּב לְהַיֵּצֶר הָרַע הָעַצְבוּת שֶׁאַחַר עֲשִׂיַּת הָעֲבֵירָה מֵהָעֲבֵירָה
גּוּפָא, כְּדֵי שֶׁיּוּכַל אַחַר כָּךְ לְהַפִּילוֹ בְּעַצְבוּת.

More than the misdeed itself, the evil inclination values the negative emotion that results from the misdeed. It hopes that this negative emotion will lead the person to enter a state of despondency.

RABBI YAAKOV YITSCHAK HALEVI HOROWITZ (THE "SEER OF LUBLIN") 1745–1815

Chasidic master and a central figure in the spread of the Chasidic movement throughout Poland in the late 18th century. He was a disciple of the Magid of Mezeritch and Rabbi Elimelech of Lizhensk and is widely known as "the Seer (*Chozeh*) of Lublin" due to his reputed clairvoyance. He is the progenitor of many modern-day Chasidic dynasties.

TEXT 10

RABBI SHMUEL SCHNEERSOHN, CITED IN *HAYOM YOM*, SIVAN 23

הַיֵּצֶר הָרַע נִקְרָא נֶפֶשׁ הַבַּהֲמִית לֹא מִפְּנֵי שֶׁהֲגָא בְּהֵמָה דַּוְקָא, כִּי לְפְעָמִים הוּא שׁוּעָל פִּקֵחַ שֶׁבַּחַיּוֹת וּצְרִיכִים לְחָכְמָה מְרֻבָּה לְהָבִין תַּחְבּוּלוֹתָיו. וְלִפְעָמִים הוּא מִתְלַבֵּשׁ בִּלְבוּשׁ צַדִּיק תָּמִים עָנָיו וּבַעַל מִדּוֹת טוֹבוֹת...

וּנְקוֹט הַאי כְּלָלָא בְּיָדְךָ וּזְכֹר אוֹתוֹ תָּמִיד, כִּי כָל דָּבָר הַמּוֹעִיל אוֹ מֵבִיא לָעֲבוֹדָה בְּפוֹעַל, הִנֵּה כָל מְנִיעָה שֶׁתִּהְיֶה לְדָבָר זֶה - אֲפִילוּ אִם הַמְּנִיעָה הִיא מִדָּבָר הַיּוֹתֵר נַעֲלֶה - הוּא רַק מִתַּחְבּוּלוֹתֶיהָ שֶׁל נֶפֶשׁ הַבַּהֲמִית.

RABBI SHMUEL SCHNEERSOHN (REBBE MAHARASH) 1834–1882

Known by the acronym "Maharash"; fourth Chabad rebbe and leader of Russian Jewry. Born in Lubavitch, Russia, he was the youngest son of Rabbi Menachem Mendel of Lubavitch (the *Tsemach Tsedek*). Much of his leadership was devoted to combating anti-Jewish policies. His discourses have been collected and published as *Likutei Torah—Torat Shmuel*.

The evil inclination is called the "animal soul" not because it necessarily behaves like a brute animal [at all times]. At times, it is a fox, the most cunning of beasts, and great wisdom is needed to see through its machinations. At other times, it disguises itself in the garb of a righteous person: sincere, humble, and of refined character. . . .

Always bear in mind and hold dear the following golden rule: If there is a course of action that is productive or leads to positive action, any opposition to it—even if it is seemingly sourced in a most noble intention—is merely a scheme of the animal soul.

TEXT 11

TANYA, CH. 26 (REPRISE)

אִם נוֹפֵל לוֹ עֶצֶב וּדְאָגָה מִמֵּילֵי דִשְׁמַיָּא בִּשְׁעַת עֲסָקָיו, בְּיָדוּעַ שֶׁהוּא תַּחְבּוּלַת הַיֵּצֶר כְּדֵי לְהַפִּילוֹ אַחַר כָּךְ בְּתַאֲווֹת חַס וְשָׁלוֹם, כַּנּוֹדָע. שֶׁאִם לֹא כֵן, מֵאַיִן בָּאָה לוֹ עַצְבוּת אֲמִיתִּית מֵחֲמַת אַהֲבַת ה' אוֹ יִרְאָתוֹ בְּאֶמְצַע עֲסָקָיו?

*Why is it that despite feeling guilt, we make the same mistakes? **Rabbi Mendel Kalmenson***'s *insightful response:*

MYJLI.COM/WARRIOR

Even while involved in commerce or other mundane matters, if we experience negative emotions or worry regarding spiritual matters, we must know that this is a ploy of the evil inclination. Its goal is well known: to subsequently lure us into following its lustful desires, G-d forbid. Were it not so, how does genuine remorse, which is derived from love or fear of G-d, come to us in the midst of our mundane activities?

QUESTION FOR DISCUSSION

Which of the following statements are true?

1 Regret leads to change.

2 Change leads to regret.

3 It can work either way.

The Penitent,
Boris Schatz,
Silver repoussé,
c. early 20th
century.
(The Magnes
Collection of
Jewish Art and
Life, Berkeley)

בעל תשובה

TEXT **12**

RABBI ELIYAHU DE VIDAS, *RESHIT CHOCHMAH*, GATE OF AWE 3 ⚇

וְאֵין לְךָ רָשָׁע שֶׁלֹּא יָבוֹאוּ לוֹ הִרְהוּרֵי תְשׁוּבָה קוֹדֶם שֶׁעוֹשֶׂה הָעֲבֵירָה, אֶלָּא שֶׁיִּצְרוֹ מְפַתֵּהוּ. וְאַחַר כָּךְ מִתְחָרֵט. וְכֵן בְּסֵפֶר חֲסִידִים אָמְרוּ: "הָרְשָׁעִים מְלֵאִים חֲרָטָה".

Before committing a wrong, all wrongdoers have reservations, and yet they are enticed to transgress. After committing the wrong, they regret their action. In *Sefer Chasidim* it is said: "The wicked are bursting with regrets."

RABBI ELIYAHU DE VIDAS
1518–1592

Born in Safed; Rabbi De Vidas is considered one of the prominent kabbalists of the 16th century. A student of Rabbi Moshe Cordovero and Rabbi Yitschak Luria, he is best known as the author of *Reshit Chochmah*, a compendium of moral teachings culled from various sources in the Talmud, Midrash, and *Zohar*. He is buried in Hebron.

Figure 3.1c

Appropriate Remorse . . .

| 1 | is only over a morally faulty *choice*. |

| 2 | is productive: |

| | a | It leads to heightened joy. |

| | b | It leads to change. |

| 3 | is a result of a genuine change of perspective and feelings. |

TEXT 13

TANYA, CH. 26 (REPRISE) 👬

וְהִנֵּה, בֵּין שֶׁנָּפְלָה לוֹ הָעַצְבוּת בִּשְׁעַת עֲבוֹדָה בְּתַלְמוּד תּוֹרָה אוֹ בִּתְפִלָּה, וּבֵין שֶׁנָּפְלָה לוֹ שֶׁלֹּא בִּשְׁעַת עֲבוֹדָה, זֹאת יָשִׂים אֶל לִבּוֹ, כִּי אֵין הַזְּמַן גְּרָמָא כָּעֵת לְעַצְבוּת אֲמִיתִּית, אֲפִלּוּ לִדְאֲגַת עֲוֹנוֹת חֲמוּרִים חַס וְשָׁלוֹם. רַק לָזֹאת צָרִיךְ קְבִיעוּת עִתִּים וּשְׁעַת הַכּוֹשֶׁר בְּיִשּׁוּב הַדַּעַת . . . וְכַמְבוֹאָר עֵת זוֹ בְּמָקוֹם אַחֵר.

"The Secret of Teshuvah," by **Mrs. Chana Slavaticki**:

MYJLI.COM/WARRIOR

Now, regardless of whether the negative emotion happens upon us while we are involved in the service of G-d—studying or praying—we must realize that now is an inappropriate time for genuine remorse, even over egregious misdeeds, G-d forbid. For genuine remorse, we need designated times, appropriate times when we have calmness of mind. . . . Elsewhere it is clarified precisely when this time should be.

The Last Prayer, Samuel Hirszenberg, 1897. (Museum of Art, Ein Harod)

TEXT 14

RABBI SHNE'UR ZALMAN OF LIADI, *SIDUR IM DACH* 18C 👥

לִהְיוֹת מִמָּארֵי דְחוּשְׁבְּנָא בְּכָל לַיְלָה בְּתִקּוּן חֲצוֹת אוֹ בִּקְרִיאַת שְׁמַע שֶׁעַל הַמִּטָּה, לִטְעוֹם מְרִירוּת בְּנַפְשׁוֹ מִכָּל מַעֲשָׂיו וְדִבּוּרָיו וּמַחְשְׁבוֹתָיו אֲשֶׁר לֹא לַה' הֵמָּה מִיּוֹם הֱיוֹתוֹ. וְיוֹסִיף דַּעַת וְהִתְבּוֹנְנוּת בִּגְדוּלַת ה', יוֹסִיף מַכְאוֹב בְּנַפְשׁוֹ עַל אֲשֶׁר בְּהֶבֶל בָּא וּבַחֹשֶׁךְ וְצַלְמָוֶת יֵלֵךְ רוֹב הַזְּמָן.

Every night, either during the *Tikun Chatsot* (midnight) prayer or the bedtime Shema, we must make a personal reckoning. We should taste the bitterness of all our unholy deeds, words, and thoughts from the moment we came into being [until the present]. The more we contemplate the greatness of G-d and increase our emotional connection with Him, the greater will be our pain over our focus on meaningless trivialities and over the fact that the preponderance of our time is spent walking in darkness and in "the shadow of death."

Figure 3.1d

Appropriate Remorse . . .

1	is only over a morally faulty *choice*.
2	is productive:
	a	It leads to heightened joy.
	b	It leads to change.
3	is a result of a genuine change of perspective and feelings.
4	is controlled and limited timewise.

QUESTION FOR DISCUSSION

What are the possible drawbacks to designating time for feeling remorse and regret?

TEXT 15

TANYA, CH.26 (REPRISE)

רַק לָזֹאת צָרִיךְ קְבִיעוּת עִתִּים וּשְׁעַת הַכּוֹשֶׁר בְּיִשּׁוּב הַדַּעַת, לְהִתְבּוֹנֵן בִּגְדוּלַת ה' אֲשֶׁר חָטָא לוֹ, כְּדֵי שֶׁעַל יְדֵי זֶה יִהְיֶה לִבּוֹ נִשְׁבָּר בֶּאֱמֶת בִּמְרִירוּת אֲמִיתִּית.

During those [designated] times, we should reflect upon the greatness of G-d against Whom we have sinned, and thereby cause our hearts to be truly broken and genuinely embittered.

TEXT 16

RABBI SHLOMO RABINOWITZ, *TIFERET SHLOMO*, HOLIDAYS, SHABBAT SHUVAH

עִנְיַן הַתְּשׁוּבָה, אֲשֶׁר הָעִיקָר הִיא הַחֲרָטָה לְהִתְמַרְמֵר בְּלִבּוֹ אֲשֶׁר הִכְעִיס לְהַבּוֹרֵא בָּרוּךְ הוּא וְגָרַם צַעַר גָּלוּת הַשְּׁכִינָה מֵחֲמַת שֶׁפָּגַם בַּעֲבֵירוֹת רַחֲמָנָא לִיצְלָן. וְלֹא יָשִׂים כָּל מְגַמָּתוֹ עַל הַצַּעַר הַפְּגָם הַנּוֹגֵעַ לְנַפְשׁוֹ, מֵעוֹנֶשׁ הַגֵּיהִנֹם וְכַדוֹמֶה.

RABBI SHLOMO HAKOHEN RABINOWITZ (*TIFERET SHLOMO*) 1801–1866
Founder of the Radomsk Chasidic dynasty. One of the great Chasidic masters of 19th-century Poland, he is known as the *Tiferet Shlomo* after the title of his book, which is considered a classic in Chasidic literature.

When repenting, our regret and bitterness should be over the fact that we have provoked the Creator and anguished Him, for our sins cause the exile of the Divine Presence. We should not overly focus on the damage we have inflicted upon our own souls, punishment in the afterlife, or the like.

Figure 3.1e

Appropriate Remorse . . .

| 1 | is only over a morally faulty *choice*. |

| 2 | is productive: |

| | a | It leads to heightened joy. |

| | b | It leads to change. |

| 3 | is a result of a genuine change of perspective and feelings. |

| 4 | is controlled and limited timewise. |

| 5 | is about the offended (not the offending) party. |

TEXT **17**

TANYA, CH. 26 (REPRISE)

מִיַּד אַחַר שֶׁנִּשְׁבַּר לִבּוֹ בָּעִתִּים קְבוּעִים הָהֵם, אֲזַי יָסִיר הָעֶצֶב מִלִּבּוֹ לְגַמְרֵי, וְיַאֲמִין אֱמוּנָה שְׁלֵמָה כִּי ה' הֶעֱבִיר חַטָּאתוֹ וְרַב לִסְלוֹחַ. וְזוֹ הִיא הַשִּׂמְחָה הָאֲמִיתִּית בַּה' הַבָּאָה אַחַר הָעֶצֶב כַּנִּזְכָּר לְעֵיל.

Is there anything that is unforgivable? **Rabbi Dov Greenberg**'s *succinct reply:*

MYJLI.COM/WARRIOR

As soon as our hearts have been broken during these designated times, we should completely remove the sorrow from our hearts and believe with a perfect faith that G-d, in His abundant forgiveness, has removed our sin. [We are then free to experience] the true joy in G-d that comes after the remorse, as mentioned above.

Jom Kippur, Georg Puschner, illustration from Peter Conrad Monath (publisher), *Juedisches Ceremoniel (Jewish Ceremonies)* (Nuremberg: 1724). (Leo Baeck Institute, Center for Jewish History, New York)

TEXT **18**

MISHNAH, BAVA KAMA 8:1–7

הַחוֹבֵל בַּחֲבֵרוֹ חַיָּב עָלָיו מִשּׁוּם חֲמִשָּׁה דְבָרִים: בְּנֶזֶק, בְּצַעַר, בְּרִפּוּי,
בְּשֶׁבֶת, וּבְבֹשֶׁת...
אַף עַל פִּי שֶׁהוּא נוֹתֵן לוֹ אֵין נִמְחַל לוֹ עַד שֶׁיְבַקֵּשׁ מִמֶּנּוּ.

One who injures another is obligated to make restitution in five ways: The attacker must pay actual damages and also pay for pain inflicted, medical bills, loss of employment, and humiliation. . . .

Even if the attacker makes these payments, G-d does not grant atonement until the offender implores the victim [for forgiveness]

MISHNAH

The first authoritative work of Jewish law that was codified in writing. The Mishnah contains the oral traditions that were passed down from teacher to student; it supplements, clarifies, and systematizes the commandments of the Torah. Due to the continual persecution of the Jewish people, it became increasingly difficult to guarantee that these traditions would not be forgotten. Rabbi Yehudah Hanassi therefore redacted the Mishnah at the end of the 2nd century. It serves as the foundation for the Talmud.

Rabbi Mordechai Dinerman discusses the halachic obligations of one who commits an offense against a fellow:

MYJLI.COM/WARRIOR

Figure 3.2

Resolving Guilt

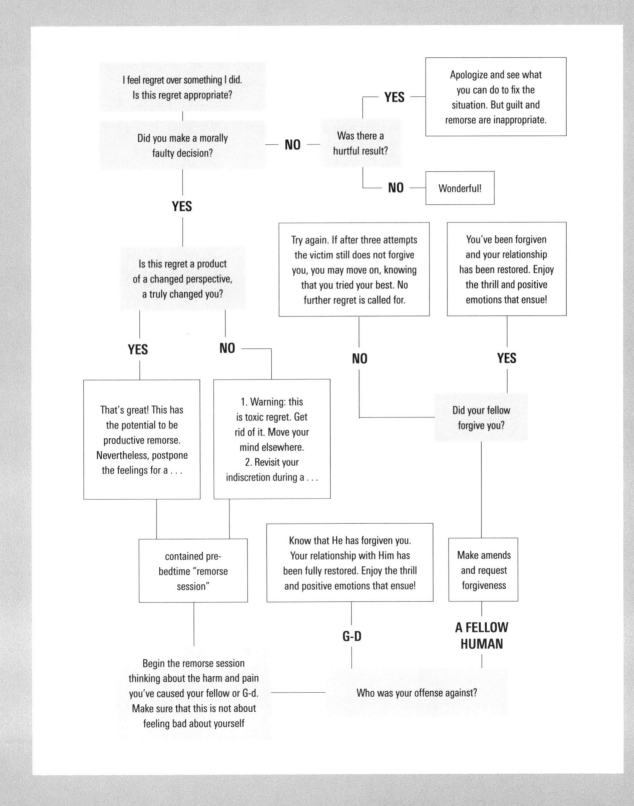

Figure 3.3

Benefits of Divine-Soul Model

AREA	RATIONALE
Negative emotions that result from feeling inauthentic	Every selfless deed is a 100 percent authentic expression of the divine soul.
Shame, feelings of inadequacy, and frustration that result from our internal struggles	These negative emotions are negated by understanding that character flaws are a gift, and our struggles are our purpose in life.
Guilt and remorse	Feelings of remorse are controlled and purposeful and lead to greater joy.

Exercise 3.4

In Exercise 3.1 you identified a past choice that has left you with significant lingering feelings of guilt. Which relevant messages from today's lesson can you implement to ensure that your remorse is productive?

KEY POINTS

1 Negative emotions, even when valid and appropriate, are never a goal unto themselves. They are merely bridges to the benefit that follows: increased joy and positive emotion.

2 It is vital that our ordinary routine runs exclusively on positive emotions. All regret and remorse must therefore be postponed for the pre-bedtime hour and contained timewise.

3 The concept of remorse is often mired in moral confusion, whereby we confuse for piety feelings that are actually toxic and expressions of self-centeredness. Remorse that flows from an unhealthy place cannot lead to a positive result—but merely perpetuates the negativity of its source.

4 These are the guidelines for legitimate, productive remorse:

(a) Remorse is appropriate only for something that legitimately calls for remorse, such as a faulty *decision*—but not a faulty *result*—because we can only control our decisions, not results.

(b) Remorse must directly lead to increased positive emotion.

(c) Remorse must trigger a change in subsequent behavior.

(d) Remorse is not a *catalyst* for true change. Rather, productive remorse is a *product* of a shift in feelings and perspective—a changed you.

(e) Healthy remorse is other-centered (caused by reflecting on how you have wronged G-d or your fellow), not self-centered (reflecting on how terrible *you* are).

5 Guilt and remorse are countered through living a life aligned with our divine soul.

Appendix

TEXT **19**

JULIEN A. DEONNA AND FABRICE TERONI, *THE EMOTIONS: A PHILOSOPHICAL INTRODUCTION*, FIRST ED. (NEW YORK: ROUTLEDGE, 2012), PP. 14–15

A first distinction that structures our intuitive grasp of the emotional domain is that between positive and negative emotions. Intuitively, sadness, fear, disgust, shame, and regret count as negative, while joy, admiration, pride, and amusement count as positive. In this context philosophers and psychologists speak of the "polarity" or "valence" of emotions. Accounting for this central aspect of emotional phenomena has typically taken one of two forms: we may approach valence in hedonic or in conative terms.

The hedonic approach has it that the various kinds of emotions are to be classed as positive or negative in virtue of "what it is like" to experience them. The idea here . . . is that each kind of emotion is among other things essentially a kind of pleasure or displeasure, pleasure and displeasure being considered as irreducible, phenomenological qualities (hence the talk in terms of the positive or negative hedonic quality of an emotion). This is perfectly compatible with the idea that certain kinds of emotions are hedonically ambivalent (e.g.,

JULIEN A. DEONNA, PHD

Assistant professor at the Department of Philosophy of the University of Geneva, Switzerland, and project leader at the Swiss Centre for Research in the Affective Sciences. Dr. Deonna works on theories of emotions and moral psychology.

FABRICE TERONI, PHD

Postdoctoral assistant at the Philosophy Department at Bern University, Switzerland, and senior researcher at the Swiss Centre for Research in the Affective Sciences. Dr. Teroni works on theories of emotions and memory.

nostalgia and scorn). A strong version of this view would then consist in claiming that each emotion-*type* essentially possesses a certain hedonic quality, i.e. it is either positive, negative, or mixed. . . .

[The] alternative approach to valence in conative terms has taken at least three forms. One can cash out the contrast between positive and negative emotions in terms of (a) motivational tendencies, where positive emotions are those that involve attraction to the object of the emotion, and negative emotions feature a kind of aversion towards it (E.G. MCLEAN, 1995), or in terms of (b) desires concerning the mental state in which one finds oneself (in positive emotions, the subject wants the intentional state she is in to continue, and in negative emotions she wants it to stop) (E.G., PRINZ 2004: 173–74), or in terms of (c) frustration or satisfaction of desires (positive emotions are those that reveal to her that a given situation is congruent with [some of] her goals, and negative emotions reveal an incongruence) (E.G., LAZARUS 1991).

TEXT 20

BARBARA L. FREDRICKSON, "THE VALUE OF POSITIVE EMOTIONS,"
AMERICAN SCIENTIST, 91 (2003), P. 332

Experiencing a positive emotion leads to states of mind and to modes of behavior that indirectly prepare an individual for later hard times. In my broaden-and-build theory, I propose that the positive emotions broaden an individual's momentary mind-set, and by doing so help to build enduring personal resources. We can test these ideas by exploring the ways that positive emotions change how people think and how they behave.

My students and I conducted experiments in which we induced certain emotions in people by having them watch short, emotionally evocative film clips. We elicited joy by showing a herd of playful penguins waddling and sliding on the ice, we elicited serenity with clips of peaceful nature scenes, we elicited fear with films of people at precarious heights, and we elicited sadness with scenes of deaths and funerals. We also used a neutral "control" film of an old computer screen saver that elicited no emotion at all. We then assessed the participant's ability to think broadly. Using global-local visual processing tasks, we measured whether they saw the "big picture" or focused on smaller details. The participant's task is to judge which of two comparison figures is more similar to a "standard" figure. Neither choice is right or wrong, but one comparison figure resembles the standard in

BARBARA L. FREDRICKSON, PHD
Social psychologist. Dr. Fredrickson is the professor of psychology at the University of North Carolina at Chapel Hill. Her main work is related to her broaden-and-build theory of positive emotions, which suggests that positive emotions lead to expansive behavior and that, over time, these actions lead to meaningful, long-term resources, such as knowledge and social relationships.

global configuration, and the other in local, detailed elements. Using this and similar measures, we found that, compared to those in negative or neutral states, people who experience positive emotions (as assessed by self-report or electromyographic signals from the face) tend to choose the global configuration, suggesting a broadened pattern of thinking.

This tendency to promote a broader thought-action repertoire is linked to a variety of downstream effects of positive emotions on thinking. Two decades of experiments by Alice Isen of Cornell University and her colleagues have shown that people experiencing positive affect (feelings) think differently. One series of experiments tested creative thinking using such tests as Mednick's Remote Associates Test, which asks people to think of a word that relates to each of three other words. So, for example, given the words mower, atomic and foreign, the correct answer is power. Although this test was originally designed to assess individual differences in the presumably stable trait of creativity, Isen and colleagues showed that people experiencing positive affect perform better on this test than people in neutral states.

TEXT 21

JOSEPH P. FORGAS, "CAN SADNESS BE GOOD FOR YOU? ON THE COGNITIVE, MOTIVATIONAL, AND INTERPERSONAL BENEFITS OF NEGATIVE AFFECT," IN W. GERROD PARROTT (ED.), *THE POSITIVE SIDE OF NEGATIVE EMOTIONS* (NEW YORK: GUILFORD PRESS, 2014), PP. 5–8

Negative affect in general, and sadness in particular . . . have important adaptive consequences by spontaneously triggering cognitive, motivational, and behavioral strategies that are well suited to dealing with the requirements of demanding social situations (FRIJDA, 1986). This is not to suggest that positive affect has no beneficial consequences, such as promoting creativity, flexibility, cooperation, and life satisfaction (FORGAS, 1994, 1998A, 1998B, 2002; FORGAS & GEORGE, 2001). Rather, a number of empirical studies now demonstrate that negative moods such as sadness may often recruit a more attentive, accommodating thinking style that produces superior outcomes whenever detailed, externally oriented, inductive thinking is required (BLESS & FIEDLER, 2006; FORGAS & EICH, 2012). . . .

Affect may . . . influence the *process* of cognition, that is, *how* people think (CLARK & ISEN, 1982; FIEDLER & FORGAS, 1988; FORGAS, 2002). . . . Negative moods call for *accommodative, bottom-up* processing, focused on the details of the external world. In contrast, positive moods recruit *assimilative, top-down* processing and

JOSEPH P. FORGAS
Social psychologist. Forgas is the Scientia Professor at the University of New South Wales, Sydney, Australia. His research interests include affect and social cognition, and interpersonal behavior.

greater reliance on existing schematic knowledge and heuristics (BLESS, 2000; BLESS & FIEDLER, 2006; FIEDLER, 2001). Thus *assimilation* involves greater reliance on preexisting internal knowledge when responding to a situation, greater use of heuristics and cognitive shortcuts, and more top-down, generative, and constructive processing strategies in general. *Accommodation*, in contrast, involves increased attention to new, external, and unfamiliar information, increased sensitivity to social norms and expectations, and a more concrete, piecemeal, and bottom-up processing style. This affectively induced assimilative–accommodative processing dichotomy has received extensive support in recent years, suggesting that moods perform an adaptive function, preparing us to respond to different environmental challenges.

Several studies suggest that such a processing dichotomy associated with good and bad moods can have significant consequences. For example, Fiedler, Asbeck, and Nickel (1991) found that people experiencing positive moods were more likely to engage in constructive processing and were more influenced by prior priming manipulations when forming judgments about people, whereas negative mood reduced this tendency. Further, negative affect, by facilitating the processing of new external information, can also reduce judgmental mistakes such as the fundamental attribution error (FORGAS, 1998A), reduce halo effects and primacy effects in impression formation (FORGAS, 2011A, 2011B), improve the quality and efficacy of persuasive arguments (FORGAS, 2007), and also improve eyewitness memory (FIEDLER, ET AL., 1991; FORGAS, VARGAS, & LAHAM, 2005).... The theory thus implies that *both* positive and negative moods can produce processing advantages, albeit in response to different situations that require different strategies.

Additional Readings

GROWING FROM PAIN

BY RABBI SHLOMA MAJESKI

Is it not important that a person experience pain when things are not working out, for this will spur him to improve? If a person never experiences pain because he constantly distracts the mind with other subjects or avoids the issue entirely, the problem—be it something physical or something spiritual—will never be dealt with.

On a physical level, physicians say that pain can be a blessing, because when a person experiences pain, it makes him aware of a problem. It motivates him to go to a physician, undergo an examination, and enable the problem to be discovered. Then, as the old *Chassidic* adage says, "the knowledge of the disease is half the cure." When a problem is defined, it can be eliminated.

If, G-d forbid, a person never experiences any pain, the disease or malfunction will continue to grow. It is possible that by the time it is discovered, it would be too late to do anything about it. Therefore, the fact that pain brings the condition to the person's attention and thus enables him to deal with it, is obviously a positive quality.

Why, then, should we avoid emotional pain? Why not say that when a person feels pain about a certain event, it is positive—that the pain is a force pushing him to change? There is tremendous inertia when it comes to changing our personalities, and without such motivation it is questionable whether a person would in fact change.

RABBI SHLOMA MAJESKI

Scholar of Chasidic philosophy. Rabbi Majeski serves as the principal of Machon L'Yahadus Women's Yeshiva in Crown Heights, Brooklyn, and is the author of *The Chassidic Approach to Joy* and *A Tzaddik and His Students*.

A *farbrengen* is a gathering where *chassidim* sit together and sing *Chassidic* songs. Usually, an elder *chassid* speaks to his younger colleagues and encourages them to improve their Divine service. Once, a group of *chassidim* were sitting together in a dark basement, wrapped up in such a gathering. Another person was walking by and heard singing. Recognizing the melody, he called out, "Where are you? Where is the *farbrengen*?"

One of the *chassidim* called back to him and told him to come down to the basement. After taking several steps down the staircase, he hesitated because it was very dark. He called down again, "How can I go down there? It is dark. I cannot see where I am going."

One of the *chassidim* sitting by the table answered him, "Do not worry, if you sit here long enough, your eyes will get used to the darkness."

The *chassid* was telling him a simple physiological fact. When we sit in darkness for a time, our pupils expand and we can see better than we could when we first entered the room. But the elder *chassid* conducting the *farbrengen* wanted to focus on a different dimension. "That is precisely the problem," he told his listeners. "If you sit in darkness long enough, you get used to it. You do not realize the need for light."

This is why it can be positive for a person to feel pain in a given situation. If something hurts him, he will know that something is wrong, and this will push him to change. If, instead, he is allowed to remain complacent, he will make his peace with the problem without trying to solve it.

Whenever a person has problems—be they physical, financial, or spiritual—it is very important for him to recognize that there is a difficulty and to do something about correcting it. Why should we tell him to divert his attention and ignore the matter? Of what permanent value is such bliss?

On the other hand, sadness and depression are not always valuable. On the contrary, they are often paralyzing influences that rob a person of vitality and prevent him from solving the problems that present themselves.

Thus, it appears that there are two types of feeling bad: one that stirs positive change, and one that reinforces negativity. How can we recognize the difference between the two? In truth, when a person is experiencing feelings of remorse, regret or hurt, he may not be able to recognize which of the two types of feeling he is experiencing. Afterwards, however, he can tell by the results.

Let us take an example: A person is up late at night and thinks to himself, "There are so many things that I wanted to get done this past month. But I did not do them. This was not done, and that was not done." The person continues along this train of thought until he comes to the conclusion, "I am a failure."

All the pressure from the entire month piles up on him, and he feels miserable and depressed. And what does he do? He decides he cannot face the world anymore. So he dives into bed, covers himself with his blankets and goes to sleep.

Perhaps this is a slight exaggeration. The point is, however, that feeling bad can leave one drained of energy with no incentive to do anything except escape from the world.

The same situation—a person sitting up at night and realizing that he has failed to accomplish anything in a month—can produce a totally different response. Instead of wanting to go to sleep, the person can feel charged with energy and filled with the resolve that he will get the job done.

What prompted these feelings? His feeling bad about his lack of accomplishment. In this instance, feeling bad generated energy and vitality.

In the *Tanya*, the Alter Rebbe differentiates between these two types of feeling bad. The depression that dulls a person's sensitivity and should be avoided is termed *atzvus*. The type of feeling bad that spurs a person towards positive activity is referred to as *merirus*, "bitterness."

To differentiate between the two, a person has to ask himself: "Why am I feeling bad? Is it concern with the past or with the future?" If the person is upset about something that has happened, and all he can think about is how bad it was, then it is *atzvus*. There is absolutely no purpose in concentrating on such thoughts; the event is over. There is nothing to do about it. What the person should do is get all thoughts of it out of his system entirely.

If, however, when thinking about a problem a person is prompted to do something about it, then it is *merirus*; it is the kind of feeling bad that is valuable. True, the person feels regret and remorse, but his feelings are channeled in the direction of change. He keeps asking himself: "What can I do to correct the situation?" and "How can I see that it does not happen again?"

There is, however, a problem. Man is not a robot, and it is hard to discern the fine line that differentiates between these positive thoughts of regret and remorse and the undesirable thoughts of depression. How can we make sure that our negative thoughts remain directed to a positive purpose?

The answer again centers on mind control. We should regulate the amount of time we spend thinking about these things. This enables us to exercise control over our thoughts, instead of allowing these thoughts to control us. Bitterness is a positive quality, but only in small doses, and only at an appropriate time.

It can be compared to an antibiotic. An antibiotic is often a helpful drug that cures disease. But people take antibiotics in very small dosages, usually a teaspoon two or three times a day.

If you are drinking apple juice or orange juice, you may drink an entire cup or even two cups. And you may drink as often as you want. But we do not take antibiotics in such large quantities, and we do not take them very often.

Why not? Because antibiotics are fundamentally a destructive agent. It is true that they destroy the germs that are causing illness. But they can—and if they are taken too frequently, they will—destroy life systems within the body that are necessary for our health.

Therefore, they are taken only in small amounts. This enables the destructive activity to be controlled and to be directed to purging the bacteria-causing illness without affecting the well-being of the body as a whole.

Similar concepts apply with regard to remorse and regret. Feeling remorse and regret is itself a negative quality. Sometimes, however, it is effective in rectifying an undesirable situation. Nevertheless, because it is fundamentally destructive, it has to be regulated and employed within certain limits. Only then will it be controlled and directed toward a positive intent. Otherwise, it will lead to depression and will drain a person's energy.

To cite an analogy: There are activities that are very good and are considered to be great *mitzvos*. Nevertheless, if these same activities are performed at the wrong time or in the wrong place, they can lose all positive value, and even become negative. For example, eating *matzah* is a very great *mitzvah*. But when? When we eat the *matzah* on the night of Passover, at the *seder*. If we eat *matzah* at any other time, it is not a *mitzvah*. And if we eat the *matzah* on the night of Yom Kippur, it is considered a sin, a very severe violation of Torah law.

The same thing is true about fasting. It is also a very great *mitzvah*. But when? On Yom Kippur, the holiest day of the year. At other times, it is not as important. And if we fast on the night of Passover, when we are supposed to be eating *matzah*, we have done something wrong.

The same idea applies with regard to thinking about problems—whether spiritual or material—that a person must correct. There is positive value to such thought and it should be encouraged. But only at the right time and in the right way. Otherwise, not only are such thoughts not positive, they can become destructive.

How can such thoughts become negative? Here we can learn an interesting concept from the Hebrew language. The Hebrew word for "sadness" is *atzvus* (עצבות). The Hebrew word for laziness is *atzlus* (עצלות). They are spelled in a very similar way. The only difference is that one contains a *beis* (ב) and the other, a *lamed* (ל).

What is the connection between depression and laziness? The connection works both ways. Depression leads to laziness. When a person is depressed, he is drained of energy. And this inactivity reinforces itself; the person becomes lazy.

The converse, however, is also true. Laziness leads to depression. A person allows himself to get depressed because it is an easier alternative. Otherwise, he would have to come to terms with the problem, to face himself and work out a solution. But that requires effort; and there is less work in lying back and feeling depressed.

Many times when a person is depressed, a friend will knock on his door and say, "Come on. We are going someplace. Do you want to join us?" And the person will refuse to go with them. The person knows that if he went along with his friend, he would definitely be able to pull himself out of his depression. He would start thinking about what is happening now, and that would take his mind off what is causing his depression. But he just cannot let go.

Why can he not let go? Because by staying depressed, he need not face the challenge of living.

When a person faces himself and confronts the problems he must deal with, it is not difficult to arrive at a solution. Many people say that they spend a lot of time thinking about a problem, but they can never arrive at a solution. Why is that so? Because at the outset, their thoughts were not directed toward finding a solution.

On the contrary, what they wanted to do—although they might not be aware of it—is to continue thinking about how devastating the situation is, and how if such and such would happen, it would be even worse.

There are times when we enjoy focusing on negativity. It is illogical. We know that these thoughts are not really relevant, that they will not bring us genuine satisfaction, nor will they lead to a practical solution. And yet we continue to think about them. Why? Because we are not ready to go out and face life. We would rather wallow in the dumps of despair instead of going out and trying to solve the problem.

If a person eliminated all that negativity and focused on one thing—how he can solve the problem he is confronting—he would be surprised to find that within a short period of time, he will conceive of several possible solutions to any given problem.

One of the *mashpi'im* (spiritual mentors) in the Lubavitcher *yeshivah* in Russia in the 1920s was R. Yechezkel Feigen. He would teach *Chassidic* thought, and from time to time, he would gather his students together and lead a *farbrengen* for them.

At one such *farbrengen*, he demanded a lot of his students. He told them that he wanted to see a deeper commitment to prayer, to study, and to personal development. His words were touched with intensity, and he addressed his students personally, showing them where they needed to concentrate their efforts.

They were deeply moved by what he said and many began to cry. Suddenly in the midst of the *farbrengen*, the person appointed as watchman came running with the news that the KGB was carrying out a search in the area.

This represented a real danger. Needless to say, such a gathering was prohibited; all of the participants could have been sent to hard-labor camps. Immediately, everyone began suggesting alternatives. One said, "Let us try to flee." Another suggested turning off the light, hoping darkness would serve as a cover. A third thought about putting newspapers and political science books on the table to show that they were involved in activities that the government would accept.

Thank G-d, the KGB never came to the room. They left the area as abruptly as they came, and the rabbi and the students were able to sit down to resume the *farbrengen*. The rabbi turned to his students and told them, "I just saw something very strange. I hope you can explain it to me."

The students looked at him quizzically and he continued, "Tell me, what affects you more, a difficulty in spiritual matters or a problem involving material things?"

The students were honest with themselves, and with him. Immediately, they replied that it was material things that affected them more.

"Why then," he asked, "was it that when I spoke to you about your spiritual well-being, everybody was crying, but when you heard that the KGB was in the area and your lives were in danger, nobody cried?"

One of the students gave him a puzzled look and replied, "What did you expect us to do, sit down and cry? What good would that do? We had to figure out a way either to get out or to hide ourselves before they came."

R. Feigen had been waiting for such an answer. "Oh, I see. When you had to act fast, you knew that crying would not help. Why, then, when it comes to spiritual things is it acceptable to cry?"

He repeated this concept and explained it until it sank in. The students understood that crying can be merely an excuse. It does not solve the problem at all. All it does is give the person catharsis. When, by contrast, a person is serious about making a change, he does not have time to cry. Every moment is precious and can be used to implement a solution. That is the way it is supposed to be.

In summary, what we are saying is that *Chassidus* teaches us that there are two ways of responding to negative factors—whether they be physical or spiritual. One is positive, *merirus*, which is translated as bitterness, and the other is negative, *atzvus*, which we have translated as depression.

There are four fundamental differences between the two:

a) *Atzvus* has no life to it; it is the type of feeling bad that leaves one drained. The person loses his incentive to do anything. *Merirus*, by contrast, spurs energy; it has dynamism and life.

b) *Atzvus* perpetuates itself. The feelings of depression continue for a long time. With *merirus*, feeling bad is temporary. The positive drive it brings produces active feelings of achievement in a very short time.

c) *Atzvus* is not directed toward a practical solution. It is not a means to an end; it is an end in itself. One becomes satisfied thinking about how terrible everything is. *Merirus*, by contrast, is future-oriented and focuses on a solution and the future. The person asks himself: what can I do about the problem?

d) *Atzvus* leads a person to be more withdrawn and self-concerned. He thinks more and more about himself. The dynamism of *merirus*, by contrast, allows a person to think about others.

There are many ramifications of the difference between these two approaches. For example, throughout the 1960s and 1970s, activists for Soviet Jewry called for adding an empty chair and setting aside an extra *matzah* at the *Seder* table as a stark reminder of the 3 million Soviet Jews who were not free to attend a *Seder*.

The Lubavitcher Rebbe disagreed with this suggestion for several reasons. Firstly, Pesach is a holiday; a time when we are not allowed to do anything that is associated with mourning and sadness. Even if he had appreciated the idea, the timing was inappropriate.

Furthermore, aside from expressing his firm belief that the move was a tactical blunder that would only serve to further alienate the Soviets, he decried the notion as fundamentally wrong.

The Rebbe emphasized that the suggestion put the focus on the negative. "So you have an empty chair," he said in the days leading up to Passover 1970. "Go out into the street where you live, and find Jews who don't know how to celebrate the *Seder*, or don't even know what a *Seder* is, and sit them down at your *Seder* table!"

The Rebbe was not just offering a different suggestion. He was showing an entirely different approach to the issue. Instead of having our thinking about the loss of Jewish freedom result in an empty chair, he wanted that the emotion aroused be directed to a positive purpose.

What can be done to compensate for the Soviet Jewry? First and foremost, something positive. Take a Jew who is free today and is on the way to total assimilation—he doesn't even seek to take part in a Pesach *Seder*—and make him feel part of the Jewish people. This counteracts Hitler's efforts and demonstrates that nothing—neither Pharaoh, nor Hitler, nor for that matter the openness of American society—can break the connection that a Jew shares with his spiritual heritage.

Let us take another example. One of the main concerns of many people who have changed their way of life and begun to observe the Torah and its *mitzvos* is *kashrus*. Once people begin keeping *kosher* and learn how important it is, many become quite upset about having eaten non-*kosher* food for so many years.

I know a number of people who wrote letters to the Lubavitcher Rebbe asking his advice regarding what they should do to atone for all the non-*kosher* food that they had eaten. They expected the Rebbe to tell them to fast a few times a week, to refrain from eating foods that gave them pleasure or to offer other suggestions of that type. The Rebbe, however, took a totally different approach. He told them to encourage and to educate other Jews to observe the laws of *kashrus*.

What the Rebbe was saying was: do not focus on the pain you are feeling because of your errors. Transform that pain into positive and productive energy. Reach out to another person and share your insights with him.

For *merirus* to be an effective tool in spurring us to improve our conduct, it cannot be left to spontaneity. Personal growth depends on a person's controlling his feelings, and that control does not happen spontaneously.

For this reason, there has to be a designated time when we think about the different problems that we have. Whether the problems are physical, financial or family oriented, we cannot allow them to haunt us all day long. Nor can we forfeit control when we think about them. We have to set aside a time when we are prepared to confront them.

Even spiritual failings should only be dealt with at a time set aside explicitly for that purpose. *Chassidus* talks about setting aside time to think about our spiritual well-being. It calls such thoughts *cheshbon hanefesh*, which literally means "making an account for the soul."

Various times are designated for this: daily—at the end of the day before going to bed; weekly—towards the end of the week, on Thursday night; monthly—on the last day of the month, which is known as *Yom Kippur Katan*, "a miniature Yom Kippur"; and yearly—at the end of the year, throughout the month of Elul.

These practices emphasize that, as mentioned above, there has to be a designated time to think about these matters. We cannot let these thoughts just barge in on us at any given time. We also see that the designated time is always at the end of the period in question.

During the day, a person should be active and productive, focusing on accomplishment. It is not a time to sit back and review situations; it is a time to act. When the day is coming to an end and he is preparing for the next day, he should stop and ask himself, "How did the day pass?" and "What can I do so that tomorrow will be better than today?"

The same concept applies to a weekly cycle, a monthly cycle and a yearly cycle. At the end, we should take stock of what we are doing, so that we are prepared for the new cycle that is approaching. But before the end of that cycle, we should be busy working, doing productive things that will benefit both ourselves and others.[1]

On this basis, we can explain the conclusion reached in the previous chapter. A person should dismiss negative thoughts from his mind, that is true—but only when he is feeling depression, not bitterness. Even if he is feeling bitterness, but it is at the wrong time, such as when he is supposed to be at work, *davening*, studying or busy with the family, these thoughts should be dismissed.

At all times, we should be in control. We should bring the undesirable matter to our attention when we want to, and deal with it in the way we know best. This is a productive approach.

Endnotes

[1] See *Likkutei Sichos*, Vol. 16, p. 272.

Rabbi Shloma Majeski, *The Chassidic Approach to Joy*
(Brooklyn: Sichos In English, 1995), ch. 8

Reprinted with permission of the author

THE FUNCTIONAL UTILITY OF NEGATIVE EMOTIONS

BY W. GERROD PARROTT, PHD

The idea that negative emotions can be functional may seem odd or even self-contradictory. Yet it is the thesis of this chapter that negative emotions can indeed be useful and even desirable, and that emotional intelligence includes recognizing and exploiting this utility. If this thesis seems strange, it is probably because of two assumptions that are often made about emotions: first, that emotions are principally feelings, and second, that people are principally hedonistic. These assumptions are fairly common; they are often made both by academics studying emotion and by laypersons in many Western societies. The assumption that emotions are feelings construes negative emotions as unpleasant feelings and positive emotions as pleasant feelings. The assumption of hedonism construes people as seeking pleasure and avoiding pain. The combination of these two assumptions yields the conclusion that people will be motivated to avoid or eliminate negative emotions and to seek or maintain positive emotions.

These two assumptions, however, are at best incomplete and are in some ways outright misleading. There is more to emotions than pleasant or unpleasant feelings, and there is more to human decision making than hedonism (Parrott, 1993). Enlarging one's conception of emotions and decision making alters one's understanding of the functions of negative emotions, and thus of emotional intelligence. Negative emotions have considerable potential to be useful. For this potential to be realized, however, these emotions must appear under the right circumstances, be expressed in ways that are productive in the current situation, be regulated so that their intensity and manifestations are appropriate, and be restrained under circumstances in which they are not helpful. Emotional

W. GERROD PARROTT, PHD

Professor of psychology at Georgetown University. Dr. Parrott's central interest is the nature of human emotion. He has published numerous scholarly articles and books.

intelligence, as it is now conceived, entails all of these determinants of functional utility.

This chapter addresses each of these points in turn. The first section describes the nature of emotions, with particular attention to negative emotions. It demonstrates that emotions entail much more than feelings: One's appraisal of one's situation, one's readiness to think and act, and one's effect on others are all modified during emotional states. The next section argues that these properties of negative emotions give them the potential to have functional utility. The rest of the chapter considers how this potential utility can best be realized. I describe a variety of factors that help determine the functional utility of emotions, and show that emotional intelligence is directly related to some of them but only indirectly related to others.

The Nature of Negative Emotions

Emotions can be understood as involving a constellation of features. These features include an appraisal, readiness to think and act in certain ways, physiological changes, and social signals and dispositions, as well as feelings. The functional utility of emotions is grounded in these changes, so understanding this utility requires appreciation of each of these aspects of emotion.

An appraisal is an assessment of how present circumstances influence one's goals and well-being. An appraisal is cognitive in the sense that it involves meaning and interpretation, but not in the sense that it need be deliberate, verbal, or symbolic. Thus, appraisal is cognitive in a way that is more like perception than like reasoning or knowledge. Appraisal also differs from other types of cognition in that it concerns the personal significance of an event, action, or object, rather than general information about it. It is the implications for one's own cares, concerns, goals, values, or well-being that are appraised (see Frijda, 1986; Lazarus, 1991; Ortony, Clore, & Collins, 1988). Theories of emotional appraisal contend that it is our interpretation of events that determines whether and in what way we become emotional. In other words, appraisals are typically the cause of emotions. Appraisal theories also typically contend that appraisals are an intrinsic part of emotions; they do not merely precede emotions. Part of what it means to have an emotion is to perceive one's circumstances along the lines of the appraisal integral to that emotion (Frijda, 1986; Lazarus, 1991).

Appraisals provide an alternative to feelings for understanding why some emotions are considered "negative" whereas others are considered "positive." Negative emotions—such as fear, sadness, shame, anger, contempt, guilt, disgust, anxiety, disappointment, embarrassment, loneliness, envy, and hatred—share the property of involving an appraisal that something is wrong. One's well-being is threatened, one's goals have to be abandoned, one lacks what one desires, one views oneself as doing wrong or as not projecting the desired appearance to others, and so on. In contrast, positive emotions—happiness, gratitude, pride, love, relief, hope, and so on—involve appraisals that one is meeting one's goals, that a bad event has not come to pass, that one is meeting or exceeding one's own standards, that one's relationship with another is secure, and so on. From this perspective, positive and negative emotions are not so much pleasant and unpleasant hedonic states as they are favorable or unfavorable assessments of one's present circumstances. For this reason even the feeling of emotion involves more than merely pleasure or pain. Emotional feelings may serve as information about one's present state of affairs and may color decision making about how to allocate one's mental and physical resources (Clore & Parrott, 1991; Oatley, 1992; Schwarz, 1990).

In addition to appraisals and feelings, emotions are associated with increased readiness to engage in various kinds of actions and thinking. For example, many negative emotions, such as anxiety and disgust, create a readiness to move away from an object or a threat. Other negative emotions, such as anger and contempt, involve a readiness to oppose or attack. Self-conscious negative emotion such as shame and embarrassment involve a tendency for social withdrawal, whereas emotions such as sadness and sorrow tend to involve giving up opposition to a disliked circumstance or abandoning a goal (Frijda, Kuipers, & ter Schure, 1989). These action tendencies are manifested in a variety of ways. There may be a lower threshold for initiating certain types of action: The fearful person is "jumpy," the irritated person is "snappish," the sad person is subdued and withdrawn. Action tendencies must be defined fairly abstractly; although there are sometimes particular actions that are primed, the tendency is often more general, such as "opposition" or "escape."

Many of the physiological aspects of emotions can be understood as aspects of action readiness. Some emotions involve activation of the sympathetic nervous system—increased heart rate and blood pressure, changes in blood flow, breathing, perspiration, and so on—and these can be understood as preparing the body for physical exertion (Cannon, 1929). Hormonal changes, such as increases in epinephrine, adrenocorticotropic hormone, or corticosteroids, mobilize energy resources and thus also prepare for action (Selye, 1956). Although there is not a clear patterning of physiology that corresponds to particular emotions, physiological changes do seem to correspond to requirements arising in coping with environmental demands and thus with preparation for action (Frijda, 1986; Ginsburg & Harrington, 1996).

Emotional action tendencies are not limited to physical actions, but include various types of mental readiness as well. The allocation of attention is one mental action that is strongly influenced by emotional states. Anxiety, for example, involves a tendency to be vigilant for threats. Attention is more quickly directed toward threatening stimuli when a person is anxious than when not (Mogg & Bradley, 1999). More generally, negative emotions allocate attention and other cognitive resources to plans and goals that need them most urgently ((Oatley, 1992). The content of thought can also be biased by emotion. Memory for past events may be skewed toward memories that are congruent with the emotional state, as when a sad person recalls unhappy times or when an angry person recalls previous transgressions (Blaney, 1986). The way a situation is interpreted may also be biased in a way that is congruent with a person's present emotional state, as when a statement or behavior is interpreted differently by sad and happy people (Bower, 1991; Forgas, 1995). Emotions influence not only attention and the content of thought, but the style of thinking as well. Negative emotions have been found to predispose people to adopt a conservative approach to problem solving: careful, methodical, and analytical. Positive emotions have been associated with a more holistic style that is less precise and detail oriented but also more creative, risky, and flexible (Isen, 2000; Schwarz & Bless, 1991).

In addition to their effects on the individuals experiencing the emotions, their effects on others can be seen as well. Emotions may be expressed by facial expression, posture, or voice, and these expressions influence other people in a variety of ways. One person's emotion can influence other people to have the same emotion, so that the emotion spreads from one person to another (Hatfield, Cacioppo, & Rapson, 1994). One person's emotion can also induce a complementary emotion in another, as when one person's anger induces another person's fear, or one person's gratitude induces another person's pride (e.g., Dimberg & Ohman, 1996).

The display of emotions is intimately intertwined with cultural norms and meanings, so many effects of emotions can be appreciated only within the context of a particular culture and social setting. Cultures tend to treat emotions objectively, in the sense that there are public standards regarding when certain emotions are allowed, reasonable, or appropriate (Sabini & Silver, 1982). To perform many jobs and social roles correctly, it is necessary to display the correct emotion in the correct manner on the correct occasion (Hochschild, 1979). For these reasons there are social costs and benefits to emotions that are specific to particular cultures and social settings, and these must be considered along with an emotion's other effects.

Although the emphasis of this argument has been to show that emotions consist of more than feelings, it is worth noting that feelings themselves may have functional utility. According to some theorists, emotional feelings function by providing feedback about one's appraisals. Although the details of the appraisals themselves may not be directly accessible to consciousness, emotional feelings may provide a conscious representation of the personal significance of events (Clore & Parrott, 1991; Schwarz, 1990). Moods and emotions may also signal whether the individual presently has the resources to cope with the demands being placed on him or her (Fredrickson, 1998; Morris 1992).

In summary, emotions modify appraisals of circumstances, preparations for various modes of action and thought, feelings, and expressions and behaviors that influence the emotions and behavior of others. Emotions thus consist of far more than feelings; in fact, many feelings of emotion may be at least partly the result of these other emotional changes (Parrott, 1995). It is because emotions affect people in so many ways that it is possible for them to have functional consequences. The next section presents an outline of these consequences and how they can be either adaptive or maladaptive.

The Functional (and Dysfunctional) Utility of Negative Emotions

Negative emotions have the potential for functional utility because there are times when the effects of negative emotions are useful. Recognizing this potential for benefit is the key to understanding why it is neither odd nor self-contradictory to claim that negative emotions can be useful or even desirable. In the simplest case, emotions will have utility if their effects tend to be beneficial under the conditions associated with each emotion's appraisal. For example, anger involves a readiness to be confrontational and antagonistic, and to the extent that confrontation and antagonism are adaptive under conditions that induce anger, this readiness will facilitate adaptive behavior. Similarly, fear involves a readiness to protect oneself and to move away from danger, and disgust involves expulsion and maintaining distance; to the extent that these actions tend to be adaptive under conditions that induce fear and disgust, these emotions too will tend to have functional utility.

The preceding examples illustrate how emotional readiness for physical action can have utility. The other effects of negative emotions also have the potential to function beneficially. For example, reallocating attention can be very functional: In anxiety it enables one to be vigilant for threats; in jealousy it leads one to monitor relationships that may have been taken for granted; in shame it can lead one to monitor others' opinions and to reestablish one's reputation. Negative emotions lead to reallocation of limited mental resources to the goals and projects that most need one's attention (Oatley, 1992).

Emotion's effects on style of thinking have the potential to be useful as well. Negative emotions occur when something has gone wrong or threaten to go wrong. They occur when there is a problem, when goals are at risk, or when resources seem inadequate. Such times may not be the best for exploring new approaches, nor are they times when one can easily afford a mistake. A careful, analytical approach that avoids risk taking may often be most appropriate in times of threat or stress (Schwarz & Bless, 1991).

The social effects of negative emotions can have a variety of potential benefits. When informing other people of an emergency, a person is more likely to obtain energetic assistance if that person expresses alarm than if he or she appears calm and matter-of-fact. It makes the urgent nature of the situation more real to others and may induce a similar emotion in them, which may in turn facilitate their actions (Hatfield, et al., 1994). Such contagion of negative emotions has the potential to produce benefits for the person initiating the social sequence.

The social effects of negative emotions can also be useful when they induce complementary emotions in others. For example, the anger expressed by a bill collector may be effective if it intimidates and scares a customer into paying a bill out of fear of legal and social consequences. Bill collectors who use anger to obtain these social effects are more effective than those who do not (Hochschild, 1983).

Finally, emotional feelings can themselves have functional utility. Their function is often conceived as one of providing information. Emotional feelings can be a source of information about something as specific as a person's attitude toward an object or individual or as general as a person's overall state of well-being (Schwarz, 1990). Although the complexity of evaluating information about a person or event may be too great to be held in conscious awareness, the outcome of one's unconscious appraisal may be learned by paying attention to resulting emotional feelings (Clore & Parrott, 1991). Just as the visual perception of size can be the result of a complex calculation yet be immediately experienced, so too may emotional feelings directly provide information about one's construal of a complex situation as it pertains to one's concerns and resources to cope (Morris, 1992).

W. Gerrod Parrott, "The Functional Utility of Negative Emotions," in Lisa Feldman Barrett and Peter Salovey (eds.), *The Wisdom in Feeling: Psychological Processes in Emotional Intelligence*, second edition (New York: The Guilford Press, 2002), pp. 341–347

Reprinted with permission of the publisher

Trauriger Frauenkopf (Sad Female Head), Ernst Ludwig Kirchner, painting, oil on canvas, c. 1928.

Lesson

4

PEERING THROUGH PAIN

ADDRESSING PAIN, ANGUISH, AND ANXIETY

Harsh reality can bring genuine suffering and sadness, swiftly deflating the most optimistic attitudes. Well-meaning reminders that time heals, or that G-d knows what is best, do little to heal the searing pain of open wounds. This lesson explores methods of shifting our internal perspectives to allow the sun to shine in our lives despite the stark reality of our suffering.

QUESTION FOR DISCUSSION

How can living a divine-soul-aligned life alleviate the emotional fallout from hardship?

Illustration, *The Jewish May*, by Ephraim Moses Lilien from the book
Lieder des Ghetto (Songs of the Ghetto) by Morris Rosenfeld (1903).

TEXT 1

RABBI YANKI TAUBER, *ONCE UPON A CHASSID* (BROOKLYN: KEHOT PUBLICATION SOCIETY, 1994), PP. 203–204

A man once came to Rabbi Dov Ber, the famed "Maggid of Mezeritch," with a question.

"The Talmud tells us," asked the man, "that 'A person is supposed to bless G-d for the bad just as he blesses Him for the good' (BERACHOT 60B). How is this humanly possible? . . . How can a human being possibly react to what he experiences as bad in exactly the *same way* he responds to what he experiences as good? How can a person be as grateful for his troubles as he is for his joys?"

Rabbi Dov Ber replied: "To find an answer to your question, you must go see my disciple, Reb Zusha of Anipoli. Only he can help you in this matter."

Reb Zusha received his guest warmly, and invited him to make himself at home. The visitor decided to observe Reb Zusha's conduct before posing his question. Before long, he concluded that his host truly exemplified the Talmudic dictum which so puzzled him. He couldn't think of anyone who suffered more hardship in his life than did Reb Zusha: a frightful pauper, there was never enough to eat in Reb Zusha's home, and his family was beset with all sorts of afflictions and illnesses. Yet Reb Zusha was always good-humored and cheerful, and

RABBI YANKI TAUBER, 1965–

Chasidic scholar and author. A native of Brooklyn, N.Y., Rabbi Tauber is an internationally renowned author who specializes in adapting the teachings of the Lubavitcher Rebbe. He is a member of the JLI curriculum development team and has written numerous articles and books, including *Once Upon a Chassid* and *Beyond the Letter of the Law.*

Dr. David Pelcovitz on dealing with stress and suffering:

MYJLI.COM/WARRIOR

constantly expressing his gratitude to the Almighty for all His kindness.

But what is his secret? How does he do it? The visitor finally decided to pose his question.

So one day, he said to his host: "I wish to ask you something. In fact, this is the purpose of my visit to you—our Rebbe advised me that you can provide me with the answer."

"What is your question?" asked Reb Zusha.

The visitor repeated what he had asked of the Maggid. "You raise a good point," said Reb Zusha, after thinking the matter through. . . .

QUESTION FOR DISCUSSION

If you were in Reb Zusha's position, how would you have responded?

Peasant Family at Home, Adriaen van Ostade, oil on oak panel, 1647. (Museum of Fine Arts, Budapest)

QUESTIONS FOR DISCUSSION

1 In your estimation, how was it possible for Reb Zusha to genuinely feel that he had never experienced suffering?

2 Reb Zusha was a holy man. Is his remarkable attitude attainable for ordinary people?

3 If yes, is this a desirable—normal and healthy—attitude for the average person?

Mrs. Sherri Mandell reflects on her son's murder and on resilience in the face of tragedy:

MYJLI.COM/WARRIOR

TEXT 2

RABBI SHNE'UR ZALMAN OF LIADI, *TANYA*, CH. 26

וְהִנֵּה עֵצָה הַיְעוּצָה לְטַהֵר לִבּוֹ מִכָּל עֶצֶב וְנִדְנוּד דְּאָגָה מִמִּילֵי דְעָלְמָא, וַאֲפִילוּ בָּנֵי חַיֵּי וּמְזוֹנֵי:

מוּדַעַת זֹאת לַכֹּל, מַאֲמַר רַזַ"ל: "כְּשֵׁם שֶׁמְּבָרֵךְ עַל הַטּוֹבָה כו'" (מִשְׁנָה, בְּרָכוֹת ט, ה), וּפֵירְשׁוּ בִּגְמָרָא (בְּרָכוֹת ס, ב), לְקַבּוֹלֵי בְּשִׂמְחָה, כְּמוֹ שִׂמְחַת הַטּוֹבָה הַנִּגְלֵית וְנִרְאֵית.

RABBI SHNE'UR ZALMAN OF LIADI (ALTER REBBE) 1745–1812

Chasidic rebbe, halachic authority, and founder of the Chabad movement. The Alter Rebbe was born in Liozna, Belarus, and was among the principal students of the Magid of Mezeritch. His numerous works include the *Tanya*, an early classic containing the fundamentals of Chabad Chasidism, and *Shulchan Aruch HaRav,* an expanded and reworked code of Jewish law.

The following is advice on cleansing one's heart of all sadness and of every trace of worry about mundane matters, even about one's family, health, and livelihood:

There is a well-known statement of our sages, "Just as we bless G-d for the good [so should we bless Him for misfortune]" (MISHNAH, BERACHOT 9:5). The Talmud (BERACHOT 60B) explains that we should accept misfortune with joy, in the same way that we rejoice over visible and overt goodness.

TEXT 3a

MALACHI 1:1–2

מַשָּׂא דְבַר ה' אֶל יִשְׂרָאֵל בְּיַד מַלְאָכִי: "אָהַבְתִּי אֶתְכֶם", אָמַר ה'.

G-d's message to Israel, delivered by Malachi: "I love you," says G-d.

TEXT 3b

JEREMIAH 31:2

מֵרָחוֹק ה' נִרְאָה לִי. וְאַהֲבַת עוֹלָם אֲהַבְתִּיךְ, עַל כֵּן מְשַׁכְתִּיךְ חָסֶד.

G-d appeared to [remind] me [of the love He showed our ancestors in Egypt] long ago, [and He instructed me to deliver the following message]:

"My love for you is eternal! I therefore extend to you My lovingkindness."

TEXT 3c

RABBI YISRAEL BAAL SHEM TOV, *KETER SHEM TOV,* P. 359

יעדער איד איז טייער ביי דעם אויבערשטן ווי אַ בן יחיד וואָס איז
געבאָרן געוואָרן ביי עלטערן לעת זקנותם, און נאָך טייערער.

G-d's love for each of us individually is comparable to
the love that elderly parents have for their only child
who was born to them in their later years—and even
greater than that.

**RABBI YISRAEL BAAL SHEM TOV
(BESHT) 1698–1760**
Founder of the Chasidic movement.
Born in Slutsk, Belarus, the Baal
Shem Tov was orphaned as a child.
He served as a teacher's assistant
and clay digger before founding
the Chasidic movement and
revolutionizing the Jewish world
with his emphasis on prayer, joy, and
love for every Jew, regardless of his
or her level of Torah knowledge.

TEXT 4

TANYA, CH. 26

וּפֵירְשׁוּ בִּגְמָרָא (בְּרָכוֹת ס, ב), לְקַבּוּלֵי בְּשִׂמְחָה, כְּמוֹ שִׂמְחַת הַטּוֹבָה
הַנִּגְלֵית וְנִרְאֵית. כִּי גַם זוּ לְטוֹבָה, רַק שֶׁאֵינָהּ נִגְלֵית וְנִרְאֵית לְעֵינֵי בָּשָׂר.

. . . The Talmud explains that we should accept misfortune with joy, in the same way that we rejoice over visible
and overt goodness. For the misfortune is likewise for
the good, although its goodness is not apparent and visible to mortal eyes.

TEXT 5

TALMUD, BERACHOT 60B–61A

תָּנָא מִשְּׁמֵיהּ דְּרַבִּי עֲקִיבָא: לְעוֹלָם יְהֵא אָדָם רָגִיל לוֹמַר: "כָּל דְּעָבִיד רַחֲמָנָא, לְטַב עָבִיד".

כִּי הָא דְּרַבִּי עֲקִיבָא דַּהֲוָה קָאָזֵיל בְּאוֹרְחָא. מְטָא לְהַהִיא מָתָא, בְּעָא אוּשְׁפִּיזָא, לֹא יָהֲבֵי לֵיהּ.

אָמַר: "כָּל דְּעָבִיד רַחֲמָנָא, לְטַב", אָזַל וּבָת בְּדַבְרָא.

וַהֲוָה בַּהֲדֵיהּ תַּרְנְגוֹלָא וַחֲמָרָא וּשְׁרָגָא. אָתָא זִיקָא, כַּבְיֵיהּ לִשְׁרָגָא. אָתָא שׁוּנָרָא, אַכְלֵיהּ לְתַרְנְגוֹלָא. אָתָא אַרְיֵה, אַכְלֵיהּ לַחֲמָרָא. אָמַר: "כָּל דְּעָבִיד רַחֲמָנָא, לְטַב".

בֵּיהּ בְּלֵילְיָא, אָתָא גְּיָיסָא שַׁבְיֵיהּ לְמָתָא. אָמַר לְהוּ: "לָאו אָמְרִי לְכוּ? כָּל מַה שֶּׁעוֹשֶׂה הַקָּדוֹשׁ בָּרוּךְ הוּא הַכֹּל לְטוֹבָה".

BABYLONIAN TALMUD

A literary work of monumental proportions that draws upon the legal, spiritual, intellectual, ethical, and historical traditions of Judaism. The 37 tractates of the Babylonian Talmud contain the teachings of the Jewish sages from the period after the destruction of the 2nd Temple through the 5th century CE. It has served as the primary vehicle for the transmission of the Oral Law and the education of Jews over the centuries; it is the entry point for all subsequent legal, ethical, and theological Jewish scholarship.

A teaching attributed to Rabbi Akiva: we should make a habit of constantly declaring, "Whatever G-d does is for the best."

[This is illustrated by an] incident in which Rabbi Akiva was traveling, and he arrived at a certain city. He sought lodging for the night, but no one was willing to host him.

"Whatever G-d does is for the best," said Rabbi Akiva, and he went to sleep for the night in a field.

He had a rooster, a donkey, and a candle. A sudden gust of wind extinguished his candle. Then a wild cat ate his rooster. Then a lion devoured his donkey.

"Whatever G-d does is for the best," Rabbi Akiva told himself.

During that night, an army attacked the city, taking all its residents captive. Rabbi Akiva [later recounted this experience and] told [his students], "Did I not tell you that whatever G-d does is for the best?"

Watchmaker, Yuri Pen, 1914. (National Art Museum of the Republic of Belarus)

TEXT 6

TALMUD, TAANIT 21A

וְאַמַּאי קָרוּ לֵיהּ "נַחוּם אִישׁ גַּם זוּ"? דְּכָל מִילְתָא דַּהֲוָה סַלְקָא לֵיהּ, אָמַר: "גַּם זוּ לְטוֹבָה".

זִמְנָא חֲדָא בָּעוּ לְשַׁדּוֹרֵי יִשְׂרָאֵל דּוֹרוֹן לְבֵי קֵיסָר. אָמְרוּ, "מַאן יֵיזִיל? יֵיזִיל נַחוּם אִישׁ גַּם זוּ, דִּמְלוּמָד בְּנִיסִין הוּא". שָׁדְרוּ בִּידֵיהּ מְלֹא סִיפְטָא דַּאֲבָנִים טוֹבוֹת וּמַרְגָּלִיּוֹת.

אֲזַל, בָּת בְּהַהוּא דִּירָה. בְּלֵילְיָא, קָמוּ הָנָךְ דִּיוֹרָאֵי וּשְׁקַלִינְהוּ לְסִיפְטֵיהּ וּמַלּוּנְהוּ עַפְרָא. לְמָחָר כִּי חַזְנְהוּ אָמַר גַּם זוּ לְטוֹבָה.

כִּי מָטָא הָתָם, שְׁרִינְהוּ לְסִיפְטָא. חָזַנְהוּ דְּמָלוּ עַפְרָא.

בָּעָא מַלְכָּא לְמִקְטְלִינְהוּ לְכוּלְּהוּ, אָמַר, קָא מְחַיְּיכוּ בִּי יְהוּדָאֵי. אָמַר: "גַּם זוּ לְטוֹבָה".

אָתָא אֵלִיָּהוּ, אִדְמֵי לֵיהּ כְּחַד מִינַּיְיהוּ. אָמַר לְהוּ: "דִּלְמָא הָא עַפְרָא מֵעַפְרָא דְּאַבְרָהָם אֲבוּהוֹן הוּא, דְּכִי הֲוָה שָׁדֵי עַפְרָא הֲווּ סַיְּיפֵיהּ, גִּילֵי הֲווּ גִּירֵי . . . ?"

הֲוָיָא חֲדָא מְדִינְתָּא דְּלָא מָצוּ לְמִיכְבְּשָׁהּ. בָּדְקוּ מִינֵּיהּ, וּכְבַשּׁוּהָ. עַיְּילוּ לְבֵי גַנְזֵיהּ וּמַלּוּהוּ לְסִיפְטֵיהּ אֲבָנִים טוֹבוֹת וּמַרְגָּלִיּוֹת וְשַׁדְּרוּהוּ בִּיקָרָא רַבָּה.

Rabbi Mordechai Dinerman on coping with anxiety and stress:

MYJLI.COM/WARRIOR

People referred to Nachum as Ish Gam Zu ("the *gam-zu* guy") because whatever happened to him, he would respond, "*Gam zu letovah*"—"This also is for the good!"

Once, the Jews needed to send a gift to the Caesar. They told each other, "Who should go [to Rome bearing the gift on our behalf]? Let us send Nachum Ish Gam Zu because he regularly experiences miracles." They sent him off with a chest filled with precious stones and jewels.

On his way, he stopped at an inn for the night. During the night, the innkeepers removed all of the precious stones and jewels and refilled the chest with soil. The next morning, Nachum realized what had happened, but he simply declared, "This is also for the good!"

When he arrived at the Caesar's palace [and presented his gift on behalf of the Jewish nation], they opened the chest and saw that it was filled with soil.

"The Jews are mocking me!" roared the Caesar. He was about to execute Nachum and the Jews who accompanied him, but Nachum simply declared, "This is also for the good!"

Elijah [the Prophet] suddenly appeared before the Caesar disguised as one of his ministers. He told [the Caesar], "Perhaps this soil is the kind that their ancestor Abraham used in battle? He threw earth [at enemy armies], and it turned into swords [that fell upon his opponents]; he threw stubble, and it turned into arrows." . . .

[The Caesar was eager to try it out.] There was a province that the Romans were unable to conquer. They tested [the soil by throwing it at their enemies] and thereby conquered that province. [In gratitude, the Caesar instructed that] Nachum's chest be refilled with precious stones and jewels from the royal treasury. They sent him [back home] with great honor.

QUESTION FOR DISCUSSION

Can you identify a distinction between these two stories—in the way in which the respective challenges resulted in positive conclusions?

TEXT 7

THE REBBE, RABBI MENACHEM MENDEL SCHNEERSON,
LIKUTEI SICHOT 2, PP. 394–395

דער חילוק פון ביידע דוגמאות איז:

ר' עקיבא האָט טאַקע געהאַט פאַרלוסט און צער. ער האָט פאַרלאָרן
דעם חמור מיטן תרנגול, געזעסן אין דער פינסטער און גענעכטיקט
אין פעלד. דאָס איז געווען **צוליב** אַ טובה, אָבער דאָס **אַליין** איז געווען
אַן ענין של צער.

ביי נחום איש גם זו איז גאָר לכתחילה קיין היזק ניט געווען, ואדרבה,
אויב ער וואָלט ברענגען אבנים טובות איז ער ווער ווייס צי ביי דעם מלך
וואָלט דאָס נתקבל געוואָרן, ווארום אין בית המלך פעלן ניט קיין אבנים
טובות, אָבער אַז ער האָט געבראַכט די ערד איז דאָס נתקבל געוואָרן.

ר' עקיבא האָט געהאַט אַ צער, נאָר דורך דעם צער איז ער ניצול געוואָרן
פון אַ גרעסערן צער. ביי נחום איש גם זו איז דאָס גופא געווען גוטב.

**RABBI MENACHEM MENDEL SCHNEERSON
1902–1994**

The towering Jewish leader of the 20th century, known as "the Lubavitcher Rebbe," or simply as "the Rebbe." Born in southern Ukraine, the Rebbe escaped Nazi-occupied Europe, arriving in the U.S. in June 1941. The Rebbe inspired and guided the revival of traditional Judaism after the European devastation, impacting virtually every Jewish community the world over. The Rebbe often emphasized that the performance of just one additional good deed could usher in the era of Mashiach. The Rebbe's scholarly talks and writings have been printed in more than 200 volumes.

There is a distinction between the stories of Rabbi Akiva and Nachum Ish Gam Zu:

Rabbi Akiva suffered loss and pain—he lost his donkey and rooster, he sat in the dark, and he spent the night in a field. True, it was *for the sake* of a positive outcome, but *the experience itself* was painful.

By contrast, Nachum Ish Gam Zu never suffered any harm. To the contrary: If he had presented precious stones and jewels, it is uncertain whether the Caesar would have valued the gift. After all, there was no shortage of precious stones in the royal treasury. The soil that he brought, on the other hand, was indeed greatly appreciated.

Rabbi Akiva endured hardship, but that hardship spared him from far greater hardship. Nachum Ish Gam Zu's experience was itself a positive one.

If pain and suffering are considered a gift from G-d, why do we pray that they go away? **Rabbi YY Jacobson** *explains:*

MYJLI.COM/WARRIOR

Figure 4.1a

The Jewish View of Hardship and Suffering

	PARADIGM A	PARADIGM B
Hindsight Understanding	Hardship leads to greater gain.	Hardship is goodness in disguise.

Figure 4.1b

The Jewish View of Hardship and Suffering—Take Two

	PARADIGM A	**PARADIGM B**
Hindsight Understanding	Hardship leads to greater gain	Hardship is goodness in disguise
Does Negativity Exist?	Yes (albeit as a vehicle for good)	No
Our Perception of Hardship	Is (mostly) correct	Is incorrect
Our Reaction to Negative Circumstances	We tolerate it	We appreciate it

Figure 4.2

The Hidden and Revealed Worlds

HIDDEN WORLD	REVEALED WORLD	
Divine Intellectual Attributes	Divine Emotional Attributes	Divine Speech
Reasons and Objectives of Creation	Energies Deployed in Creation	Power of Creation

TEXT **8**

TANYA, CH. 26 ⊕

| ...כִּי גַם זוֹ לְטוֹבָה, רַק שֶׁאֵינָהּ נִגְלֵית וְנִרְאֵית לְעֵינֵי בָשָׂר, כִּי הִיא מֵעַלְמָא
דְאִתְכַּסְיָא שֶׁלְמַעֲלָה מֵעַלְמָא דְאִתְגַלְיָא.

. . . For "this is also for the good," except that it is
not apparent and visible to mortal eyes because it
stems from the Hidden World that is higher than the
Revealed World.

Figure 4.1c

The Jewish View of Hardship and Suffering — Take Three

	PARADIGM A	**PARADIGM B**	**PARADIGM C**
Hindsight Understanding	Hardship leads to greater gain	Hardship is goodness in disguise	Hardship is a greater good in disguise
Does Negativity Exist?	Yes (albeit as a vehicle for good)	No	No
Our Perception of Hardship	Is (mostly) correct	Is incorrect	Is incorrect
Our Reaction to Negative Circumstances	We tolerate it	We appreciate it	We rejoice because of it

TEXT 9

TANYA, IBID.

הַשִּׂמְחָה הִיא מֵאַהֲבָתוֹ קִרְבַת ה' יוֹתֵר מִכָּל חַיֵּי הָעוֹלָם הַזֶּה, כְּדִכְתִיב, "כִּי טוֹב חַסְדְּךָ מֵחַיִּים וגו'" (תְּהִילִים סג, ד). וְקִרְבַת ה' הִיא בְּיֶתֶר שְׂאֵת וּמַעֲלָה לְאֵין קֵץ בְּעָלְמָא דְאִתְכַּסְיָא.

The joy [a person experiences due to suffering] is a consequence of one's desiring G-d's closeness more than anything offered by life in this world, as it is written, "For Your lovingkindness is dearer than life. . . ." (PSALMS 63:4)—and the nearness of G-d is infinitely stronger and more sublime in the Hidden World.

*As a thirteen-year-old, **Mrs. Lynda Fishman** lost her mother and siblings to a plane crash. A beautiful, bittersweet account of suffering and survival:*

MYJLI.COM/WARRIOR

King David, illustration from the *Passover Haggadah*, Jakob Steinhardt, woodcut, Berlin, 1921. (The Jewish Museum, Berlin)

TEXT 10

"ANAH EMTSAACHA," *SEFER HANIGUNIM* 213 👥

רבונו של עולם! איך וויל דיר אַ דודעלע שפילען.
רבונו של עולם! איך וויל דיר אַ דודעלע זינגען.

אנה אמצאך, רבונו של עולם? ואנה לא אמצאך, רבונו של עולם?
אַוו זאל איך דיר געפינען, רבונו של עולם? און אַוו זאל איך דיר נישט
געפינען, רבונו של עולם?

אַז מעלה דו, מטה דו, מזרח דו, מערב דו, דרום דו, צפון דו.
דו, דו, דו, דו.

אַז עס איז גוט, איז דאָך דו.
חלילה ניט, אויך דו.
און אַז דו, איז דאָך גוט.
דו, דו, דו, דו.

SEFER HANIGUNIM

A published collection of Chabad songs and melodies. Edited by Rabbi Shmuel Zalmanov (1903–1975), the 2-volume series contains the musical notations for 347 compositions, as well as the writings of Rabbi Yosef Yitschak Schneersohn, the sixth Lubavitcher Rebbe, on the mystical significance of music.

Master of the universe!
I'd like to sing You a song all about You.
Master of the universe!
I'd like to play You a melody all about You.

Where are You to be found, O G-d?
Where are you *not* to be found, O G-d!

Up? There You are! Down? That's You! To the east?
It's You! To the west? You! To the north? You! To the south? You!

You, You, You . . .

When things are good, that's You!
And when they're not, that's also You!
But since it's You, it *is* good—

You, You, You . . .

TEXT 11

RABBI ADIN EVEN-ISRAEL (STEINSALTZ), *THE LONG SHORTER WAY: DISCOURSES ON CHASIDIC THOUGHT* (NEW MILFORD, CT: MAGGID BOOKS, 2014), P. 182

RABBI ADIN EVEN-ISRAEL (STEINSALTZ) 1937–

Talmudist, author, and philosopher. Rabbi Even-Israel (Steinsaltz) is considered one of the foremost Jewish thinkers of the 20th century. Praised by *Time* magazine as a "once-in-a-millennium scholar," he has been awarded the Israel Prize for his contributions to Jewish study. He lives in Jerusalem and is the founder of the Israel Institute for Talmudic Publications, a society dedicated to the translation and elucidation of the Talmud.

To say, "This too is for the best," is hardly the same thing as superficial optimism. It is a recognition of the reality of pain and evil and an attempt to get to the root of suffering, to get beyond the fact that everything bad has something good in it, and that salvation often emerges from tribulation. There is no longer any consideration of the ultimate profit or hidden goodness in the reality of suffering. Besides, what kind of release or consolation resides in the thought that the pain will pass? One who is in agony of body or spirit can hardly be made to feel better by philosophic or religious ideas.

The Jew who sincerely faces suffering does not seek an accounting with G-d—he does not reproach Divine justice or defend his own innocence. Nor does he seek ways of reaping some advantage. He relates entirely to the present, to that which is now, not to what was in the past, or what is liable to be in the future. No solace is sought or vain imaginings. If G-d wills it, the situation will improve; otherwise, it's none of my business. The argument is that since suffering is something that comes from G-d, it is in the nature of a gift, or at least something that is given. Because, to be sure, not everything that is given can, at first sight, be recognized as something positive. And this takes a lot of time, a great deal of tumultuous repudiation before one reaches a relatively peaceful state of equilibrium.

Figure 4.1d

The Jewish View of Hardship and Suffering—Take Four

	PARADIGM A	PARADIGM B	PARADIGM C	PARADIGM D
Hindsight Understanding	Hardship leads to greater gain	Hardship is goodness in disguise	Hardship is a greater good in disguise.	Hardship constitutes intimacy with G-d
Does Negativity Exist?	Yes (albeit as a vehicle for good)	No	No	No
Our Perception of Hardship	Is (mostly) correct	Is incorrect	Is incorrect	Is irrelevant
Our Reaction to Negative Circumstances	We tolerate it	We appreciate it	We rejoice because of it	It is dearer than life itself

Figure 4.3

Benefits of the Divine-Soul Model

AREA	RATIONALE
Negative emotions that result from feeling inauthentic	Every selfless deed is a 100 percent authentic expression of the divine soul.
Shame, feelings of inadequacy, and frustration that result from our internal struggles	These negative emotions are negated by understanding that character flaws are a gift, and our struggles are our purpose in life.
Guilt and remorse	Feelings of remorse are controlled and purposeful and lead to greater joy.
Anxiety and worry over material matters	When one's focus is nearness to G-d, one can be happy despite—and even because of—hardship.

CLASS DISCUSSION

*A moving lecture by **Rabbi Dr. Abraham J. Twerski** on pain, happiness, and growth:*

MYJLI.COM/WARRIOR

In today's lesson, we explored four different perspectives on hardship and suffering. What obstacles might we face in applying these perspectives to our own lives?

After the Pogrom, Maurycy Minkowski, oil on canvas, c. 1910. (The Jewish Museum, New York)

TEXT 12

RABBI SHALOM DOVBER SCHNEERSOHN, *BESHAAH SHEHIKDIMU* 5672:1, P. 527

עִנְיָן "הַשְּׂמֵחִים בְּיִסּוּרִים שׁוֹמְעִים חֶרְפָּתָם וְאֵינָם מְשִׁיבִים כו'", דְּאֵין
הַכַּוָּונָה שֶׁאֵינוֹ מַרְגִּישׁ הַיִּסּוּרִים אוֹ הַחֶרְפָּה וְלֹא אִיכְפַּת לוֹ כְּלָל, דְּאִם כֵּן,
אֵין זֶה יִסּוּרִים וְחֶרְפָּה כְּלָל, וְאֵינוֹ שַׁיָּיךְ לוֹמַר הַשְּׂמֵחִים כו'.

וְגַם אֵין הַדַּעַת סוֹבֵל עִנְיָן הַחֶרְפָּה רַחֲמָנָא לִיצְלַן, וְרַק הַשּׁוֹטֶה וַחֲסַר דַּעַת
לֹא יַרְגִּישׁ בְּחֶרְפָּה וְיִסּוּרִים רַחֲמָנָא לִיצְלַן, מִפְּנֵי שֶׁהוּא כִּבְהֵמָה כו'.

אֲבָל הָאָדָם בַּאֲשֶׁר הוּא אָדָם יַרְגִּישׁ הַיִּסּוּרִים וְהַחֶרְפָּה וְלֹא טוֹב לוֹ מִזֶּה
כו'. וּמִכָּל מָקוֹם הוּא שָׂמֵחַ כו', שֶׁזֶּהוּ רַק מִפְּנֵי הָאֱמוּנָה וְהַדַּעַת הָאֱלֹקִי
שֶׁיֵּשׁ בָּזֶה טוֹבָה גְדוֹלָה בְּהֶעְלֵם...

וְעִם הֱיוֹתוֹ שָׂמֵחַ, מִכָּל מָקוֹם לֹא טוֹב לוֹ הַיִּסּוּרִים.

RABBI SHALOM DOVBER SCHNEERSOHN (RASHAB) 1860–1920

Chasidic rebbe. Rabbi Shalom Dovber became the fifth leader of the Chabad movement upon the passing of his father, Rabbi Shmuel Schneersohn. He established the Lubavitch network of *yeshivot* called Tomchei Temimim. He authored many volumes of Chasidic discourses and is renowned for his lucid and thorough explanations of kabbalistic concepts.

When our sages speak [in praise] of "those who rejoice in their suffering, who hear themselves vilified and do not respond" they do not mean that one does not feel the afflictions or the shame and that these experiences do not bother the person at all. Were that so, these experiences would not be forms of suffering or shame at all; we would not be able to say, "Those who rejoice in their *suffering*."

Besides, the mind cannot bear being disgraced, G-d forbid, and only a fool or someone with a deficiency of mind would not feel shame and suffering, G-d forbid—for such a person is similar to an animal in this regard.

Rather, as human beings, we experience suffering and shame, and we do not consider them pleasant experiences. Nonetheless, we rejoice. This is only due to the G-dly faith and knowledge that there is tremendous goodness hidden within these experiences. . . .

We rejoice but, at the same time, experience these realities as suffering.

KEY POINTS

1 Hardship and pain easily trigger a host of negative emotions that can cripple us emotionally, spiritually, and practically. To maintain our cheerfulness and avoid negative emotions, we must shift our perspective on suffering.

2 G-d loves each of us infinitely, eternally, and unconditionally. G-d is also omnipotent, in complete control. Therefore, He does not allow anything bad to happen to us. Whatever He allows us to experience falls into two categories of goodness: undisguised good and disguised good.

3 There are various ways of understanding the goodness hidden in hardship:

(a) As a means to an end: all pain and inconvenience lead to a greater good.

(b) Direct goodness: all hardship is, itself, goodness in disguise.

(c) Ultimate goodness: hidden good is *greater* because it is goodness on G-d's terms, a goodness that is so great that we cannot possibly appreciate it.

(d) Bonding: Covert goodness involves a greater degree of intimacy with G-d. In this paradigm, we no longer look for gifts, but for love.

4 Living in alignment with our divine soul allows us to value closeness to G-d over personal gratification.

Appendix

TEXT **13**

GEORGE A. BONANNO, "LOSS, TRAUMA, AND HUMAN RESILIENCE: HAVE WE UNDERESTIMATED THE HUMAN CAPACITY TO THRIVE AFTER EXTREMELY AVERSIVE EVENTS?" *AMERICAN PSYCHOLOGIST,* 59:1 (2004), P. 20

Most people are exposed to at least one violent or life-threatening situation during the course of their lives (OZER, BEST, LIPSEY, & WEISS, 2003). As people progress through the life cycle, they are also increasingly confronted with the deaths of close friends and relatives. Not everyone copes with these potentially disturbing events in the same way. Some people experience acute distress from which they are unable to recover. Others suffer less intensely and for a much shorter period of time. Some people seem to recover quickly but then begin to experience unexpected health problems or difficulties concentrating or enjoying life the way they used to. However, large numbers of people manage to endure the temporary upheaval of loss or potentially traumatic events remarkably well, with no apparent disruption in their ability to function at work or in close relationships, and seem to move on to new challenges with apparent ease. This article is devoted to the latter group and to the question of resilience in the face of loss or potentially traumatic events.

A key feature of the concept of adult resilience to loss and trauma . . . is its distinction from the process of recovery.

GEORGE A. BONANNO, PHD

Psychologist. Dr. Bonanno is a professor of clinical psychology at Columbia University. He is known as a pioneering researcher in the field of bereavement and trauma and is a leading expert on resilience.

The term recovery connotes a trajectory in which normal functioning temporarily gives way to threshold or subthreshold psychopathology (e.g., symptoms of depression or posttraumatic stress disorder [PTSD]), usually for a period of at least several months, and then gradually returns to pre-event levels. Full recovery may be relatively rapid or may take as long as one or two years. By contrast, resilience reflects the ability to maintain a stable equilibrium. In the developmental literature, resilience is typically discussed in terms of protective factors that foster the development of positive outcomes and healthy personality characteristics among children exposed to unfavorable or aversive life circumstances (E.G., GARMEZY, 1991; LUTHAR, CICCHETTI, & BECKER, 2000; MASTEN, 2001; RUTTER, 1999; WERNER, 1995). Resilience to loss and trauma . . . pertains to the ability of adults in otherwise normal circumstances who are exposed to an isolated and potentially highly disruptive event, such as the death of a close relation or a violent or life-threatening situation, to maintain relatively stable, healthy levels of psychological and physical functioning. A further distinction is that resilience is more than the simple absence of psychopathology. Recovering individuals often experience subthreshold symptom levels. Resilient individuals, by contrast, may experience transient perturbations in normal functioning (e.g., several weeks of sporadic preoccupation or restless sleep) but generally exhibit a stable trajectory of healthy functioning across time, as well as the capacity for generative experiences and positive emotions (BONANNO, PAPA, & O'NEILL, 2001).

TEXT 14

STEVEN M. SOUTHWICK AND DENNIS S. CHARNY, "THE SCIENCE OF RESILIENCE: IMPLICATIONS FOR THE PREVENTION AND TREATMENT OF DEPRESSION," *SCIENCE* 338:5, 2012, P. 80

How can what we currently know about resilience be applied to the prevention and treatment of depression? There are several areas that have been studied.

Genetics and environment. Research in genetics and epigenetics suggests that putative vulnerability genes or "risk alleles" operate in a dynamic interplay with the environment and that resilience may be promoted, in some cases, by changing the biological and/or psychosocial environment.

Child rearing. To protect against learned helplessness and depression, as well as to promote resilience, it is critical to provide children with a supportive and loving environment that fosters healthy attachment, protects

STEVEN M. SOUTHWICK, M.D.

Psychiatrist. Dr. Southwick is a recognized expert on the psychological and neurobiological effects of extreme psychological trauma. He is a professor of psychiatry, posttraumatic stress disorder, and resilience at the Yale Medical School and medical director of the Clinical Neurosciences Division of the National Center for Posttraumatic Stress Disorder.

DENNIS S. CHARNY, M.D.

Biological psychiatrist and researcher. Dr. Charny is one of the world's leading experts in the neurobiology and treatment of mood and anxiety disorders. He is the author of *Neurobiology of Mental Illness, The Physician's Guide to Depression and Bipolar Disorders,* and *Molecular Biology for the Clinician,* as well as the author of over 500 original papers and chapters. He is currently dean of Icahn School of Medicine at Mount Sinai in New York City.

them from repeated experiences of uncontrollable stress, and provides them with ample opportunities to master life challenges. Such mastery can contribute to stress inoculation with reduced overall reactivity to future stressors and enhanced mastery of future challenges.

Social support. Low levels of social support have been associated with depression, PTSD, and medical morbidity, whereas high levels of social support have been positively associated with active problem-focused coping, sense of control and predictability in life, self-esteem, motivation, optimism, enhanced immune function, dampened neuroendocrine and cardiovascular responses to stress, resilience, and lower levels of depression.

Cognitive and/or psychological interventions. When individuals believe that the demands of a stressful situation exceed their personal capabilities and external resources, they tend to appraise the situation as a threat and as out of their control, which negatively affects their emotional and behavioral response and increases the likelihood of developing depression. On the other hand, if the individual believes that they have the skills, experience, and resources needed to successfully deal with an adverse situation, they are more likely to appraise the situation as a challenge.

TEXT **15**

STEVEN M. SOUTHWICK AND DENNIS S. CHARNY, *RESILIENCE: THE SCIENCE OF MASTERING LIFE'S GREATEST CHALLENGES (2ND ED.)* (CAMBRIDGE, U.K.: CAMBRIDGE UNIVERSITY PRESS, 2018), PP. 232–252

In the scientific literature, acceptance has been cited as a key ingredient in the ability to tolerate highly stressful situations. This has been true both among survivors of extreme environmental hardships and threats to life (SIEBERT, 1996), among highly successful learning-disabled adults (GERBER & GINSBERG, 1990) and among individuals with a variety of medical and mental disorders (SIROIS & HIRSH, 2017; CASIER ET AL., 2011; HUSTON ET AL., 2016; THOMPSON ET AL., 2011). Acceptance has also been associated with better psychological and physical health in many different groups of people. In a nationwide survey of individuals shortly after the terrorist attacks of September 11, 2001, researchers found reduced levels of posttraumatic stress symptoms in those who accepted the situation (SILVER ET AL., 2002). In a study of mothers whose children had life-threatening cancer diagnoses and were undergoing bone transplants—a painful and highly invasive procedure—Sharon Manne and colleagues (2002) found that those who accepted their situation reported fewer symptoms of depression. Acceptance has also been recommended as a coping mechanism for families of children with cancer (KAZAK ET AL., 1999) and for family members of adults with serious mental illness (ZAUSZNIEWSHI ET AL., 2015). Further, the most commonly used scale to measure resilience, the Connor-Davidson Resilience Scale, includes a question about positive acceptance of change. . . .

In psychological research, studies have [also] found that having a clear and valued purpose, and committing fully to a mission, can markedly strengthen one's resilience. University of Missouri psychologist Laura A. King and her colleagues (KING, HEINTZELMAN & WARD, 2016) proposed methods for defining and measuring feelings of meaning and the degree to which individuals experience their lives as meaningful. They argue that far from being "the icing on the cake of psychological well-being" (p. 211), living a meaningful life is a basic human need, without which we can easily fall into despair, alienation, or even violent acts against others or against ourselves. . . .

In a study of bus drivers, Paul Bartone (1989) found that those who were high in hardiness (a construct related to resilience) were generally proud of their work and found it to be meaningful. When faced with work-related stressors, these individuals fared better than those for whom driving a bus was "just a job." Similarly, in a 12-year longitudinal study of employees at Illinois Bell

Telephone, Salvatore Maddi (1987) found that workers who reported a purposeful direction in their community, school, and work activities were more resilient during an organizational crisis than were workers who lacked such direction.

Additional Readings

THE MEANING OF SADNESS, PART II

BY RABBI ADIN EVEN-ISRAEL (STEINSALTZ)

What about the incessant problems of existence—besides the daily cares of eating and sleeping and money—the worry about life and love and death and children?

There has never been an easy answer, and it is known to be far more difficult in the doing than in the saying. Consider the story of Rabbi Meizlish of Cracow and Warsaw, who was a well-to-do merchant before he became a rabbi. Even then, when he was sending timber along the river to Germany to be sold there at a profit, he was famous for his erudition, and he used to teach brilliant pupils at the yeshivah. Once the news came that the timber rafts were wrecked in a storm, and the whole of the rabbi's fortune was lost in one day. They did not know how to tell the rabbi and chose one of his favorite pupils to do so. The young man selected a passage in the Talmud and came to the rabbi with his question: "It says here that one has to thank G-d with blessings for the evil that befalls one as well as for the good. How can this be done?" The rabbi explained the matter in terms of its hidden meaning as well as in straightforward theology. To this the pupil replied, "I am not sure I understand. And if my rabbi were to learn that all his timber rafts were wrecked on the river, would he dance for joy?" The rabbi said, "Yes, of course."

RABBI ADIN EVEN-ISRAEL (STEINSALTZ), 1937–

Talmudist, author, and philosopher. Rabbi Even-Israel (Steinsaltz) is considered one of the foremost Jewish thinkers of the 20th century. Praised by *Time* magazine as a "once-in-a-millennium scholar," he has been awarded the Israel Prize for his contributions to Jewish study. He lives in Jerusalem and is the founder of the Israel Institute for Talmudic Publications, a society dedicated to the translation and elucidation of the Talmud.

"Well then," said the pupil, "you can dance—all the rafts are lost!" Upon hearing this, the rabbi fainted. When he came to, he said, "Now I must confess I no longer understand this Talmud passage."

In other words, there is a difference between theoretically knowing that G-d is always present and knowing it when one is crushed. To be sure, there are many saints, and even ordinary men, who are able to bless the evil as well as the good, not only to receive it without complaint, but also to accept it with joy. The capacity to do so is a function of deeper comprehension as well as of faith or certainty in the wisdom of the hidden workings of G-d. Hence we understand the meaning of the verse: "Happy is the man whom Thou, O G-d, chasteneth . . ." (Psalms 94:12).

To be sure, everything is good, in the sense that it comes from G-d. On the other hand, there can be no denying that suffering exists and that the cause of suffering is something that may be called evil. In this case, the good is hidden, and several levels have to be excavated in order to get to it. On the simplest level, one can sometimes see it quite directly—my cow broke a leg, and I found a treasure at that spot. Or there is the story of Rabbi Akiva who, traveling, could not get lodging at the inn. He had, however, a candle to read by, a donkey to take him to the forest where he could sleep, and a cock to wake him in the morning. So, he was pleased and said, "This too is for the best." Then a lion came and killed his donkey; a cat devoured his cock, and the wind snuffed out his candle. "This too is for the best," he said, and he curled up in a tree and slept soundly. In the morning, he learned that a band of wild robbers had come to the inn, looted and taken captive all who were there. Had his donkey neighed or his cock crowed, or had the robbers seen his candle, he too would have been plundered, so he was able to say again with conviction, "This too is for the best."

Of course, in most instances the matter is far more complex. There may be a considerable time gap, as in the case of Joseph and his brothers. Or the true nature of evil may never be made evident to the outer eye. Even a very cursory reflection upon the events of one's life can often lead one to contemplate the relative nature of what were once considered calamities. This notwithstanding, we are still confronted with the existence of evil.

Whatever it is, evil is not the same as what many would classify as unmitigated wickedness. As in most things, a certain education of the moral sense allows one to see things differently. In matters of taste—the bitterness of certain beverages, like beer, has to be cultivated in order to be enjoyed, in contrast to the obvious sweetness of sugary things, which is almost always enjoyed. Or consider the whole gamut of sophisticated taste in art, as well as in culinary matters. The development of "good taste" requires time.

So too, it is easy to bless that which is universally good. It is difficult to comprehend the true nature of suffering, and even more so, to "enjoy it." For the truth of things is hidden, and the true good is on a higher level of reality, making it less available to our understanding. That is to say, suffering comes from the revealed aspects of the Divine (the letters *yud, heh*). A more profound happiness comes from the hidden aspects of Divine reality (the letters *vav, heh*).

To be sure, most men are willing to renounce this Divine chastening, preferring to receive the good portion of the simple man. Thus, in praying we say: "May it be Thy will to forgive and wipe away our sins, but not by suffering and affliction." Also, it is written in the Talmud: "L-rd of the Universe, truly Thy gifts are good and sufferings are among the greatest gifts, for nothing truly valuable comes without suffering, and no man attains to the Promised Land or to Torah or to the life in the next world, except through suffering, from the earliest breath. . . ." Nevertheless, we do pray, in all humility, in all simplicity, for release from suffering.

The relation, however, between the evil person and suffering is rather puzzling. Obviously, the wicked should receive the just deserts of their actions and suffer the consequences. But life is more likely to be the paradox of the sick person getting all sorts of delicacies to eat while the healthy person has to suffice with whatever is available. Or the disobedient child getting much more attention than the obedient one. If suffering can be seen as a gift from G-d, how can we accept punishment as the evil effects of sin? Do the wicked have it good from all sides?

The answer is that suffering is, of course, not always the same thing. To the wicked, suffering often comes as a means of release from a certain constriction. And the real punishment lies not in the virulent reaction of life and society against the sinner, but in the exemption from suffering—when the one who has sinned is discharged before he has made right his evil deed. Like in the explanation given concerning G-d's punishment of the snake for tempting Eve in the Garden of Eden, the snake is made to crawl in the dust of the earth to "eat of the dust all the days of thy life." This means that, in contrast to man's punishment— "Cursed is the ground for thy sake; in sorrow shalt thou eat of it all the days of thy life"—the snake always has enough to eat, and he can survive without effort no matter where he is. "Not much of an affliction," one may say. The real punishment is that G-d is ridding Himself of all responsibility; the snake can go and do what it likes; it doesn't even have to pray to G-d for anything. And this disconnection from the Divine is the worst that can happen to any creature; it is the nature of Hell.

Suffering is then a means of restoring a person to G-d. As we have said, there are many who will never awaken to holiness without some life crisis. Just as it is interesting to observe the effects of what is considered "success." Not only does success often bring a certain crassness and insensitivity, but it also brings a forgetting of how to be grateful.

It is written in the Talmud that were it not for the sins of Israel, only the five books of the Torah and the Book of Joshua would have been given and no more. If so, we have to thank the sins of our fathers for much of the wisdom, poetry, and prophecy in the Bible; their recurrent wrongdoing apparently demanded that much more Divine care and intervention.

Another way of looking at it is that man oscillates between periods of spiritual soaring and periods of rest from the spirit, when he is content with the simple things of life. Also, there seems to be some danger in all extremes. Riches lead to one sort of temptation, poverty to another.

Thus, while the wicked get G-d's attention, causing Him to occupy Himself with them, the saintly are privileged to suffer as their portion, and the mediocre are usually happy to avoid either extreme and are satisfied to live out their lives in tranquil dullness and insensitivity. However, since nothing shakes them, there is no thrust forward or awakening to another world. And indeed, suffering is often "wasted" on the complacently mediocre. This is a very different sort of thing from the "wasting" of suffering on the saintly who simply do not see it as something evil. For the conscious person, the gift of suffering comes as a test, an opportunity to learn something and to progress into an acceptance of suffering as a hidden blessing.

The point is that man needs to see suffering as something given to him for his own benefit, whether as instruction or as a bitter medicine. If it is so hidden that one fails to see it, something very serious and complicated happens to one's relationship with G-d—a kind of destructive bitterness. On the other hand, the person who is ready to receive the Divine chastisement is the one who is closest to G-d, even though He is hidden. In chastisement, G-d is closer than in correct or formal relations. As is true in ordinary human associations, rebuke is a part of genuine cherishing.

Moreover, the person who is prepared to accept chastisement is not simply passive and obedient. The problem is far deeper than that. If a person is sick, he should not merely take medicine and lie in bed in order to be able to enjoy the chastisement of suffering, nor does the poor man have to resign himself to poverty. The problem is: What is one to do with the suffering that is inflicted? Is it in the nature of a calamity or a revelation? The only answer lies in the certainty that no matter what the nature of the situation, one is always interrelating with G-d. If there is suffering, He is contending with me, bringing me to some new appraisal of things. He may be right or He may be wrong, in my opinion; but at least I can argue the matter with Him. That is what G-d wants—a living relationship.

Ordinarily, men see the world through a thick veil—and the image of the sun coming out of its covering represents a real event of revelation. In the resultant brightness, the Tzadik will be healed, and the wicked will be burned. The Tzadik, or saintly person, who was ready to accept G-d in His hiddenness, in the darkness of suffering, will be able to receive the greater light and be healed, while the one who wished only to avoid G-d or any kind of Divine interference in his life, is consumed by the revelation.

To say, "This too is for the best" is hardly the same thing as superficial optimism. It is a recognition of the reality of pain and evil and an attempt to get to the root of suffering, to get beyond the fact that everything bad has something good in it, and that salvation often emerges from tribulation. There is no longer any consideration of the ultimate profit or hidden goodness in the reality of suffering. Besides, what kind of release or consolation resides in the thought that the pain will pass? One who is in agony of body or spirit can hardly be made to feel better by philosophic or religious ideas.

The Jew who sincerely faces suffering does not seek an accounting with G-d—he does not reproach Divine justice or defend his own innocence. Nor does he seek ways of reaping some advantage. He relates entirely to the present, to that which is now, not to what was in the past, or what is liable to be in the future. No solace is sought or vain imaginings. If G-d wills it, the situation will improve; otherwise, it's none of my business. The argument is that since suffering is something that comes from G-d, it is in the nature of a gift, or at least something that is given. Because, to be sure, not everything that is given can, at first sight, be recognized as something positive. And this takes a lot of time, a great deal of tumultuous repudiation before one reaches a relatively peaceful state of equilibrium. In other words, the Chasidic teacher tells us that his wisdom cannot really remove the pain or resolve the sadness. It can only eliminate the anxiety, the tension, the fear, and the uncertainty.

The problem becomes focused on the nature of passivity in the spiritual life. First, there is the simple situation of a certain distress, whether of a greater or a lesser degree—a lack of money or illness or a calamity of tragic proportions or despondency. The distress is genuine enough, and there is no point in claiming that one should be glad about it, or that one should not do everything possible to eliminate it. The usual way of relating to distress is to experience a certain drop of spirit, a sadness, or bitterness, which can be interpreted as stemming from an attitude that one does not deserve the pain and sorrow, that one has somehow been unfairly or wrongly treated. And it is this that can be remedied by seeing the suffering, not as punishment for some wrongdoing, that one may or may not have done, but as a sort of reward—which is not immediately apparent as such. It takes a while to distinguish it.

The second part of the problem lies in the nature of whatever causes distress. What if it gets worse? What if no good comes of it? The hiddenness of the Divine necessarily brings on its wretchedness and suffering. G-d does not appear to the one who is in misery in the same way as to the same person in ordinary life, when the evil and the pain come from outside oneself, from the structure of the created world.

In other words, the problem focuses on the fact of suffering as a trial. For suffering can lead to many things. Some rise; others fall. Suffering is the test. Can a person receive it without sliding into hatred? Can he grow from experiencing it? And if he can, is he able to persist and reach a world illuminated like the "sun emerging"?

In other words, the sun comes out of its sheath or covering gradually; it is a process that one has to pass through. Otherwise it would consume one instead of heal. The revelation would be too much for anyone who is unprepared. It is necessary to become accustomed to, or rather, made able to absorb the light. Like any learning process, there is the need to make mistakes, the need to repeat and exercise the correct action or word or concept. Nothing in life, or comparatively little, comes of itself. And the light of G-d is made available through a growing process, a learning through hardship, an exercising of one's ability to accept suffering, to receive it as a gift from G-d. This gift does not carry any obligations beyond the requirements, perhaps, to relinquish self-pity, the sweet solace of feeling sorry for oneself. And not to worry about repairing G-d's world for Him, leaving Him to care for it.

This does not mean that there is nothing for a man to do. On the contrary, a person has to try to do the maximum possible in the way of fixing himself and the world, which is all in the realm of the World of Action. After that, he is released from all anxiety and sadness. Because anxiety and sadness come from a certain lack of proportion, from the fact that a person thinks G-d is able to do wrong, or that it is up to me to set Him right. Suffering by itself is not a matter of being mistreated by life; it is something given that has to be received, sometimes as a gift. I have to relate realistically and not become sad or downhearted. Pain and sadness are two very different qualities. Sadness is a state of mind in which a person perceives himself as rather justified and decent, and G-d as rather unfair. Thus, one should avoid falling into anxiety and sadness.

Rabbi Adin Even-Israel (Steinsaltz), *The Long Shorter Way* (Jerusalem: Koren Publishers Jerusalem, 2014), pp. 177–184

Reprinted with permission of the publisher

THE ROAD TO RESILIENCE

How do people deal with difficult events that change their lives? The death of a loved one, loss of a job, serious illness, terrorist attacks and other traumatic events: these are all examples of very challenging life experiences. Many people react to such circumstances with a flood of strong emotions and a sense of uncertainty.

Yet people generally adapt well over time to life-changing situations and stressful conditions. What enables them to do so? It involves resilience, an ongoing process that requires time and effort and engages people in taking a number of steps.

What Is Resilience?

Resilience is the process of adapting well in the face of adversity, trauma, tragedy, threats or significant sources of stress—such as family and relationship problems, serious health problems or workplace and financial stressors. It means "bouncing back" from difficult experiences.

Research has shown that resilience is ordinary, not extraordinary. People commonly demonstrate resilience. One example is the response of many Americans to the September 11, 2001 terrorist attacks and individuals' efforts to rebuild their lives.

Being resilient does not mean that a person doesn't experience difficulty or distress. Emotional pain and sadness are common in people who have suffered major adversity or trauma in their lives. In fact, the road to resilience is likely to involve considerable emotional distress.

Resilience is not a trait that people either have or do not have. It involves behaviors, thoughts and actions that can be learned and developed in anyone.

Factors in Resilience

A combination of factors contributes to resilience. Many studies show that the primary factor in resilience is having caring and supportive relationships within and outside the family. Relationships that create love and trust, provide role models and offer encouragement and reassurance help bolster a person's resilience.

Several additional factors are associated with resilience, including:

- The capacity to make realistic plans and take steps to carry them out.
- A positive view of yourself and confidence in your strengths and abilities.
- Skills in communication and problem solving.
- The capacity to manage strong feelings and impulses.

All of these are factors that people can develop in themselves.

Strategies for Building Resilience

Developing resilience is a personal journey. People do not all react the same to traumatic and stressful life events. An approach to building resilience that works for one person might not work for another. People use varying strategies.

Some variation may reflect cultural differences. A person's culture might have an impact on how he or she communicates feelings and deals with adversity—for example, whether and how a person connects with significant others, including extended family members and community resources. With growing cultural diversity, the public has greater access to a number of different approaches to building resilience.

Some or many of the ways to build resilience in the following pages may be appropriate to consider in developing your personal strategy.

Ten Ways to Build Resilience
1. Make connections.

Good relationships with close family members, friends or others are important. Accepting help and support from those who care about you and will listen to you strengthens resilience. Some people find that being active in civic groups, faith-based organizations, or other local groups provides social support and can help with reclaiming hope. Assisting others in their time of need also can benefit the helper.

2. Avoid seeing crises as insurmountable problems.
You can't change the fact that highly stressful events happen, but you can change how you interpret and respond to these events. Try looking beyond the present to how future circumstances may be a little better. Note any subtle ways in which you might already feel somewhat better as you deal with difficult situations.

3. Accept that change is a part of living.
Certain goals may no longer be attainable as a result of adverse situations. Accepting circumstances that cannot be changed can help you focus on circumstances that you can alter.

4. Move toward your goals.
Develop some realistic goals. Do something regularly—even if it seems like a small accomplishment—that enables you to move toward your goals. Instead of focusing on tasks that seem unachievable, ask yourself, "What's one thing I know I can accomplish today that helps me move in the direction I want to go?"

5. Take decisive actions.
Act on adverse situations as much as you can. Take decisive actions, rather than detaching completely from problems and stresses and wishing they would just go away.

6. Look for opportunities for self-discovery.
People often learn something about themselves and may find that they have grown in some respect as a result of their struggle with loss. Many people who have experienced tragedies and hardship have reported better relationships, greater sense of strength even while feeling vulnerable, increased sense of self-worth, a more developed spirituality and heightened appreciation for life.

7. Nurture a positive view of yourself.
Developing confidence in your ability to solve problems and trusting your instincts helps build resilience.

8. Keep things in perspective.
Even when facing very painful events, try to consider the stressful situation in a broader context and keep a long-term perspective. Avoid blowing the event out of proportion.

9. Maintain a hopeful outlook.
An optimistic outlook enables you to expect that good things will happen in your life. Try visualizing what you want, rather than worrying about what you fear.

10. Take care of yourself.
Pay attention to your own needs and feelings. Engage in activities that you enjoy and find relaxing. Exercise regularly. Taking care of yourself helps to keep your mind and body primed to deal with situations that require resilience.

Additional ways of strengthening resilience may be helpful.
For example, some people write about their deepest thoughts and feelings related to trauma or other stressful events in their life. Meditation and spiritual practices help some people build connections and restore hope.

The key is to identify ways that are likely to work well for you as part of your own personal strategy for fostering resilience.

Learning from Your Past
Focusing on past experiences and sources of personal strength can help you learn about what strategies for building resilience might work for you. By exploring answers to the following questions about yourself and your reactions to challenging life events, you may discover how you can respond effectively to difficult situations in your life.

Consider the following:
- What kinds of events have been most stressful for me?
- How have those events typically affected me?
- Have I found it helpful to think of important people in my life when I am distressed?

- To whom have I reached out for support in working through a traumatic or stressful experience?
- What have I learned about myself and my interactions with others during difficult times?
- Has it been helpful for me to assist someone else going through a similar experience?
- Have I been able to overcome obstacles, and if so, how?
- What has helped make me feel more hopeful about the future?

Staying Flexible

Resilience involves maintaining flexibility and balance in your life as you deal with stressful circumstances and traumatic events. This happens in several ways, including:

Letting yourself experience strong emotions, and also realizing when you may need to avoid experiencing them at times in order to continue functioning. Stepping forward and taking action to deal with your problems and meet the demands of daily living, and also stepping back to rest and reenergize yourself. Spending time with loved ones to gain support and encouragement, and also nurturing yourself. Relying on others, and also relying on yourself.

Continuing on Your Journey

To help summarize several of the main points in this brochure, think of resilience as similar to taking a raft trip down a river.

On a river, you may encounter rapids, turns, slow water and shallows. As in life, the changes you experience affect you differently along the way.

In traveling the river, it helps to have knowledge about it and past experience in dealing with it. Your journey should be guided by a plan, a strategy that you consider likely to work well for you.

Perseverance and trust in your ability to work your way around boulders and other obstacles are important. You can gain courage and insight by successfully navigating your way through white water. Trusted companions who accompany you on the journey can be especially helpful for dealing with rapids, upstream currents and other difficult stretches of the river.

You can climb out to rest alongside the river. But to get to the end of your journey, you need to get back in the raft and continue.

Acknowledgments

APA gratefully acknowledges the following contributors to this publication:

Lillian Comas-Diaz, PhD, Director, Transcultural Mental Health Institute, Washington, D.C.

Suniya S. Luthar, PhD, Teachers College, Columbia University, New York City, N.Y.

Salvatore R. Maddi, PhD, The Hardiness Institute, Inc., University of California at Irvine, Newport Beach, Calif.

H. Katherine (Kit) O'Neill, PhD, North Dakota State University and Knowlton, O'Neill and Associates, Fargo, N.D.

Karen W. Saakvitne, PhD, Traumatic Stress Institute/Center for Adult & Adolescent Psychotherapy, South Windsor, Conn.

Richard Glenn Tedeschi, PhD, Department of Psychology, University of North Carolina at Charlotte

"The Road to Resilience," online brochure, American Psychological Association, Psychology Help Center: https://www.apa.org/helpcenter/road-resilience

Lesson 5

LIVING JOYFULLY
FINDING HAPPINESS AND FULFILLMENT

Despite considering ourselves successful in terms of health, finances, and relationships, we sometimes fall into a funk, feeling unexplainably lackadaisical or unhappy. This lesson explores the inner workings of happiness and examines our instinctive methods of securing satisfaction. It then delivers a shift in perspective that sets a workable goal of inner contentment and fulfillment.

Exercise 5.1

Oxford Happiness Questionnaire*

Indicate the degree to which you agree or disagree with the following statements. After each statement, enter a number in the blank according to the following scale:

1 - Strongly disagree   4 - Slightly agree
2 - Moderately disagree   5 - Moderately agree
3 - Slightly disagree   6 - Strongly agree

QUESTIONS

1. I don't feel particularly pleased with the way I am. (R)	
2. I am intensely interested in other people.	
3. I feel that life is very rewarding.	
4. I have very warm feelings toward almost everyone.	
5. I rarely wake up feeling rested. (R)	
6. I am not particularly optimistic about the future. (R)	
7. I find most things amusing.	
8. I am always committed and involved.	
9. Life is good.	
10. I do not think that the world is a good place. (R)	

---

* Hills, P., and Argyle, M., "The Oxford Happiness Questionnaire: A Compact Scale for the Measurement of Psychological Well-Being," *Personality and Individual Differences*, 33 (2002), pp. 1073–1082.

11. I laugh a lot.	
12. I am well satisfied about everything in my life.	
13. I don't think I look attractive. (R)	
14. There is a gap between what I would like to do and what I have done. (R)	
15. I am very happy.	
16. I find beauty in some things.	
17. I always have a cheerful effect on others.	
18. I can fit in (find time for) everything I want to.	
19. I feel that I am not especially in control of my life. (R)	
20. I feel able to take anything on.	
21. I feel fully mentally alert.	
22. I often experience joy and elation.	
23. I don't find it easy to make decisions. (R)	
24. I don't have a particular sense of meaning and purpose in my life. (R)	
25. I feel I have a great deal of energy.	
26. I usually have a good influence on events.	
27. I don't have fun with other people. (R)	
28. I don't feel particularly healthy. (R)	
29. I don't have particularly happy memories of the past. (R)	

CALCULATE YOUR SCORE

1. Items marked (R) should be scored in reverse: If you gave yourself a "1," cross it out and change it to a "6."

   Reversed Scores: 1=6   2=5   3=4   4=3   5=2   6=1

2. Add the numbers for all 29 questions. (Use the converted numbers for the 12 items that are reverse scored.)

3. Divide by 29. Your happiness score = the total (from step 2) divided by 29.

Total Score _____

Exercise 5.2

I would be happier if . . .

1	
2	
3	

Figure 5.1

Contending with Negative Emotions

NEGATIVE EMOTION	NATURAL-SOUL APPROACH	DIVINE-SOUL APPROACH
Inauthenticity	Be more authentic and/or stop doing things that cause us to feel inauthentic.	Understand that every good deed is 100 percent authentic.
Shame and inadequacy	Address and fix our character flaws.	Understand that character flaws are a gift. Our struggles against them are our life's purpose.
Guilt	Forgive ourselves and move on.	Experience controlled and purposeful remorse.
Anxiety, worry, and sadness	Manage the feelings.	Understand that non-revealed good is actually greater good.

Exercise 5.3

Describe three of the ways in which the natural soul achieves happiness and positive emotions:

1	
2	
3	

TEXT 1

ED DIENER (ED.), *THE SCIENCE OF WELL-BEING: THE COLLECTED WORKS OF ED DIENER* (NEW YORK: SPRINGER SCIENCE+BUSINESS MEDIA, 2009), P. 104

People briefly react to good and bad events, but in a brief time they return to neutrality. Thus, happiness and unhappiness are merely short-lived reactions to changes in people's circumstances. People continue to pursue happiness because they incorrectly believe that greater happiness lies just around the next corner in the next goal accomplished, the next social relationship obtained, or the next problem solved. Because new goals continually capture one's attention, one constantly strives to be happy without realizing that in the long run such efforts are futile.

ED DIENER, PHD
1946–

Psychologist and professor. Dr. Diener is a leading researcher in positive psychology who coined the expression "subjective well-being," or SWB, as the aspect of happiness that can be empirically measured. Noted for his research on happiness, he has earned the nickname "Dr. Happiness."

"The Pursuit of Happiness: A Jewish Perspective," by **Mrs. Miriam Lipskier**:

MYJLI.COM/WARRIOR

TEXT 2

THE REBBE, RABBI MENACHEM MENDEL SCHNEERSON,
IGROT KODESH 17, PP. 32–33

צומח, ווען אַלעס וואָס איז נויטיג צום וואַקסן, ערד, וואַסער, לופט
א.ד.ג. איז צוגעשטעלט געוואָרען אין דער פולער מאָס - איז דער
צומח "באַפרייט" פון אַלע זיינע "זאָרג" און שטערונגען. און כאָטש ער
קען ניט אַוועק פון זיין אָרט, ער איז "פאַראָרטייילט" צו בלייבן דאָרט
זיינע אַלע יאָרן–האָט ער די פולע פרייהייט פון אַ צומח. כל זמן ער איז
ניט מער ווי אַ צומח - איז ער באמת פריי.

אָבער אַ **חי**, ווען ער איז אפילו באַזאָרגט מיט אַלע זיינע באַדערפענישען
פון עסען, טרינקען און אזוי ווייטער, אָבער ער איז געצוואונגען צו
זיין אויף איין אָרט, איז דאָס בַא אים די גרעסטע באַשרענקונג - אַ
תפיסה, די שרעקליכסטע תפיסה, ווייל עס פעלט עם דער **עיקר** פון
זיין מהות (וועזן).

אַ מענש, וואָס ער איז דאָך אַ שכלי, אפילו אַז ער האָט די פולע
פרייהייט פון בעוועגונג, אָבער אַז מען שליסט עם אָפּ פון שכל-לעבן
- געפינט ער זיך אין תפיסה, אין אַ תפיסה וועלכע באַרויבט עם פון
זיין **עיקר מהות.**

**RABBI MENACHEM MENDEL SCHNEERSON
1902–1994**

The towering Jewish leader of the 20th century, known as "the Lubavitcher Rebbe," or simply as "the Rebbe." Born in southern Ukraine, the Rebbe escaped Nazi-occupied Europe, arriving in the U.S. in June 1941. The Rebbe inspired and guided the revival of traditional Judaism after the European devastation, impacting virtually every Jewish community the world over. The Rebbe often emphasized that the performance of just one additional good deed could usher in the era of Mashiach. The Rebbe's scholarly talks and writings have been printed in more than 200 volumes.

When a plant is fully provided with all that it requires for growth—earth, water, air, etc.—it is liberated from all of its worries and concerns, so to speak. Although it is immobile, doomed to remain rooted in place for its entire lifespan, it nevertheless enjoys the full freedom that a plant can experience. As long as it remains no more than a plant, it is truly free—despite its lack of mobility.

An animal, however, is a different story. Even if its needs for food, drink, etc., were to be provided, it would feel horribly restricted—imprisoned in the harshest manner—if it were to be immobilized and forced to forever remain in one place. For it would be denied one of the primary features of its existence.

The primary feature of a human being is its intelligence. Humans would feel imprisoned even if granted full freedom of mobility if they were denied their primary aspect of being—the freedom to utilize their intelligence and live mindfully.

Le saoul (The Drunkard), Marc Chagall, oil on canvas, Paris, 1912.

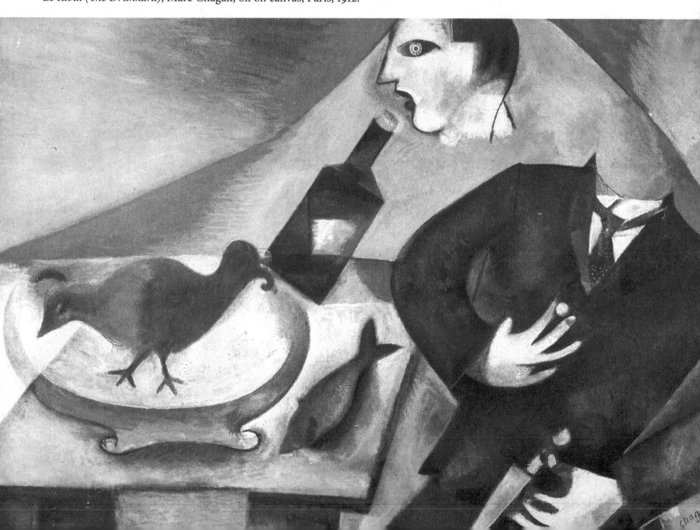

TEXT 3

RABBI SHNE'UR ZALMAN OF LIADI, *MAAMAREI ADMUR HAZAKEN, HAKETSARIM*, P. 553

כָּל חַיּוֹת וּבְהֵמוֹת הֵם תָּמִיד בְּשִׂמְחָה, כִּי אֵין הַגּוּף מַסְתִּיר לְהַחַיּוּת, רַק כְּפִי שֶׁנִּבְרָא הַחַיּוּת כַּךְ הוּא אֵצֶל כָּל בְּהֵמָה בְּלִי שׁוּם הוֹסָפָה וְגִירָעוֹן.

אָכֵן בָּאָדָם, שֶׁנֶּאֱמַר בּוֹ, מִי יוֹדֵעַ רוּחַ הָאָדָם הָעוֹלָה לְמַעְלָה וְרוּחַ הַבְּהֵמָה יֹרֶדֶת לְמַטָּה (קֹהֶלֶת ג, כא), שֶׁאֶפְשָׁר שֶׁיִּהְיֶה בְּחִינַת מְדַבֵּר שֶׁלּוֹ בְּתוֹךְ מַאֲסַר הַגּוּף.

RABBI SHNE'UR ZALMAN OF LIADI (ALTER REBBE) 1745–1812

Chasidic rebbe, halachic authority, and founder of the Chabad movement. The Alter Rebbe was born in Liozna, Belarus, and was among the principal students of the Magid of Mezeritch. His numerous works include the *Tanya*, an early classic containing the fundamentals of Chabad Chasidism, and *Shulchan Aruch HaRav*, an expanded and reworked code of Jewish law.

Wild beasts and animals are always happy because their spiritual life force is compatible with their bodies—to a degree neither greater nor less than how they are created.

Not so humans, regarding whom it is stated, "How many understand that the [sacred] spirit of the human being soars higher, while the spirit of the beast [within the human] descends lower?" (ECCLESIASTES 3:21). The [incompatible desires] create the possibility that the unique human spirit will find itself suffering incarceration within the corporeal body [that drags the person lower].

Is Happiness a Choice?
Rabbi Yitzchak Schochet
has a brief response:

MYJLI.COM/WARRIOR

Exercise 5.4

List three things that, at one point in your life, brought
you considerable happiness:

1	
2	
3	

TEXT 4

MIDRASH, *KOHELET RABAH* 1:13

אֵין אָדָם יוֹצֵא מִן הָעוֹלָם וַחֲצִי תַּאֲוָתוֹ בְּיָדוֹ.

אֶלָּא אִן אִית לֵיהּ מְאָה, בָּעֵי לְמֶעֱבַד יַתְהוֹן תַּרְתֵּין מָאוָן. וְאִן אִית לֵיהּ תַּרְתֵּי מָאוָן, בָּעֵי לְמֶעֱבַד יַתְהוֹן אַרְבְּעָה מְאָה.

No one leaves this world with even half of their cravings fulfilled.

Rather, one who has one hundred [coins] longs to turn it into two hundred, and one who indeed attains the two hundred longs to turn it into four hundred.

KOHELET RABAH

A Midrashic text on the Book of Ecclesiastes. Midrash is the designation of a particular genre of rabbinic literature. The term "Midrash" is derived from the root *d-r-sh*, which means "to search," "to examine," and "to investigate." This particular Midrash provides textual exegeses and develops and illustrates moral principles. It was first published in Pesaro, Italy, in 1519, together with 4 other Midrashic works on the other 4 biblical *Megilot*.

TEXT 5

RABBI SHNE'UR ZALMAN OF LIADI, *MAAMAREI ADMUR HAZAKEN, HAKETSARIM*, P. 553

בְּמִי וָואשׁ דֶער אִיךְ נֶעמְט אַרוּם, אֲזַי הוּא יוֹתֵר בְּעַצְבוּת. כִּי כָּל מַה שֶׁהוּא
יוֹתֵר גָּדוֹל אוּן עֶר לִיגְט נִידֶעְריק הַדָּבָר גָּדוֹל יוֹתֵר בְּעַצְבוּת.

רַק לְמַעַן הַשֵּׁם, נִיט צוּ נֶעמִין הַשִּׂמְחָה מִיט דֶעם אִיךְ! בֶּדַאֲרְף הָאבִּין
הַשִּׂמְחָה, רַק לְקַבֵּל הַשִּׂמְחָה מֵחֲמַת הָאֱמֶת שֶׁאֵין הַהַסְתָּרָה מְהַוֶּת כְּלַל
בֶּאֱמֶת, וּמִמֵּילָא נוֹפֵל הַשִּׂמְחָה כְּשֶׁאֵין מַסְתִּיר הַיֵּשׁ.

"The Road to Happiness," a lecture by **Dr. Rona Novick**:

MYJLI.COM/WARRIOR

One who is consumed with self-focus is more miserable. For the more important a person considers himself, the more misery he experiences at his preoccupation with lowly matters.

For heaven's sake, do not attempt to attain happiness through focusing on yourself. We must be happy, but the happiness must flow from connection to the unconcealed truth of the soul. When the ego no longer conceals the soul, joy is automatic.

TEXT 6

RABBI SHNE'UR ZALMAN OF LIADI, *TANYA*, CH. 41

וְהִנֵּה כָּל כַּוָּנָתוֹ בִּמְסִירַת נַפְשׁוֹ לַה' עַל יְדֵי הַתּוֹרָה וְהַתְּפִלָּה לְהַעֲלוֹת נִצּוֹץ אֱלֹקוּת שֶׁבְּתוֹכָהּ לִמְקוֹרוֹ, תְּהֵא רַק כְּדֵי לַעֲשׂוֹת נַחַת רוּחַ לְפָנָיו יִתְבָּרֵךְ, כְּמָשָׁל שִׂמְחַת שִׂמְחַת הַמֶּלֶךְ בְּבוֹא אֵלָיו בְּנוֹ יְחִידוֹ בְּצֵאתוֹ מִן הַשִּׁבְיָה וּבֵית הָאֲסוּרִים, כַּנִּזְכָּר לְעֵיל.

וְהִנֵּה כַּוָּנָה זוֹ הִיא אֲמִתִּית בֶּאֱמֶת לַאֲמִתּוֹ לְגַמְרֵי בְּכָל נֶפֶשׁ מִיִּשְׂרָאֵל בְּכָל עֵת וּבְכָל שָׁעָה, מֵאַהֲבָה הַטִּבְעִית שֶׁהִיא יְרֻשָּׁה לָנוּ מֵאֲבוֹתֵינוּ.

Rabbi Manis Friedman discusses the correlation between happiness and the Chasidic movement:

MYJLI.COM/WARRIOR

When we study Torah and pray, we surrender our souls to G-d; meaning, we elevate the spark of G-dliness within us to its Source. Our intention in doing so should be solely for the sake of causing G-d gratification. The pleasure we cause G-d can be compared to the joy that a king experiences when his only child, who was in captivity or imprisonment, is released and returns to him (as we discussed earlier).

Every Jewish soul truly and authentically aspires [to please G-d] at all times, by virtue of the natural love [for G-d] that we inherited from our ancestors.

TEXT 7

TANYA, CH. 33 😇

וְזֶהוּ שֶׁכָּתוּב: "יִשְׂמַח יִשְׂרָאֵל בְּעֹשָׂיו" (תְּהִלִּים קמט, ב). פֵּירוּשׁ: שֶׁכָּל
מִי שֶׁהוּא מִזֶּרַע יִשְׂרָאֵל יֵשׁ לוֹ לִשְׂמוֹחַ בְּשִׂמְחַת ה' אֲשֶׁר שָׂשׂ וְשָׂמֵחַ
בְּדִירָתוֹ בַּתַּחְתּוֹנִים.

The meaning of the verse "Let Israel rejoice with its Maker" (PSALMS 149:2) is that whoever is of Jewish stock ought to rejoice in G-d's own joy, for He rejoices and is happy to dwell in the lowest realm [our physical world].

Vintage New Year greeting card depicting the holiday of Simchat Torah. Germany, c. 1910. (New York: Williamsburg Art Company) (Center for Jewish History Museum Collections)

TEXT 8

TANYA, CH. 46 🈁

וְזֶהוּ שֶׁאוֹמְרִים "אֲשֶׁר קִדְּשָׁנוּ בְּמִצְוֹתָיו", כְּאָדָם הַמְקַדֵּשׁ אִשָּׁה לִהְיוֹת
מְיֻחֶדֶת עִמּוֹ בְּיִחוּד גָּמוּר, כְּמוֹ שֶׁכָּתוּב "וְדָבַק בְּאִשְׁתּוֹ וְהָיוּ לְבָשָׂר אֶחָד"
(בְּרֵאשִׁית ב, כד).

כָּכָה מַמָּשׁ וְיֶתֶר עַל כֵּן לְאֵין קֵץ הוּא יִחוּד נֶפֶשׁ הָאֱלֹקִית הָעוֹסֶקֶת בַּתּוֹרָה
וּמִצְוֹת, וְנֶפֶשׁ הַחִיּוּנִית וּלְבוּשֵׁיהֶן הַנִּזְכָּרִים לְעֵיל, בְּאוֹר אֵין סוֹף בָּרוּךְ הוּא.

וְלָכֵן הִמְשִׁיל שְׁלֹמֹה עָלָיו הַשָּׁלוֹם בְּשִׁיר הַשִּׁירִים יִחוּד זֶה לְיִחוּד חָתָן
וְכַלָּה בִּדְבֵיקָה חֲשִׁיקָה וַחֲפִיצָה בְּחִבּוּק וְנִשּׁוּק.

The phrase *asher kideshanu bemitsvotav*, "Who has sanctified us with His commandments," implies that [our bond with G-d is] like a man who betroths a woman so that she may be united with him in a perfect bond—as it is written, "And he shall cleave to his wife, and they shall be one flesh" (GENESIS 2:24).

Exactly so, and to an infinitely greater degree, is our divine soul (along with our natural soul and its faculties) united with G-d's infinite light when we engage in Torah study and the *mitzvot*.

For that reason, Solomon, in his Song of Songs, compared our union with G-d to the union of a bridegroom and bride in [all its particulars,] with attachment, desire, pleasure, embracing, and kissing.

TEXT 9

WILLIAM E. HICKSON, *THE SINGING MASTER*
(LONDON: TAYLOR AND WATSON, 1840), P. 106

'Tis a lesson you should heed:
Try, try, try again.

If at first you don't succeed,
Try, try, try again.

WILLIAM E. HICKSON
1803–1870

British educational writer. Hickson
was a noted author on the subject
of elementary education and later
became the editor and owner of
The Westminster Review, which
championed legislative and
educational reform. In 1836, he
published *The Singing Master*,
featuring his composition "G-d Bless
Our Native Land," verses from which
are included in the British national
anthem, "G-d Save the Queen."

Candle Blessing on Sabbath Eve,
illustrated Rosh Hashanah
greeting card, c. 1910. (The
Magnes Collection of Jewish
Art and Life, Berkeley)

Figure 5.2

Benefits of the Divine-Soul Model

AREA	RATIONALE
Negative emotions that result from feeling inauthentic	Every selfless deed is a 100 percent authentic expression of the divine soul.
Shame, feelings of inadequacy, and frustration that result from our internal struggles	These negative emotions are negated by understanding that character flaws are a gift and our struggles are our purpose in life.
Guilt and remorse	Feelings of remorse are controlled and purposeful and lead to greater joy.
Anxiety and worry over material matters	When one's focus is nearness to G-d, one can be happy despite—and even because of—hardship.
Happiness	Happiness is not contingent on personal attainments.

TEXT 10

EXODUS 14:5–8

וַיֻּגַּד לְמֶלֶךְ מִצְרַיִם כִּי בָרַח הָעָם. וַיֵּהָפֵךְ לְבַב פַּרְעֹה וַעֲבָדָיו אֶל הָעָם,
וַיֹּאמְרוּ: "מַה זֹּאת עָשִׂינוּ, כִּי שִׁלַּחְנוּ אֶת יִשְׂרָאֵל מֵעָבְדֵנוּ?"

וַיֶּאְסֹר אֶת רִכְבּוֹ וְאֶת עַמּוֹ לָקַח עִמּוֹ . . . וַיִּרְדֹּף אַחֲרֵי בְּנֵי יִשְׂרָאֵל.

Pharaoh was told that the people [of Israel] had fled. Pharaoh and his servants experienced a change of heart regarding the people, and they exclaimed, "What have we done? Why have we released Israel from serving us?"

So Pharaoh harnessed his chariot and took his people with him . . . and he chased after the Children of Israel.

TEXT 11a

TANYA, CH. 31

דְּלִכְאוֹרָה הוּא תָּמוּהַּ, לָמָּה הָיְתָה כָּזֹאת? וְכִי אִילוּ אָמְרוּ לְפַרְעֹה לְשַׁלְּחָם
חָפְשִׁי לְעוֹלָם, לֹא הָיָה מוּכְרָח לְשַׁלְּחָם?

This seems puzzling. Why was this [manipulation] necessary? If they would have simply told Pharaoh to set them free permanently, would he not have been compelled to let them go regardless?

TEXT **11b**

TANYA, IBID. 🈂

אֶלָּא מִפְּנֵי שֶׁהָרַע שֶׁבְּנַפְשׁוֹת יִשְׂרָאֵל עֲדַיִין הָיָה בְּתָקְפּוֹ בֶּחָלָל הַשְּׂמָאלִי,
כִּי לֹא פָּסְקָה זוּהֲמָתָם עַד מַתַּן תּוֹרָה. רַק מַגַּמָתָם וְחֶפְצָם הָיְתָה לָצֵאת
נַפְשָׁם הָאֱלֹקִית מִגָּלוּת הַסִּטְרָא אַחֲרָא, הִיא טוּמְאַת מִצְרַיִם, וּלְדָבְקָה
בּוֹ יִתְבָּרֵךְ, וּכְדִכְתִיב: "ה' עֻזִּי וּמָעֻזִּי וּמְנוּסִי בְּיוֹם צָרָה" (יִרְמְיָהוּ טז, יט).

At that time, the Jewish nation still harbored in their
hearts the full force of the natural soul's untamed ego.
For their natural impurity did not disappear until the
giving of the Torah. Nevertheless, their striving and
desire was to set their divine souls free from their exile
within the forces of evil—[which was represented by]
the Egyptian impurity—and to attach to G-d, as it is
stated, "G-d is my strength and my fortress, my refuge
on a day of distress" (JEREMIAH 16:19).

TEXT 12

TANYA, IBID. 🔄

זֹאת יָשִׁיב אֶל לִבּוֹ לְנַחֲמוֹ בְּכִפְלַיִם... לֵאמֹר לְלִבּוֹ:

אֱמֶת הוּא כֵן בְּלִי סָפֵק, שֶׁאֲנִי רָחוֹק מְאֹד מֵה' בְּתַכְלִית וּמְשׁוּקָץ וּמְתוֹעָב כו'. אַךְ כָּל זֶה הוּא אֲנִי לְבַדִּי, הוּא הַגּוּף עִם נֶפֶשׁ הַחִיּוּנִית שֶׁבּוֹ. אֲבָל מִכָּל מָקוֹם יֵשׁ בְּקִרְבִּי חֵלֶק ה' מַמָּשׁ, שֶׁיֶּשְׁנוֹ אֲפִילוּ בְּקַל שֶׁבְּקַלִּים, שֶׁהִיא נֶפֶשׁ הָאֱלֹקִית עִם נִיצוֹץ אֱלֹקוּת מַמָּשׁ הַמְלוּבָּשׁ בָּהּ לְהַחֲיוֹתָהּ; רַק שֶׁהִיא בִּבְחִינַת גָּלוּת.

וְאִם כֵּן אַדְּרַבָּה, כָּל מַה שֶׁאֲנִי בְּתַכְלִית הָרִיחוּק מֵה' וְהַתִּיעוּב וְהַשִּׁיקוּץ, הֲרֵי נֶפֶשׁ הָאֱלֹקִית שֶׁבִּי בְּגָלוּת גָּדוֹל יוֹתֵר, וְהָרַחֲמָנוּת עָלֶיהָ גְּדוֹלָה מְאֹד.

וְלָזֶה, אָשִׂים כָּל מַגַּמָּתִי וְחֶפְצִי לְהוֹצִיאָהּ וּלְהַעֲלוֹתָהּ מִגָּלוּת זֶה לַהֲשִׁיבָהּ אֶל בֵּית אָבִיהָ כִּנְעוּרֶיהָ, קוֹדֶם שֶׁנִּתְלַבְּשָׁה בְגוּפִי, שֶׁהָיְתָה נִכְלֶלֶת בְּאוֹרוֹ יִתְבָּרַךְ וּמְיוּחֶדֶת עִמּוֹ בְּתַכְלִית.

וְגַם עַתָּה כֵן תְּהֵא כְּלוּלָה וּמְיוּחֶדֶת בּוֹ יִתְבָּרַךְ, כְּשֶׁאָשִׂים כָּל מַגַּמָּתִי בַּתּוֹרָה וּמִצְוֹת, לְהַלְבִּישׁ בָּהֶן כָּל עֶשֶׂר בְּחִינוֹתֶיהָ כַּנִּזְכָּר לְעֵיל. וּבִפְרָט בְּמִצְוַת תְּפִלָּה, לִצְעוֹק אֶל ה' בַּצַּר לָהּ מִגָּלוּתָהּ...

וְזֹאת תִּהְיֶה עֲבוֹדָתוֹ כָּל יָמָיו בְּשִׂמְחָה רַבָּה, הִיא שִׂמְחַת הַנֶּפֶשׁ בְּצֵאתָהּ מֵהַגּוּף הַמְתוֹעָב וְשָׁבָה אֶל בֵּית אָבִיהָ כִּנְעוּרֶיהָ בְּשְׁעַת הַתּוֹרָה וְהָעֲבוֹדָה... וְאֵין לְךָ שִׂמְחָה גְדוֹלָה כְּצֵאת מֵהַגָּלוּת וְהַשִּׁבְיָה. כְּמָשָׁל בֶּן מֶלֶךְ שֶׁהָיָה בַּשִּׁבְיָה וְטוֹחֵן בְּבֵית הָאֲסוּרִים וּמְנֻוָּל בָּאַשְׁפָּה, וְיָצָא לַחָפְשִׁי אֶל בֵּית אָבִיו הַמֶּלֶךְ.

וְאַף שֶׁהַגּוּף עוֹמֵד בְּשִׁיקוּצוֹ וְתִיעוּבוֹ, וּכְמוֹ שֶׁכָּתוּב בַּזֹּהַר דְּנִקְרָא "מַשְׁכָא דְחִוְיָא", כִּי מַהוּתָהּ וְעַצְמוּתָהּ שֶׁל הַנֶּפֶשׁ הַבַּהֲמִית לֹא נֶהְפַּךְ לְטוֹב לִיכָּלֵל בִּקְדוּשָׁה, מִכָּל מָקוֹם, תִּיקַר נַפְשׁוֹ בְּעֵינָיו לִשְׂמוֹחַ בְּשִׂמְחָתָהּ יוֹתֵר מֵהַגּוּף הַנִּבְזֶה, שֶׁלֹּא לְעַרְבֵּב וּלְבַלְבֵּל שִׂמְחַת הַנֶּפֶשׁ בְּעִצְּבוֹן הַגּוּף.

To gain a powerful dose of consolation, we should take to heart and tell ourselves:

It is undoubtedly true: I am extremely distant from G-d; I am loathsome, repulsive, and so on [due to my naturally lowly spiritual stature]. But that is only my body and its attached natural soul. Despite all that, there [also] exists within me an actual part of G-d—for even the most worthless have it—the divine soul, which harbors a spark of actual G-dliness that gives it its life. Unfortunately, however, it languishes in a state of exile [within me].

In that case, I should shift my focus [from feeling crushed at my lowly spiritual stature] to the contrary: The more that I am distant from G-d and consider myself despicable and repulsive as a result, the more intensely is my divine soul mired in exile within me; how tremendously is she to be pitied!

I will therefore throw my every effort and determination into extracting her and lifting her out of this exile, to restore her to her Father's house as in her youth—meaning [to restore her to the state that she enjoyed] before she was installed within my body. Back then, she was absorbed in G-d's blessed light and was completely united with Him.

That is exactly what will happen now as well because I will invest all my efforts and all the faculties of my natural soul into the Torah and *mitzvot*, and especially in prayer, during which time I will [allow expression

*Laughter has been scientifically proven to boost happiness and the immune system. **Mrs. Nira Berry** on how to experience the benefits of laughter:*

MYJLI.COM/WARRIOR

to my divine soul so that she can] cry out to G-d over her distress at her state of exile. . . .

With this approach, we serve G-d with tremendous joy throughout our lives, rejoicing with our Divine Soul as it is [repeatedly] rescued from the loathsome body and is restored to her Father's home as in her [pristine] youth each time we engage in Torah study and the service of G-d. . . . There is no greater joy than being rescued from exile and captivity. It has been compared to the tremendous joy of a prince who languished in captivity, where he was forced to labor at grinding with a millstone in prison while wallowing in repulsive filth—and he is then set free and returned to the palace of his father, the king.

Our body will remain in its repulsive and loathsome state—indeed, the *Zohar* refers to the corporeal body as "serpent's skin"—because the core essence of our natural soul will not have been converted to good nor merged into holiness. Nevertheless, our soul will be far more precious to us than our despised body, and we will therefore share in her joy. We will not allow the misery of our body to disturb or confuse the joy of our soul.

Exercise 5.5

I will be happier because I will . . .

1	
2	
3	

TEXT 13

PSALMS 126:2

שִׁיר הַמַּעֲלוֹת, בְּשׁוּב ה' אֶת שִׁיבַת צִיּוֹן, הָיִינוּ כְּחֹלְמִים.

אָז יִמָּלֵא שְׂחוֹק פִּינוּ, וּלְשׁוֹנֵנוּ רִנָּה.

אָז יֹאמְרוּ בַגּוֹיִם, "הִגְדִּיל ה' לַעֲשׂוֹת עִם אֵלֶּה".

הִגְדִּיל ה' לַעֲשׂוֹת עִמָּנוּ, הָיִינוּ שְׂמֵחִים.

A song of ascents. When G-d will return the exiles of Zion, we will have been like dreamers.

Then our mouth will be filled with laughter and our tongue with songs of joy. Then they will say among the nations, "G-d has done great things for these [people]."

G-d has done great things for us; we were joyful.

Illustration (detail) from the *Venice Haggadah* depicting the final redemption as described in the hymn, "Adir Hu" (Great is G-d, may He rebuild His House quickly in our days). Venice, 1609.

KEY POINTS

1 Our natural soul's self-centered perspective is inconducive to positive emotions and happiness for two reasons:

(a) Self-centeredness smothers our divine soul and its calling. However, our divine soul is a critical and defining element of our deepest selves. If we deny ourselves complete self-expression, we will find it impossible to experience real happiness.

(b) A self-oriented mind-set focuses on ourselves and our own desires. This leaves us perpetually unsatisfied; we never have enough and constantly crave more.

2 Happiness is a direct function of the divine soul and the consequence of a life aligned with its perspective for two reasons:

(a) The divine soul has no self-interest; it is entirely devoted to its divine mission. Therefore, it does not have grandiose plans or desires that it needs fulfilled before experiencing happiness. It is fully satisfied with embracing each moment and circumstance because the ability to serve always exists.

(b) If we live a divine-soul lifestyle, G-d's happiness is the source of our happiness: our joy flows from the knowledge that our efforts make G-d happy.

3 Living a divine-soul life is challenging because the natural soul is the default human state, whereas the divine-soul attitude is unnatural. The only alternative, however, is to continue pursuing happiness via the natural-soul approach—which has been consistently proven to fail!

4 If we feel overwhelmed by the enormity of the specter of living a divine-soul life, we should recall that we do *not* have to feel ready in order to embark on the journey—a truth illustrated by our ancestors' "escape" from Egypt.

Appendix

TEXT **14**

DANIEL KAHNEMAN AND ANGUS DEATON, "HIGH INCOME IMPROVES EVALUATION OF LIFE BUT NOT EMOTIONAL WELL-BEING," *PROCEEDINGS OF THE NATIONAL ACADEMY OF SCIENCE OF THE UNITED STATES OF AMERICA*, 107:38 (2010), PP. 16489–16492

The question of whether "money buys happiness" comes up frequently in discussions of subjective well-being in both scholarly debates and casual conversation. . . . No single article can settle this complex question definitively, but data recently collected by the Gallup Organization in the Gallup-Healthways Well-Being Index (GHWBI) provide a rich source of observations, as well as an unusually detailed measurement of well-being. We analyzed the responses of more than 450,000 US residents surveyed in 2008 and 2009 to several questions about their subjective well-being. . . .

We defined positive affect by the average of three dichotomous items (reports of happiness, enjoyment, and frequent smiling and laughter) and what we refer to as "blue affect"—the average of worry and sadness. Reports of stress (also dichotomous) were analyzed separately (as was anger, for which the results were similar but not shown). . . . Fig. 1 [in this excerpt, Figure 5.3] presents averages over eight income groups for the

DANIEL KAHNEMAN, PHD
1934–

Psychologist and economist. Raised in Paris, Dr. Kahneman spent his childhood running from the Nazis until his family immigrated to Israel. He studied psychology and mathematics at Hebrew University and went on to receive his doctorate at UC Berkeley. Kahneman is most noted for his work on the psychology of decision-making and behavioral economics, for which he was awarded the 2002 Nobel Memorial Prize in Economic Science. He is professor emeritus of psychology and public affairs at Princeton University, and the author of *Thinking, Fast and Slow* (2011).

SIR ANGUS DEATON, PHD
1945–

Economist. Dr. Deaton is a Senior Scholar in the Woodrow Wilson School of International Affairs at Princeton University. Born in Scotland, he received his doctorate at the University of Cambridge in 1975. In 2015, he was awarded the Nobel Prize in Economics for his analysis of the effects of poverty and consumption on welfare, a topic on which he has authored numerous books and scholarly articles.

three aspects of emotional well-being. . . . Here blue affect and stress are converted to their complements, not blue and stress-free, so that higher values in the figure always refer to better psychological outcomes. Income is converted to an annual basis and plotted on a log scale. . . .

Fig. 1 shows that for all measures of experienced well-being, individuals in the lower-income groups do worse on average than those above them, but that those in the top two groups do not differ. . . . This observation implies that emotional well-being satiates somewhere in the third category of income from the top. We infer that beyond about $75,000/y, there is no improvement whatever in any of the three measures of emotional well-being. . . . Below $75,000, many factors become gradually worse, at least on average. For example, the emotional pain associated with ill health depends on income; for those reporting a monthly income of at least $3,000 (about two-thirds of households), the fractions reporting blue affect with and without headaches are 38% and 19%, respectively, a difference of 19 percentage points. The corresponding values for those with a monthly income of <$1,000 (about 10% of households) are 70% and 38%, a difference of 32%. [Indeed,] the pain of some of life's misfortunes, including asthma, divorce, and being alone, is significantly exacerbated by poverty; even the benefits of the weekend are less for the poor. Similar results apply to stress and positive affect. . . .

The data for positive and blue affect provide an unexpectedly sharp answer to our original question. More money does not necessarily buy more happiness, but less money is associated with emotional pain. Perhaps $75,000 is a threshold beyond which further increases in income no longer improve individuals' ability to do what matters most to their emotional well-being, such as spending time with people they like, avoiding pain and disease, and enjoying leisure. . . . It also is likely that when income rises beyond this value, the increased ability to purchase positive experiences is balanced, on average, by some negative effects. A recent psychological study using priming methods provided suggestive evidence of a possible association between high income and a reduced ability to savor small pleasures.

Figure 5.3

Effects of Income on Emotional Well-Being

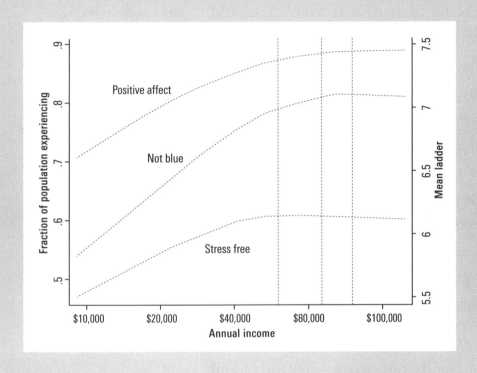

TEXT **15**

SONJA LYUBOMIRSKY, *THE MYTHS OF HAPPINESS*
(LONDON: PENGUIN PRESS, 2008), PP. 168–170

Being well off can bring numerous conveniences and advantages—besides offering us the ability to afford more stuff, it helps us meet potential mates and provides security and stability—but an unavoidable fact is that we get used to it. For example, economists have found that two-thirds of the benefits of a raise in income are erased after just one year, in part because our spending and new "needs" rise alongside it and because we begin to associate with people in a higher income bracket. Furthermore . . . having more money . . . has little if any impact on the daily positive and negative emotions and the uplifts and hassles that we experience.

In the beginning, greater wealth brings us a higher standard of living, and the extra comforts and extravagances bring extra pleasure. Then, we get used to—and perhaps even "addicted" to—the higher standard of living, to the extent that we are not satisfied unless we up the dosage by acquiring even more. However, those of us not *au courant* with the latest findings from psychology and economics fail to anticipate this development and end up assuming that increases in wealth should bring more happiness than

SONJA LYUBOMIRSKY, PHD

Leading expert in positive psychology. Dr. Lyubomirsky is professor of psychology at the University of California, Riverside. Originally from Russia, she received her PhD in social/personality psychology from Stanford University. Her research on the possibility of permanently increasing happiness has been honored with various grants, including a million-dollar grant from the National Institute of Mental Health. She has authored *The How of Happiness* and, more recently, *The Myths of Happiness*.

we actually get. Furthermore, when we don't obtain the expected pleasure, we presume that the fault lies not with human nature but with our failure to purchase the right object, steering us right back to the mall, realtor, or car dealer. . . .

[In addition,] it appears that what our peers are making determines our happiness even more than what *we* are making, no matter how generous it is. In other words, the average person . . . cares more about social comparison, about status, about rank, and about so-called positional goods than about the absolute value of his bank account or reputation. A famous 1998 study showed that people prefer to live in a world in which they receive an annual salary of $50,000 (when others are pulling in $25,000) than an annual salary of $100,000 (when others are making $200,000). Similarly, researchers in the United Kingdom have demonstrated that people would rather give away some of their own money if it means that others would have less. In sum, the reasons that we get used to having money are many, and the consequences unwelcome.

TEXT 16

ELIZABETH W. DUNN, ET AL., "IF MONEY DOESN'T MAKE YOU HAPPY THEN YOU PROBABLY AREN'T SPENDING IT RIGHT," *JOURNAL OF CONSUMER PSYCHOLOGY*, 21:2 (2011), P. 117

Human beings are the most social animal on our planet. . . .

Because of this, almost anything we do to improve our connections with others tends to improve our happiness as well—and that includes spending money. Dunn, Aknin, and Norton (2008) asked a nationally representative sample of Americans to rate their happiness and to report how much money they spent in a typical month on (1) bills and expenses, (2) gifts for themselves, (3) gifts for others, and (4) donations to charity. The first two categories were summed to create a personal spending composite, and the latter two categories were summed to create a prosocial spending composite. Although personal spending was unrelated to happiness, people who devoted more money to prosocial spending were happier, even after controlling for their income. Another experiment revealed a similar pattern of results (DUNN, AKNIN, & NORTON, 2008). Researchers approached individuals on the University of British Columbia (UBC) campus, handed them a $5 or $20 bill, and then randomly assigned them to spend the money on themselves or on others by the

ELIZABETH W. DUNN, PHD

Professor of psychology at the University of British Columbia. Dr. Dunn's research focuses on how time, money, and technology shape human happiness. She has recently coauthored *Happy Money: The Science of Happier Spending* with fellow happiness researcher Dr. Michael Norton.

end of the day. When participants were contacted that evening, individuals who had been assigned to spend their windfall on others were happier than those who had been assigned to spend the money on themselves. The benefits of prosocial spending appear to be cross-cultural. Over 600 students attending universities in Canada and in the East African nation of Uganda were randomly assigned to reflect on a time they had spent money on themselves or on others (AKNIN, ET AL., 2010). Participants felt significantly happier when they reflected on a time they had spent money on others, and this effect emerged consistently across these vastly different cultural contexts—even though the specific ways in which participants spent their money varied dramatically between cultures. The emotional rewards of prosocial spending are also detectable at the neural level. Participants in an MRI were given the opportunity to donate money to a local food bank. Choosing to give money away—or even being forced to do so—led to activation in brain areas typically associated with receiving rewards (HARBAUGH, MAYR, & BURGHART, 2007).

Additional Readings

LAUGHING BELOW, DANCING ABOVE

BY RABBI YERACHMIEL TILLES

Once, while the *Baal Shem Tov* was sitting at the Shabbos night dinner table, he suddenly started to laugh heartily. After a few minutes, the Rebbe started laughing again. A short while later, the Rebbe laughed a third time!

The disciples who were present that night couldn't imagine what could cause their Rebbe to burst into such laughter—and three times, no less!—but they didn't dare to ask. However, Saturday night, after the *Havdalah* ("end of Shabbos") ceremony, they asked one of their veteran members, Rabbi Ze'ev-Wolff Kitzis (who was also the Baal Shem Tov's brother-in-law), to query the Rebbe about this seemingly strange behavior. They knew it was his custom to visit the Baal Shem Tov at his home on Saturday nights while the Rebbe was smoking his pipe.

The Baal Shem Tov's response was to tell him, "Why don't you and the rest of the *chevreh* (the group of his close followers) accompany me on a journey now, and I will reveal to you what made me laugh."

The Baal Shem Tov then asked his gentile coach-driver, Alexi, to prepare the wagon and horses for a trip. The excursion lasted the entire night.

As the sky began to lighten, they arrived at a large town, which they soon found out was Apta. After praying in a local synagogue, the Baal Shem Tov went over to the leader of the congregation and asked him to send for Reb Shabsi the bookbinder. "And tell him to please bring his wife too," he added.

RABBI YERACHMIEL TILLES

Cofounder of Ascent of Safed. Rabbi Tilles is the managing editor of Kabbalah Online, and has published hundreds of stories about kabbalah sages, Chasidic masters, and other Jewish heroes.

When they arrived, the Baal Shem Tov addressed Shabsi, "Please tell us what went on in your home on Shabbos night. Don't leave out anything."

Shabsi's jaw dropped in shock. After opening and closing his mouth several times, he began. "Rebbe, I'm sorry. If I've sinned, please instruct me how to rectify it." Then, after a glance at his wife, he related what happened.

"All my life I worked binding books, and thank G-d, it supported all my needs. My custom was that every Thursday I buy everything needed for Shabbos, and had everything ready for Shabbos long before midday on Friday. At midday, already dressed for Shabbos, I go to *shul*. There I review the weekly reading and read Song of Songs until it is time for the *Mincha* (afternoon prayer) and Welcoming the Shabbos prayers. Then I go home, pour a cup of wine and recite *Kiddush*.

"This was my practice for more than forty years. Lately however, since I became old, I don't have the strength to work as much. As a result, I slowly became impoverished. I rarely have the means to buy everything we need for Shabbos. Still, I maintain my custom to go to *shul* at midday on Friday, already prepared for the holy day.

"This past Friday was especially difficult. I had no money at all to buy anything for Shabbos. When midday came, I told my wife that I nevertheless was going to go to *shul* as always, and I asked her to promise not to go to the neighbors to borrow anything for Shabbos—no oil for lighting candles, nor food nor wine nor flour to bake *challah*. Even if they offered to give she should not take. I felt in total agreement with the statement of our sages, 'It is better to make Shabbos like a weekday, than to be dependent on others.'

"I went to *shul* as usual and learned and prayed, yet feeling uneasy knowing that my house was dark and empty of anything for Shabbos. After completion of the Shabbos night prayers, I waited till everyone else left before I set out for home. I didn't want to answer their questions if they should notice through our window that no candles were burning.

"I was still a short distance from home when I noticed that there was bright light coming from my front window! I could barely trust my eyes. I knew there was no oil or candles in the house.

"I felt bad, realizing that my wife certainly wasn't able to stand up to the test and had gone to the neighbors to borrow candles. And perhaps food too!

"When I went inside, I saw the table was set beautifully, and the whole house smelled of delicious food! For a moment I became angry; I had told my wife to promise me that she wouldn't borrow anything, and clearly she didn't keep her word.

"Nevertheless, I decided I was not going to say anything so as not to cause any arguments and thereby spoil the peace and harmony of Shabbos. I understood it must have been difficult for her.

"Instead, I sang Shalom Aleichem and Eishes Chayil (the two traditional pre-Kiddush hymns) as usual. However, when my wife brought over the wine for Kiddush and covered the beautiful challahs, I was unable to hold back, and I asked her as gently as I could why she broke her promise.

"Did she surprise me! She stated that she didn't break her word. She quickly explained that after I left for shul she didn't know what to do: there was no food to prepare and she had already cleaned the house. So, she decided that instead of sitting idle, she would busy herself cleaning out the storage chest and refolding the old clothes in it.

"Inside the chest was an old coat, and in its pockets she discovered a pair of matching gloves that had been missing for many years, on which the buttons and decorative flowers—the fashion decades ago—were made of pure silver! She snipped them off and rushed to a silversmith in the marketplace, who willingly purchased them for a tidy sum. With the money, she went to the nearby stalls of the food and beverage sellers, and purchased everything we could possibly need for Shabbos, in her excitement sparing no expense.

"Hearing this, I also became excited, and very happy and grateful. I recited Kiddush with great joy. We washed our hands and said the blessing for bread over the two fresh challahs, and as soon as I finished chewing my first bite, I thanked my wife for what she had done, and when she served the gefilte fish I told her how lucky we were to have such a blessing from the Creator, that He saved us from poverty and taking charity and enabled us to honor the Shabbos properly.

"In our joy, we both got up and danced energetically like a young chatan and kallah (bride and groom) on the day of their wedding! After a while we sat back down and ate chicken soup and roasted meat and other delicious foods.

"I couldn't contain my great happiness, though, so I took her by the hand and we danced again! Finally, we got tired. We returned to the table and ate a rich selection of fruits and desserts, which led to our getting up and dancing a third time! We were so happy and so thankful to G-d for how he helped us, that dancing seemed to be the only way we could show Him our joy and gratitude!"

The elderly bookbinder completed his words by repeating, "Rebbe, I'm sorry. If I've sinned, please instruct me how to rectify it."

The Baal Shem Tov beamed at Shabsi, and turned to the eagerly listening chasidim. "Each of the three times Reb Shabsi and his wife danced around the Shabbos table last night, the angels in heaven too rejoiced and danced! This was what delighted me and made me laugh three times."

Turning back to Shabsi and his wife, Perle, the Baal Shem Tov addressed the woman directly. "In the merit of your great Shabbos efforts and the extraordinary rejoicing of you both, you are to be granted a special blessing. Would you like that you live the rest of your days in great wealth, or do you want a blessing to have a child in your old age?"

Perle answered instantly. "What good will riches do us? We are old, in our sixties, and childless, Rebbe. Please bless me and my husband to have a good son." Shabsi nodded his head vigorously at hearing her choice.

The Baal Shem Tov said "Amen," and declared that by this time next year, Reb Shabsi and his wife would have a son. He also said that he would attend the *brit milah* circumcision ceremony and be the *sandek* (the man who holds the baby on his lap during the physical circumcision), and that their son would be a bright light for them in the World of Truth.

And that's what happened. Before twelve months, the elderly couple had a baby boy! Rabbi Yisrael Baal Shem Tov was the *sandek* at the *brit*, and they named the infant "Yisrael" after him.

This child grew up to be a great Torah scholar and a leading chasidic *rebbe* in his own right. He was none other than Rabbi Yisrael, the famed "*Maggid* ('Preacher') of Kozhnitz"!

Biographic Note:
Rabbi Yisrael ben Eliezer [of blessed memory: 18 Elul 5458–6 Sivan 5520 (Aug. 1698–May 1760 C.E.)], the Baal Shem Tov ["Master of the Good Name"—often referred to as "the Besht" for short], a unique and seminal figure in Jewish history, revealed his identity as an exceptionally holy person on his 36th birthday, 18 Elul 5494 (1734 C.E.), and made the until-then underground Chasidic movement public. He wrote no books, although many works claim to contain his teachings. One available in English is the excellent annotated translation of *Tzava'at Harivash*, published by Kehos.

Rabbi Yisroel Haupstein [5497–14 Tishrei 5575 (1737–Sept. 1814 C.E.)], the "Maggid" (preacher) of Kozhnitz was a major disciple of the Rebbe Reb Elimelech of Lyzhensk and, along with the "Seer" of Lublin, the main spreader of the Chasidic movement to Poland-Galitzia. He acquired his position in Kozhnitz at age 28, and lived there for the rest of his life, known for his passionate prayer and many miracles. He is the author of the chassidic-kabbalistic work, *Avodas Yisrael* and fifteen other kabbalistic books. His miraculous birth to an elderly couple is the subject of a famous Baal Shem Tov story.

Adapted by Yerachmiel Tilles, from *Why the Baal Shem Tov Laughed*, by Shternah Citron (Lanham, Md.: Rowman & Littlefield, 1993), with some additions based on the lengthier rendition in the Hebrew classic, *Sipurei Chasidim*, by Rabbi S. Y. Zevin (Jerusalem: Beit Hillel, 1995), and a few supplementary biographical notes from *Chasidic Masters*, by Rabbi Aryeh Kaplan (Brooklyn: Moznaim Publishing Corp., 1984).

www.ascentofsafed.com

Reprinted with permission of the author

LIBERATION OF THE SELF

BY RABBI ADIN EVEN-ISRAEL (STEINSALTZ)

Spiritual joy is of the nature of the Exodus from Egypt—it has been said that the Exodus represents the emergence of the self from the narrow place of restriction, the breaking out from the gloomy darkness into joy. It is not a matter of ignoring the existence of evil that surrounds and is within one, but rather of using the evil and transforming it in the process of living.

Think not that this is the essential purpose of life; in the endeavor to build up one's own soul, there may not be ample opportunity to stop and repair all the evil one meets on the way. The important thing is to provide the Divine Soul both with powers of adaptation to deal with these forces and with the light needed to make its way. In this respect, too, the process is in the nature of an "exodus"—full of questions and doubts. Why did the Children of Israel have to wait for Pharaoh's permission, even if he was forced to grant it? Why could they not have just gone forth with head held high, under the glory and power of G-d, instead of relying on all sorts of stratagems—such as requesting to go for a period of ceremonial worship? The point is that the evil in the soul of the Children of Israel was still active in the left chamber of the heart, and its force continued to be felt until the giving of the Torah. Only then, when they were standing before G-d at Sinai, did the evil in the soul of Israel cease to have any effect.

For the state of slavery in Egypt is not only a banishment from the Holy Land; it is also a matter of participating in the "defilement of Egypt," which is said to be equivalent to the abomination of the earth. To get out of this state of defilement and to cleave to the holiness of G-d was, therefore, in the nature of a flight, of running away, not only from Pharaoh, but also from one's own uncleanness. There was no thought of solving the problem in its entirety. Thus, too, when the soul is struggling against the body, it usually has no time to answer all the questions of the *self*; all it wants to do is escape, as well it may, to the saving hands of G-d. Hence too, in the future, when the spirit of G-d will begin to sweep away all the defilement of the earth, there won't be opportunity to do much else but make one's escape. The difference is that in that future, there will no longer be any need to hasten; one will be able to walk. Because the Exodus from Egypt was also an exodus from some inner servitude—which cannot be done at leisure (the Torah relates many occasions when the people complained that the journey was too much for them and they wanted to go back). Whereas in the future redemption, it will be possible to walk to Divine holiness with the feeling of wholeness and with the happiness that follows the sadness of despair.

True, the person who reaches this spiritual joy following dejection knows that he has not achieved a high level of holiness and that he is hardly able to be a messenger of G-d. Nevertheless, he does feel that he has a great task in the world, that it is a matter of expressing joy and overcoming the sadness of the body, of being a penitent in the deep sense of one who "returns." This means an ever increasing amplification of the great joy by embracing the elements of knowledge and understanding. The purpose is to sharpen intellectual comprehension, after having made a thorough reckoning of one's life, in order to be able to see the shallowness or disinterestedness of one's previous efforts.

RABBI ADIN EVEN-ISRAEL (STEINSALTZ), 1937–

Talmudist, author, and philosopher. Rabbi Even-Israel (Steinsaltz) is considered one of the foremost Jewish thinkers of the 20th century. Praised by *Time* magazine as a "once-in-a-millennium scholar," he has been awarded the Israel Prize for his contributions to Jewish study. He lives in Jerusalem and is the founder of the Israel Institute for Talmudic Publications, a society dedicated to the translation and elucidation of the Talmud.

Rabbi Adin Even-Israel (Steinsaltz), *The Long Shorter Way* (Jerusalem: Koren Publishers Jerusalem, 2014), pp. 211–213

THE CURIOUS AND POWERFUL PHENOMENON OF HEDONIC ADAPTATION

BY SONJA LYUBOMIRSKY, PHD

When I am in New York, I want to be in Europe, and when I am in Europe, I want to be in New York.
—Woody Allen

One of the great ironies of our quest to become happier is that so many of us focus on changing the circumstances of our lives in the misguided hope that those changes will deliver happiness. In an attempt to allay unhappiness, a recent college graduate may choose a high-paying job in a distant city, a middle-aged divorcee may undergo beautifying cosmetic surgery, or a retired couple may buy a condominium with a view. Unfortunately, all these individuals will likely become only temporarily happier. An impressive body of research now shows that trying to be happy by changing our life situations ultimately will not work.

Why do life changes account for so little? Because of a very powerful force that psychologists call hedonic adaptation.

Human beings are remarkably adept at becoming rapidly accustomed to sensory or physiologic changes. When you walk in from the bitter cold, the warmth of the crackling fire feels heavenly at first, but you quickly get used to it and may even become overheated. When a mild but conspicuous odor dwells in our apartment, you may completely fail to notice it

SONJA LYUBOMIRSKY, PHD

Leading expert in positive psychology. Dr. Lyubomirsky is professor of psychology at the University of California, Riverside. Originally from Russia, she received her PhD in social/personality psychology from Stanford University. Her research on the possibility of permanently increasing happiness has been honored with various grants, including a million-dollar grant from the National Institute of Mental Health. She has authored *The How of Happiness* and, more recently, *The Myths of Happiness*.

until you have left for a while and returned. This experience is labeled physiological or sensory adaptation. The same phenomenon, however, occurs with hedonic shifts—that is, relocations, marriages, job changes—that make you happier for a time but only a short time. To give a concrete example, I had laser eye surgery at age thirty-six after a lifetime of near blindness, discomfort with contact lenses, and loathing of glasses. The result was miraculous. For the first time in memory, I could read street signs, tell time when waking in the middle of the night, and see my toes in the shower. The surgery made me wonderfully happy. Remarkably, however, after about two weeks I was completely and perfectly adapted to my new 20/20 vision, and it no longer provided the happiness boost it had on that memorable first day. Nearly everyone has stories like this: about moving into a bigger house, securing a promotion or a pay raise, getting a makeover, or flying first class. Research psychologists have even tried to bottle this experience by investigating it systematically—for example, asking whether people show hedonic adaptation to such significant life events as marriage, sudden wealth, or chronic illness. It turns out they do.

The Altar, the Lottery, and a House in the 'Burbs

Any happy newlywed will wonder how it could be possible to adapt to the benefits of matrimony. Indeed, every married person reading this undoubtedly grasped the enormous, life-changing impact of marriage. In fact, studies show that married people are significantly happier than their single peers. Numerous anecdotal examples, including mine, prove the point: Getting married was one of the best things that I have ever done, and I am absolutely convinced that I am happier now than before.

Yet psychological researchers have evidence to prove me wrong. In a landmark study, residents of West Germany and East Germany, including citizens, immigrants, and foreigners—25,000 in all—were surveyed every year for fifteen years. Over the course of the study, 1761 individuals got married and stayed married. Using this spectacular data set, scientists showed that alas, marriage has only a temporary effect on happiness. It appears that after the wedding husband and wife get a happiness boost for about two years and then simply return to their baseline in happiness, their set point. It seems wise not to share this bit of news with newlyweds.

Several lines of research suggest that a similar phenomenon occurs with the attainment of money and possessions. In a classic study conducted back in the 1970s, psychologists interviewed some lucky individuals who had won between fifty thousand and one million dollars (in 1970s dollars) in the Illinois State Lottery. Strikingly, less than a year after receiving the potentially life-changing news of winning the lottery, they reported being no more happy than regular folks who had not experienced the sudden windfall. Indeed, the lottery winners mused that they now derived less enjoyment from day-to-day activities such as watching television or going out to lunch, relative to the nonwinners.

Why does hedonic adaptation occur? The two biggest culprits are rising aspirations (e.g., the bigger house you buy after your windfall feels natural after a while; you experience a sort of "creeping normalcy" and begin to want an even bigger one) and social comparison (e.g., your new friends in the neighborhood are driving BMWs and you feel you should too). As a result, even as people amass more of what they want with every year, their overall happiness tends to stay the same. To paraphrase the Red Queen in *Through the Looking-Glass*, "We're running faster and faster, but we seem to end up in exactly the same place."

My friend Dianna is a walking case study in hedonic adaptation. When she married her husband, he was still a graduate student, and for a year they shared a single tiny dormitory room, lacking a kitchen, with their new baby and Dianna's mother. I remember thinking how insanely difficult this must have been: her husband laboring to finish his dissertation, the baby crying in the middle of the night, a mother-in-law sleeping a couple of feet away. Years later the family, now with three beautiful girls, moved to a tidy bedroom community north of San Diego, with a neighborhood pool and an excellent public school. Their house is lovely and new—two stories, four bedrooms, family room, enormous yard with playground set. A few months after they settled in, Dianna called to tell me about a house three doors down from them that had just gone on the market. It was identical to theirs, but it had an extra bedroom and an extra patio where one could mount a barbecue. She was obsessed with this house, ruminating about every possible way that it was superior to theirs. Could they afford to buy it? Maybe they could. Could they? Maybe somehow they could. . . .

So the bad news about hedonic adaptation is that it ultimately dampens your happiness and satisfaction after any positive event or uplift. But there is good news too. I would argue that human beings are actually lucky to have the ability to adapt quickly to changing circumstances, as it's extremely useful when *bad* things happen. Some studies of hedonic adaptation show, for instance, that we have a phenomenal ability to recover much of our happiness after a debilitating illness or accident.

Do you think that having end-stage kidney disease would reduce your capacity for happiness? Imagine having to endure *nine hours* of hemodialysis per week, during which you are attached to a machine filtering your blood. Imagine having to adhere to a strict diet, limiting meat, salt, and even daily fluids. Most people are positive that this situation would make them quite unhappy. Researchers put their belief to empirical test. Two groups of people—healthy participants and dialysis patients—were asked to carry for a week Palm Pilots that would beep them randomly every ninety minutes. After each beep, the participant was required to punch in the mood that he happened to be experiencing at that very moment (pleased? joyful? anxious? unhappy?). The average of a person's mood ratings gathered over the course of a week happens to be an excellent indicator of his general well-being because such ratings are unlikely to be edited, filtered, or otherwise biased. It turned out that the renal disease patients were just as happy as the healthy controls. It seems that they adapted quite well to their condition.

But the healthy participants truly believed that they would be less happy if they had to undergo regular dialysis, and even the patients themselves lacked insight into their own miraculous capacity for hedonic adaptation; they were certain they'd be happier if they had not had to endure the disease.

Amazing as it may seem, people show a great deal of adaptation to disabilities like paralysis and blindness and other conditions that involve losing an important capacity or function. Consider a multiple sclerosis patient whose disease, as it developed, was transformed from something frightening to something manageable. Although with time Ernest could no longer drive, run, walk, or even stand, these things "lost much of their importance. . . . [They] are no longer within the sphere of possibility and are therefore not missed as though they were possible." He explained his change in perspective this way: "Gradual changes have taken place in my outlooks, in my likes and dislikes, in what I feel to be a natural part of my life and in what I had always regarded as a necessity for happiness. . . . Probably had I known in 1956 what would be the symptoms that have appeared by now, I would have been anxious about and discouraged by the prospect of the future. Now that I actually find myself here, however, it seems that things are not nearly so bad as I would have thought then."

Summing Up

We cannot and will not adapt to everything. But the evidence for hedonic adaptation, especially with regard to positive events, is very strong. Human beings adapt to favorable changes in wealth, housing, and possessions, to being beautiful or being surrounded by beauty, to good health, and even to marriage.

Sonja Lyubomirsky, PhD, *The How of Happiness* (New York: The Penguin Press, 2007), pp. 48–52

Reprinted with permission of the author

Lesson

6

REFRESHING RELATIONSHIPS
REMODELING OUR APPROACH TO LOVE AND RELATIONSHIPS

An Old Man and Woman, artist unknown, cut paper with wash, America, c. 19th century. (Metropolitan Museum of Art, New York)

Relationships are the most rewarding and challenging features of human life. Healthy relationships are critical to positive emotions, but they are highly elusive. This lesson introduces a significant shift in the way we view the foundation upon which all of our relationships are based. This new perspective empowers us to enjoy better, lasting, and more genuine relationships, even with individuals with whom we share little in common.

Exercise 6.1

(a) Think of an individual in your life with whom you would appreciate applying the relationship insights you will gain in this session.

(b) Record three things you have in common with this individual:

1	
2	
3	

Record three of the most obvious differences between you:

1	
2	
3	

QUESTION FOR DISCUSSION

Theoretically, are any two random people capable of having a good relationship with each other?

TEXT **1a**

TALMUD, SOTAH 2A

> אֵין מְזַוְּוגִין לוֹ לְאָדָם אִשָּׁה אֶלָּא לְפִי מַעֲשָׂיו . . . וְקָשִׁין לְזַוְּוגָן כִּקְרִיעַת יַם
> סוּף, שֶׁנֶּאֱמַר: "אֱלֹקִים מוֹשִׁיב יְחִידִים בַּיְתָה, מוֹצִיא אֲסִירִים בַּכּוֹשָׁרוֹת"
> (תְּהִלִּים סח, ז).
>
> אִינִי? וְהָא אָמַר רַב יְהוּדָה אָמַר רַב: אַרְבָּעִים יוֹם קוֹדֶם יְצִירַת הַוָּלָד בַּת
> קוֹל יוֹצֵאת וְאוֹמֶרֶת: "בַּת פְּלוֹנִי לִפְלוֹנִי . . . "?
>
> לֹא קַשְׁיָא: הָא בְּזוּג רִאשׁוֹן הָא בְּזוּג שֵׁנִי.

BABYLONIAN TALMUD

A literary work of monumental proportions that draws upon the legal, spiritual, intellectual, ethical, and historical traditions of Judaism. The 37 tractates of the Babylonian Talmud contain the teachings of the Jewish sages from the period after the destruction of the 2nd Temple through the 5th century CE. It has served as the primary vehicle for the transmission of the Oral Law and the education of Jews over the centuries; it is the entry point for all subsequent legal, ethical, and theological Jewish scholarship.

Heaven matches a woman to a man only according to his deeds. . . . [Therefore,] it is as difficult to [successfully] match a couple as it was to split the Red Sea [when rescuing the Jews from Egypt]. As it is stated, "G-d settles solitary individuals [together] in a home; He brings out those who were imprisoned in chains" (PSALMS 68:7).

Is that true? Did Rabbi Yehudah not repeat in the name of Rav: "Forty days before an embryo is formed, a Divine Voice declares, 'This woman is destined to marry this man . . . '"?

Nevertheless, the original statement is not problematic, for the latter teaching speaks of a first marriage, whereas the former statement speaks of a second marriage.

QUESTION FOR DISCUSSION

Does this Talmudic reading shed light on the question of compatibility between random individuals?

Wedding Ceremony, Edouard Moyse, oil on canvas, France, c. 1860. (The Jewish Museum, New York)

TEXT 1b

RABBI YEHUDAH LOWE, *CHIDUSHEI AGADOT*, AD LOC.

וְקָאָמַר "וְקָשֶׁה לְזַוְּגָם כִּקְרִיעַת יַם סוּף", רְצוֹנוֹ לוֹמַר כְּשֵׁם שֶׁהוּא פֶּלֶא גָדוֹל לִקְרוֹעַ דָּבָר שֶׁהוּא אֶחָד כְּמוֹ הַיָּם שֶׁהוּא אֶחָד, וְקָשֶׁה הוּא לְחַלֵּק וּלְהַפְרִידוֹ לִשְׁנַיִם, וְכָךְ הוּא פֶּלֶא גָדוֹל לְחַבֵּר שְׁנֵי דְבָרִים שֶׁהֵם בְּעַצְמָם מְחֻלָּקִים.

כְּדִכְתִיב, "מוֹשִׁיב יְחִידִים בַּיְתָה", כְּלוֹמַר יְחִידִים שֶׁהֵם מְחֻלָּקִים וּמְפֻזָּרִים, לְהוֹשִׁיב אוֹתָם לְחַבֵּר אוֹתָם הוּא כְּמוֹ קְרִיעַת יַם שֶׁהוּא חָלוּק דָּבָר שֶׁהוּא אֶחָד (כָּזֶה). כִּי חִלּוּק דָּבָר שֶׁהוּא אֶחָד וְלְגַמְרֵי הוּא קָשֶׁה כְּמוֹ לְחַבֵּר וְלַעֲשׂוֹת אֶחָד דָּבָר שֶׁהוּא מְחֻלָּק בְּעַצְמוֹ כְּמוֹ אִישׁ וְאִשָּׁה.

וְעוֹד תֵּדַע שֶׁקָּשֶׁה לְזַוְּגָם כִּקְרִיעַת יַם סוּף, כִּי קְרִיעַת יַם סוּף הָיָה נֵס שֶׁלֹּא כְּסֵדֶר הָעוֹלָם, וְכָךְ הַחִבּוּר הַזֶּה הוּא שֶׁלֹּא מִמַּדְרֵיגַת הָעוֹלָם הַזֶּה, כִּי בְּטִבְעָם הֵם מְחֻלָּקִים, וְאִי אֶפְשָׁר שֶׁיִּזְדַּוְּוגוּ וְיִתְאַחֲדוּ רַק שֶׁלֹּא מִמַּדְרֵיגַת עוֹלָם הַזֶּה.

RABBI YEHUDAH LOWE (MAHARAL OF PRAGUE) 1525–1609

Talmudist and philosopher. Maharal rose to prominence as leader of the famed Jewish community of Prague. He is the author of more than a dozen works of original philosophic thought, including *Tiferet Yisrael* and *Netsach Yisrael*. He also authored *Gur Aryeh*, a supercommentary to Rashi's biblical commentary, and a commentary on the nonlegal passages of the Talmud. He is buried in the Old Jewish Cemetery of Prague.

Mrs. Mina Sputz, a director of disabilities for a special education center, on the art of understanding others and strengthening relationships:

MYJLI.COM/WARRIOR

Successfully pairing a couple is as difficult as splitting the Red Sea. It requires a tremendous feat to split an entity that is intrinsically one, such as a sea, into two distinct parts. It is a similarly spectacular feat to join two entities that are in essence distinct.

The quoted verse states, "G-d settles *yechidim* (solitary individuals) together in a home." The term *yechidim* implies singularity—each is utterly dissimilar and distinct from the other. Nevertheless, G-d settles them together and merges them into a single entity. Just as sea-splitting sunders something indivisibly singular, so is it equally challenging to create a unified entity out of entities that are as essentially distinct as a man and a woman.

In addition, splitting the Red Sea contradicted the laws of nature. Similarly, pairing couples is entirely unnatural, for by nature, they are distinct to the point that pairing and uniting requires supernatural input.

*How real and lasting is your love? A 2-minute animated clip by **Rabbi David Aaron**:*

MYJLI.COM/WARRIOR

TEXT 2

ETHICS OF THE FATHERS 5:16

כָּל אַהֲבָה שֶׁהִיא תְּלוּיָה בְדָבָר, בָּטֵל דָּבָר, בְּטֵלָה אַהֲבָה. וְשֶׁאֵינָהּ תְּלוּיָה בְדָבָר, אֵינָהּ בְּטֵלָה לְעוֹלָם.

אֵיזוֹ הִיא אַהֲבָה שֶׁהִיא תְּלוּיָה בְדָבָר? זוֹ אַהֲבַת אַמְנוֹן וְתָמָר.

וְשֶׁאֵינָהּ תְּלוּיָה בְדָבָר? זוֹ אַהֲבַת דָּוִד וִיהוֹנָתָן.

ETHICS OF THE FATHERS (PIRKEI AVOT)

A 6 chapter work on Jewish ethics that is studied widely by Jewish communities, especially during the summer. The first 5 chapters are from the Mishnah, tractate Avot. Avot differs from the rest of the Mishnah in that it does not focus on legal subjects; it is a collection of the sages' wisdom on topics related to character development, ethics, healthy living, piety, and the study of Torah.

Any love that is dependent on something—when the thing ceases, the love also ceases. But a love that is not dependent on anything never ceases.

What is [an example of] a love that is dependent on something? The love of Amnon for Tamar.

And [what is an example of a love] that is not dependent on anything? The love of David and Jonathan.

TEXT 3

ELLIOT D. COHEN, "HOW COMPATIBLE ARE YOU WITH YOUR
SIGNIFICANT OTHER?" *PSYCHOLOGY TODAY*, MARCH 21, 2013

Two people who are ego-centered are not likely to get along. An ego-centered person is one who believes that what he or she wants, desires, prefers, values, or believes is good, right, and true; and therefore, that others should share the same subjective states as he or she does. If one individual is ego-centered while the other is not, there is a greater chance that the relationship will last but it is not likely to be a very functional relationship. This is because, sooner or later, even very tolerant people tend to become wary of constantly appeasing a self-centered person.

ELLIOT D. COHEN, PHD
1951–

Philosopher, ethicist, and political analyst. Author of 26 books and numerous articles, Dr. Cohen is editor-in-chief of the *International Journal of Applied Philosophy*. He is also president of the Logic-Based Therapy and Consultation Institute and writes a popular blog for *Psychology Today* called *What Would Aristotle Do?*

TEXT 4

RABBI SHNE'UR ZALMAN OF LIADI, *TANYA*, CH. 32

וְהִנֵּה עַל יְדֵי קִיּוּם הַדְּבָרִים הַנִּזְכָּרִים לְעֵיל, לִהְיוֹת גּוּפוֹ נִבְזֶה וְנִמְאָס בְּעֵינָיו, רַק שִׂמְחָתוֹ תִּהְיֶה שִׂמְחַת הַנֶּפֶשׁ לְבַדָּהּ, הֲרֵי זוֹ דֶרֶךְ יְשָׁרָה וְקַלָּה לָבֹא לִידֵי קִיּוּם מִצְוַת "וְאָהַבְתָּ לְרֵעֲךָ כָּמוֹךָ" (וַיִּקְרָא יט, יח) לְכָל נֶפֶשׁ מִיִּשְׂרָאֵל, לְמִגָּדוֹל וְעַד קָטָן.

כִּי מֵאַחַר שֶׁגּוּפוֹ נִמְאָס וּמְתוֹעָב אֶצְלוֹ, וְהַנֶּפֶשׁ וְהָרוּחַ, מִי יוֹדֵעַ גְּדוּלָּתָן וּמַעֲלָתָן בְּשָׁרְשָׁן וּמְקוֹרָן בֵּאלֹקִים חַיִּים. בְּשֶׁגַּם שֶׁכֻּלָּן מַתְאִימוֹת וְאָב אֶחָד לְכוּלָּנָה, וְלָכֵן נִקְרְאוּ כָּל יִשְׂרָאֵל אַחִים מַמָּשׁ, מִצַּד שׁוֹרֶשׁ נַפְשָׁם בַּה' אֶחָד. רַק שֶׁהַגּוּפִים מְחוּלָּקִים.

וְלָכֵן הָעוֹשִׂים גּוּפָם עִיקָר וְנַפְשָׁם טְפֵלָה, אִי אֶפְשָׁר לִהְיוֹת אַהֲבָה וְאַחֲוָה אֲמִתִּית בֵּינֵיהֶם, אֶלָּא הַתְּלוּיָה בְּדָבָר לְבַדָּהּ.

RABBI SHNE'UR ZALMAN OF LIADI (ALTER REBBE) 1745–1812
Chasidic rebbe, halachic authority, and founder of the Chabad movement. The Alter Rebbe was born in Liozna, Belarus, and was among the principal students of the Magid of Mezeritch. His numerous works include the *Tanya*, an early classic containing the fundamentals of Chabad Chasidism, and *Shulchan Aruch HaRav*, an expanded and reworked code of Jewish law.

Acting on the suggestion mentioned above—to view one's body with scorn and contempt and to find joy in the joy of the soul alone—is a direct and easy way to fulfill the commandment, "Love your fellow as yourself" (LEVITICUS 19:18), toward every soul of Israel, from the greatest to the smallest.

For [physical and material considerations no longer erect barriers between us] now that we disdain and loathe the body. And as for [spiritual disparities caused by variations in] the soul and spirit, well—who can even know their [true] greatness and worth, as they are rooted and sourced in the Living G-d! Moreover, all souls are [truly] equal, and all have one Father, to the point that all Jews are referred to as actual brothers—because of the [single] source of their souls: the One G-d. It is *only* our bodies that separate us.

Consequently, those who prioritize their bodies while considering their souls to be less significant cannot experience true love and brotherhood; [they can] only [experience love] that is contingent on [nonessential] factors.

TEXT 5

RABBI YOEL KAHN, *SUGYOT BECHASIDUT* (JERUSALEM: MAAYANOTECHA PUBLISHING, 2012), PP. 57–58

If my primary identity is the "I"—my sense of tangible being—then I cannot experience true unity with my fellows. However, if my life and sense of self are in accordance with my *essential* identity, my divine soul, then I love my fellow just as I love myself, literally, because the other isn't an "other"—he or she is me.

As a result, the more I sense *myself*, the greater the barrier between me and my fellows. Conversely, the more I sense my *soul*, the more I will love others.

That is why the commandment to love our fellows is the one mitzvah which is most reflective and expressive of a person's general spiritual state.

RABBI YOEL KAHN
1930-

Lead expert on Chabad philosophy. Rabbi Kahn served as the leader of the team that would memorize and transcribe the Rebbe's talks and discourses that were delivered on Shabbat and holidays, when audio recordings and taking notes are proscribed. A leading authority on Chabad philosophy and the Rebbe's teachings, he is in the midst of publishing a comprehensive encyclopedia on Chabad Chasidism, of which 8 volumes have already appeared. He also serves as the senior educator of Chasidic teachings at the central Lubavitcher yeshiva.

*"The Kabbalah of Love," an insightful lecture by **Mrs. Gheula Nemni**:*

MYJLI.COM/WARRIOR

Figure 6.1

Benefits of Divine-Soul Model

AREA	RATIONALE
Negative emotions that result from feeling inauthentic	Every selfless deed is a 100 percent authentic expression of the divine soul.
Shame, feelings of inadequacy, and frustration that result from our internal struggles	These negative emotions are negated by understanding that character flaws are a gift, and our struggles are our purpose in life.
Guilt and remorse	Feelings of remorse are controlled and purposeful and lead to greater joy.
Anxiety and worry over material matters	When one's focus is nearness to G-d, one can be happy despite—and even because of—hardship.
Happiness	Happiness is not contingent on personal attainments.
Relationships	**Focusing on our essential divine bond makes us ultimately compatible.**

TEXT **6**

THE REBBE, RABBI MENACHEM MENDEL SCHNEERSON,
SICHOT KODESH 5733:2, PP. 145–146

RABBI MENACHEM MENDEL SCHNEERSON
1902–1994

The towering Jewish leader of
the 20th century, known as "the
Lubavitcher Rebbe," or simply as "the
Rebbe." Born in southern Ukraine,
the Rebbe escaped Nazi-occupied
Europe, arriving in the U.S. in June
1941. The Rebbe inspired and guided
the revival of traditional Judaism
after the European devastation,
impacting virtually every Jewish
community the world over. The
Rebbe often emphasized that the
performance of just one additional
good deed could usher in the era
of Mashiach. The Rebbe's scholarly
talks and writings have been printed
in more than 200 volumes.

ער ברײַנגט אױף אַ דוגמא פֿון אמנון און תמר, װאָס דאָס איז
בדוגמא צו אַן אהבה שתלויה בדבר, דאָס הײסט, אַז נישט קוקנדיק
אױף דעם װאָס בעצם דאָרטן איז דער אהבה אינה תלוי' בדבר, װאָרום,
אמנון און תמר זײַנען געװען ברודער און שװעסטער . . . במילא איז
מצד דערױף װאָס זײ זײַנען געװען במשפחה אחת, האָבן זײ געדאַרפֿט
זײַן נאָנט אײנעם צום צװײטן און האָבן אַן אהבה שאינה תלויה
בדבר . . . פֿונדעסטװעגן, װײבאַלד בגלוי דאָס װאָס עס איז געװען אַן
אהבה בינֵיהם איז דאָס געװען מצד יופֿי, תלוי בדבר, דעריבער איז
געװען לאחר װאָס עס איז בטל געװאָרן דער דבר, איז בטל געװאָרן
די אהבה . . . זעט מען פֿון דעם אַז עס איז נישט נוגע דאָס װאָס עס
ברײַנגט צו צום אהבה, עס איז נוגע װי דער ענין איז איצטער . . .

און דערנאָך ברײַנגט ער דעם צװײטן דוגמא פֿון דוד מיט יהונתן װאָס
דאָרטן איז עס געװען פֿאַרקערט. בנוגע דעם אהבה פֿון יהונתן צו
דוד, בעצם האָט זיך נישט געמאָנט . . . איז דער גאָנצע אהבה געװען
אַ חיצוניות'דיקע. פֿונדעסטװעגן האָט מען געזען אַז נאָך דעם איז
דער אהבה אױסגעקומען אױף אַ עצם'דיקע אופֿן ביז, װי ער האָט
געזאָגט, אַז "נפֿשו קשורה בנפֿשו" (שמואל א יח, א) און נאָכמער. ביז
דאָס האָט גאָר אָנגערירט בנוגע דער ענין המלוכה - אַז ער האָט מװתּר
געװען אַז די מלוכה זאָל קומען צו אים און עס זאָל גײן צו דוד! . . .
נישט קוקנדיק אױף די אַלע עילום, האָט יהונתן מצד זײַן גרױסן
אהבה צו דוד המלך מװתּר געװען אױף דעם, װײַל זײַן אהבה איז געװען
אַ אהבה עצמית.

װאָס דאָ זעט מען אין דעם צװײטן קצה . . . הגם בתחלה איז עס
געקומען פֿון אַ סיבה, װאָרום מען קאָן דאָ נישט ליב האָבן צװײטן
גלײַך אױפֿן אָרט, נאָר דאָס גײט מיט אַ סֵדר - ערשט דאַרף מען
באַקאָנען זיך, דערנאָך רעדט מען, ביז עס קומט צו אַזאַ אהבה װאָס
איז נישט תלוי בדבר - במילא איז הגם בתחלה איז עס געקומען נישט
מצד העצם, דאָס הײסט, אַז דאָס איז אַ באה מדבר, פֿונדעסטװעגן קאָן
אָבער דערנאָך אַרױסקומען דער אהבה באַן אופֿן אַז דאָס איז נישט תלוי
אין קײן זאַך נישט.

Our sages cite the case of Amnon and Tamar as an example of love based on specific considerations. In truth, there was an essential love present in that case as well because Amnon and Tamar were siblings. As close family members, they should have experienced a closeness for each other that was independent of any particular consideration. Nevertheless, the love expressed in that incident was dependent on a consideration, namely physical beauty. As a result, when the reason for that contingent love was removed, the love vanished altogether, taking the natural sibling bond along with it. This demonstrates that the critical factor is not the origins of the love but, rather, *the form that the love assumes at the present moment.*

Our sages then cite the case of David and Jonathan, which presents an opposite scenario because the love between them was originally an external friendship. Despite that, we observe that once the bond deepened to the point that it became an essential love, the verse (I SAMUEL 18:1) describes it as a bond of soul to soul. Why, it even affected Jonathan's kingship, for he readily gave up his role as the future king to David. Despite all the greatness associated with monarchy, he abdicated in favor of David because his love was an essential one.

This illustrates the opposite extreme: They were originally attracted to each other's specific qualities, for one cannot love a person instantaneously upon first meeting; genuine bonding is a process. The parties must first become acquainted, then sit down to talk, and eventually they can develop their relationship to the point that it is *no longer reliant* on particular considerations. *For even a nonessential love can blossom into a nondependent love.*

Israeli stamp inscribed with the verse "Love your neighbor as yourself." Issued: December 10, 1958. (Israeli Postage Stamp Catalog)

TEXT 7

THE REBBE, RABBI MENACHEM MENDEL SCHNEERSON,
SEFER HASICHOT 5751:1, PP. 266–267 ⚏

אין דער מהדורא **קמא** פון ספר התניא (כנראה אין די כתבי יד וכו') איז
ניטאָ דער פרק לב (ביאור ענין אהבת ישראל), נאָר פון פרק לא גייט
גלייך בהמשך אחד צו פרק לג. אָבער אין דער מהדורא בתרא פון תניא
- דער ספר התניא שלפנינו - האָט דער אלטער רבי מוסיף געווען דעם
פרק לב ענין אהבת ישראל ובביאור.

וויבאַלד אַז יעדער זאַך איז בהשגחה פרטית, און די השתלשלות
הדברים איז אָנגעקומען צו אונז - איז זיכער פאַראַן אין דעם אַ לימוד
והוראה, בגודל ההדגשה בתורת החסידות בענין אהבת ישראל:

טאָמער איינער וועט מיינען אַז ס'איז דאָ אַ קא סלקא דעתך אַז דער
ענין פון אהבת ישראל דאַרף ניט זיין בהדגשה בכל מקום ומקום, והראי'
אַז אין דער מהדורא קמא פון תניא איז דאָס ניט אַרייַנגעשטעלט
געוואָרן לכתחילה, און מ'האָט געקענט לערנען דעם תניא אָן דעם
פרק - האָט מען דעם לימוד דערפון וואָס אין דער מהדורא שלאחרי
זה ובפרט - בתרא האָט דער אלטער רבי דאָס צוגעגעבן, - און "הכל
הולך אחר החיתום". . . אַז איצטער איז ניטאָ קיין אָרט און קיין קא
סלקא דעתך כלל וכלל באופן אחר. ואדרבה.

As evidenced from the original manuscripts, chapter
thirty-two of *Tanya*, which explains the concept of
loving one's fellow, *did not exist* in the *Tanya*'s original
draft. Rather, the text flowed uninterrupted from [what
is now] chapter thirty-one directly into [what is now]
chapter thirty-three. Only in the final draft, the printed
edition of the *Tanya*, did the Alter Rebbe insert chapter
thirty-two to explain the concept of loving one's fellow.

Everything occurs by divine design. Since the process by which this chapter was included was made known to us, it must provide us with a message and directive, namely that Chasidism demands tremendous emphasis on loving one's fellow.

Someone might assume that loving one's fellow need not be overly emphasized in every situation—as indicated by the initial draft of *Tanya* not devoting a chapter to this topic. This seemingly implies that the *Tanya* can be studied appropriately *without* focusing on love for one's fellow. Therefore the Alter Rebbe pointedly included this topic in his later version (his *final* version, and the final conclusion is binding). . . . By doing so, he absolutely negated this misunderstanding, clarifying that it is unthinkable *not* to emphasize love for our fellows at all times.

QUESTION FOR DISCUSSION

When might hatred be legitimately justified? Can you think of specific examples?

TEXT **8a**

EXODUS 23:5

כִּי תִרְאֶה חֲמוֹר שֹׂנַאֲךָ רֹבֵץ תַּחַת מַשָּׂאוֹ, וְחָדַלְתָּ מֵעֲזֹב לוֹ? עָזֹב תַּעֲזֹב עִמּוֹ.

If you see your enemy's donkey lying under its burden, would you refrain from helping him? You shall surely help along with him.

TEXT 8b

TALMUD, PESACHIM 113B

מַאי שׂוֹנֵא? . . . וּמִי שָׁרְיָא לְמִסְנֵיהּ? וְהָכְתִיב "לֹא תִשְׂנָא אֶת אָחִיךָ
בִּלְבָבֶךָ" (וַיִּקְרָא יט, יז)? . . . אֶלָּא לָאו כִּי הַאי גְוֹנָא דְחַזְיָא בֵּיהּ אִיהוּ
דְּבַר עֶרְוָה?

רַב נַחְמָן בַּר יִצְחָק אָמַר: מִצְוָה לִשְׂנֹאתוֹ, שֶׁנֶּאֱמַר "יִרְאַת ה', שְׂנֹאת רָע"
(מִשְׁלֵי ח, יג).

*Is hate for another ever okay? Hear what **Rabbi Simon Jacobson** thinks:*

MYJLI.COM/WARRIOR

What is the meaning of "your enemy"? . . . Is one permitted to hate a fellow? Isn't it written, "You shall not hate your brother in your heart" (LEVITICUS 19:17)? . . . This verse clearly refers to an instance wherein one saw a fellow doing something inappropriate.

Rabbi Nachman, the son of Yitschak, said that it is a mitzvah to hate such an individual, as it is stated, "The fear of G-d is to hate evil" (PROVERBS 8:13).

TEXT 9

TANYA, CH. 32

> וְגַם . . . שֶׁמִּצְוָה לִשְׂנֹאותָם, מִצְוָה לְאַהֲבָם גַּם כֵּן!
>
> וּשְׁתֵּיהֶן הֵן אֱמֶת: שִׂנְאָה מִצַּד הָרַע שֶׁבָּהֶם, וְאַהֲבָה מִצַּד בְּחִינַת הַטּוֹב הַגָּנוּז שֶׁבָּהֶם, שֶׁהוּא נִיצוֹץ אֱלֹקוּת שֶׁבְּתוֹכָם הַמְחַיֶּה נַפְשָׁם הָאֱלֹקִית.
>
> וְגַם, לְעוֹרֵר רַחֲמִים בְּלִבּוֹ עָלֶיהָ, כִּי הִיא בִּבְחִינַת גָּלוּת בְּתוֹךְ הָרַע מִסִּטְרָא אַחֲרָא הַגּוֹבֵר עָלֶיהָ בָּרְשָׁעִים. וְהָרַחֲמָנוּת מְבַטֶּלֶת הַשִּׂנְאָה וּמְעוֹרֶרֶת הָאַהֲבָה.

Even with regard to those . . . whom one is enjoined to hate, there still remains the duty to love them also!

And both are true: hatred, because of the wickedness in them; and love, on account of the hidden good in them, the divine spark that animates their divine soul.

We need to awaken pity in our hearts for [the divine soul], for in wicked people, she is held captive by the evil and unholiness that triumphs over her. Compassion nullifies the hatred and awakens love.

Exercise 6.2

Negative Emotions

At the outset of this course, we presented the following list of negative emotions and asked which you would like to resolve or reduce as a consequence of the course:

Anger	Hypocrisy
Anxiety	Inauthenticity
Despair	Loneliness
Disappointment	Negative self-image
Fear	Sadness
Grief	Shame
Guilt	Worry
Hate	Other _____

Refer back to your response on page 6. Have you gained a new perspective and helpful tools that enable you to better overcome or subdue these feelings?

Positive Emotions

We also asked which of the following positive emotions you hoped this course might help you foster and strengthen:

Alacrity	Love
Enthusiasm	Optimism
Excitement	Positive self-image
Fulfillment	Self-confidence
Gratitude	Serenity
Hope	Zeal
Joy	Other _____

Refer back to your response on page 7. Have you gained a new perspective and helpful tools that enable you to strengthen these feelings?

Exercise 6.3

What are some practical activities or behaviors that you can introduce into your lifestyle that will help you have a more divine-soul-oriented perspective?

1	
2	
3	

Practically, how do we live our everyday lives with a divine-soul focus and view? Five scholars' responses:

MYJLI.COM/WARRIOR

TEXT **10**

MODEH ANI, PRAYER UPON WAKING

מוֹדֶה אֲנִי לְפָנֶיךָ מֶלֶךְ חַי וְקַיָּם, שֶׁהֶחֱזַרְתָּ בִּי נִשְׁמָתִי בְּחֶמְלָה. רַבָּה אֱמוּנָתֶךָ.

I offer thanks to You, living and enduring King, for You have mercifully restored my soul within me; Your faithfulness is great.

SIDDUR TEHILAT HASHEM

One of the prayer books that follow the tradition of the Arizal, as established by Rabbi Shne'ur Zalman of Liadi. It was first published in New York in 1945.

Synagogue clock used to indicate the times for the daily prayers. Bohemia, c. 1860. (Jewish Museum in Prague)

KEY POINTS

1 Establishing and sustaining strong and healthy relationships is key to maintaining positive emotions.

2 It is incredibly difficult—miraculous—for two individuals to form a harmonious relationship. Each person is a universe of his or her own, and two universes cannot become one.

3 Most relationships are contingent, based on common ground—shared interests or views—held by the parties, or they are based on superficial appeal. Contingent relationships risk eventual deterioration or collapse.

4 The miracle of a true and lasting relationship is based on essential, noncontingent love. The most effective way to build a lasting relationship on a non-ego model is to activate our divine-soul perspective.

5 The divine soul is perfectly primed for relationships for two reasons: (a) It is focused on G-d's plan, not its own. Therefore, another's personality and disposition do not contradict or compete with its own. (b) Our divine souls are parts of a single, divine whole.

6 To improve our relationships, instead of focusing on our attitude toward the *other party,* we should focus on how we view *ourselves*: Do we identify more with the natural or divine soul? By changing our self-perspective, the nitty gritty of most relationships becomes less relevant.

7 Switching to divine-soul mode requires a monumental shift in perspective of how one views oneself and one's place in the world. It is imperative to introduce into our daily life behaviors and deeds that assist us in making the shift and staying focused on it.

Appendix

Exercise 6.4

Instructions

Take a moment to think of someone you know person-ally. This can be a person you have a close relationship with, such as a family member or friend, or just a casual acquaintance.

After viewing the seven images in Figure 6.2, ask your-self: Which image best describes my relationship with this person?

Repeat this process for another two or three people you know.

Figure 6.2

The Inclusion of Other in the Self (IOS) Scale*

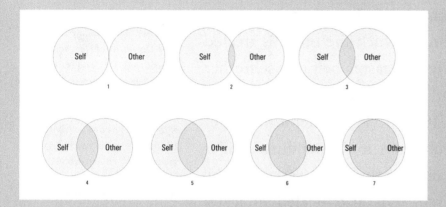

---

* Adapted from Aron, Arthur, et al., "Inclusion of Other in the Self Scale and the Structure of Interpersonal Closeness," *Journal of Personality and Social Psychology*, 63 (1992), pp. 596–612.

TEXT **11**

ARTHUR ARON AND ELAINE ARON, ET AL., "CLOSE RELATIONSHIPS AS INCLUDING OTHER IN THE SELF," *JOURNAL OF PERSONALITY AND SOCIAL PSYCHOLOGY*, 60:2 (1991), PP. 242–243

Much of our cognition about the other in a close relationship is cognition in which the other is treated as self . . . the underlying reason being a self/other merging or, as Aron and Aron (1986) put it, "including others in the self" (p. 19). . . . This general notion of overlapping selves involves an understanding similar to what Greenwald and Pratkanis (1984) call the "collective" aspect of self. It is also related to Ickes, Tookc, Stinson, Baker, and Bissonnette's (1988) idea of "intersubjectivity," which Ickes and his colleagues made vivid by citing Merleau-Ponty's (1945) description of a close relationship as a "double being" and Schutz's (1970) reference to two people "living in each other's subjective contexts of meaning" (p. 167). In a similar vein, Bakan (1966) wrote about "communion" in the context of his expansion on Buber's (1937) "I-thou" relationship.

The principle is that in a close relationship, the person acts as if some or all aspects of the partner are partially the person's own. (There may in addition be some sense of a general increase of fusion of self and other.) Aron and Aron (1986) emphasized that three aspects of self seem to be involved in this process: resources, perspectives, and characteristics. This categorization relies in part

ARTHUR ARON, PHD (1945–)

Professor of psychology at the State University of New York at Stony Brook, Dr. Aron is a leading researcher on the psychology of love and close relationships. He is married to fellow psychologist, Elaine Aron, with whom he often collaborates. His innovations in psychology include the "self-expansion" model of motivation and cognition in relationships, the Inclusion of Other in Self Scale for measuring relationship closeness, and the 36 questions for falling in love.

ELAINE ARON, PHD (1944–)

Psychotherapist. Dr. Aron earned her PhD in clinical psychology from the Pacifica Graduate Institute and frequently collaborates with her husband, Arthur Aron, on relationship research. She is the author of *The Highly Sensitive Person*, *The Highly Sensitive Person in Love*, and *The Highly Sensitive Child*.

on James's (1890/1948) influential division of the "empirical self" into material, social, and spiritual—the latter meaning typical styles of thinking. . . . Specifically, to the extent a partner is perceived as part of one's self, allocation of resources is communal (because benefiting other is benefiting self), actor/observer perspective differences are lessened, and other's characteristics become one's own. . . .

More generally still, a wide variety of thinkers on close relationships use metaphors such as union and attachment. Bataille (1962) expressed it dramatically: "Between one being and another there is a gulf, a discontinuity" (p. 12). "What we desire is to bring into a world founded on discontinuity all the continuity such a world can sustain" (p. 19). Jung (1925/1959) emphasized the role of relationship partners as providing unavailable aspects of self, so as to help make the self whole. Maslow (1967) took it for granted that "beloved people can be incorporated into the self" (p. 103). And McCall (1974) described attachment as "incorporation of . . . [the other's] actions and reactions . . . into the content of one's various conceptions of the self" (p. 219). Finally, the related notion of "possessing" the other (you are mine; I am yours) has been part of classic systematic treatments of love (E.G., BERL, 1924; FREUD, 1921/1951; GRANT, 1976).

TEXT **12**

ARTHUR ARON AND ELAINE ARON, ET AL., "INCLUDING OTHERS IN THE SELF,"
EUROPEAN REVIEW OF SOCIAL PSYCHOLOGY, 15 (2004), PP. 102–114

It seems to us that close relationships are so very central because they are intricately linked to the self, the core of human experience and behavior. . . . Specifically, in a close relationship, each includes to some extent in his or her self the other's resources, perspectives, and identities. . . .

In the first direct test of this principle of treating others' [resources] as one's own (ARON, ARON, TUDOR, & NELSON, 1991, EXPERIMENT 1 AND FOLLOW-UPS 1 AND 2), participants took part in an allocation game in which they made a series of decisions allocating money to self, best friend, or another person or persons (friendly acquaintance, stranger, or disliked other). . . . Allocations to best friend were consistently similar to those for self (the small and inconsistent differences between self and close friend hovered around 0). However, allocations to others consistently favoured self. . . . Importantly, these results held up whether or not the other would know one was responsible for the allocations. . . .

[A] dramatic illustration of the impact of including a close other's perspective in the self is a series of studies adapting a paradigm developed by Lord (1980, 1987). This paradigm focuses on the conceptual perspective of seeing oneself as background to experience while seeing other people as figural. Participants are presented with a series of 60 nouns, for each of which they are to form a vivid, elaborated image of a particular person (self or someone else) interacting with the object the noun represents. Later, participants are given a free recall test for the nouns. As predicted from his model of self as background to experience, Lord found consistently *fewer* nouns recalled that were imaged with self as compared to nouns imaged with media personalities. In our studies using this paradigm (ARON ET AL., 1991; EXPERIMENT 2 AND FOLLOW-UP), in addition to self and a familiar non-close other, participants also imaged nouns with a close other, their mother. Our results replicated Lord's for self and non-close other. But *also* . . . we found that nouns imaged with the close other (i.e., the participant's mother) were recalled about the same as for those imaged with self. . . . Further, in the replication study we included a measure of closeness to mother. This degree of the effect . . . correlated strongly . . . with the measure of closeness. . . . We tentatively concluded from these studies that just as one's perspective as self is as a background to experience, one's perspective with regard to close others is also experienced as a background to experience; and the closer they are, the more this is the case. . . .

However, our model also posits . . . that the self changing [is] such that the self includes the other in its very make-up. For example, the model implies that one's own and a close-other's traits may actually be confused or interfere with each other. To test this idea, we evaluated the patterns of response latencies in making me/not decisions (that is, "does the trait describe me?") about traits previously rated for their descriptiveness of self and spouse (ARON ET AL., 1991, EXPERIMENT 3 AND FOLLOW-UP). We found that for traits on which the self matched the partner (the trait was true of both or false of both), me/not-me responses were faster and had fewer errors than when a trait was mismatched for self and partner (was true for one but false for the other). . . . Further, Aron and Fraley (1999) found that the degree of this match-mismatch response-time . . . significantly correlates with self-report measures of relationship quality, including significantly predicting increases in subjective closeness over a 3-month period. . . . Smith and colleagues eloquently articulated why such patterns may result: "if mental representations of two persons . . . overlap so that they are effectively a single representation, reports on attributes of one will be facilitated or inhibited by matches and mismatches with the second" (p. 873). . . . In sum, these various data suggest that one way in which close others may shape the self is that these others become part of the self, with elements of the cognitive representation of the partner being incorporated in the cognitive representation of the self.

Additional Readings

ULTERIOR MOTIVE

BY RABBI YANKI TAUBER

Hillel would say: Be of the disciples of Aaron—a lover of peace, a pursuer of peace, one who loves his fellow creatures and draws them close to Torah.
—Ethics of the Fathers 1:12

"Love your fellow as yourself,"[1] never an easy task for the human heart, proves even more difficult when applied to one's "inferiors"—to those who are spiritually and morally lesser than oneself. How can one honestly perceive another as his equal when his fellow's character and behavior are so obviously corrupt? More specifically, throughout the ages a most divisive issue has been: How is a Jew to regard a fellow Jew who has strayed from the path of Torah?

In the first chapter of the *Ethics of the Fathers,* the great sage Hillel directs, "Love your fellow creatures and draw them close to Torah." "Creatures" *(beri'ot)* is the lowliest of the several Hebrew terms for "man"; it connotes the lowest common denominator of the human race—the fact that we are all G-d's creations. Says Hillel: Love also the creatures, also those whose only redeeming quality is that they are G-d's creations, and lovingly draw them to the ethos and ideals of Torah.

But Hillel's policy seems to raise more questions than it answers. What does it mean to "love G-d's creatures and draw them close to Torah"? Is this the unconditional love of tolerance and acceptance, or a love with an ulterior motive, albeit a most selfless and

RABBI YANKI TAUBER, 1965–

Chasidic scholar and author. A native of Brooklyn, N.Y., Rabbi Tauber is an internationally renowned author who specializes in adapting the teachings of the Lubavitcher Rebbe. He is a member of the JLI curriculum development team and has written numerous articles and books, including *Once Upon a Chassid* and *Beyond the Letter of the Law.*

honorable motive? Is this "Love your fellow as yourself" or "Love your fellow, so that you can turn him into yourself"?

A Chassid's Approach

Rabbi Schneur Zalman of Liadi, founder of Chabad Chassidism, applies Hillel's saying in the following manner:

> *Also those who are far from G-d's Torah and His service . . . one must draw them close with strong cords of love—perhaps one might succeed in bringing them to Torah and the service of G-d. And even if one fails, one has still merited the rewards of the fulfillment of the precept "Love your fellow."*[2]

Yet also Rabbi Schneur Zalman's words require clarification—he seems to adopt *both* of these apparently conflicting definitions of "love." In his closing words, he clearly establishes that the precept of loving one's fellow exists independently and regardless of the positive influence it may bring: even if one's efforts accomplish nothing, one has still fulfilled the Torah's injunction to "Love your fellow." On the other hand, Rabbi Schneur Zalman writes that "one must draw them close with strong cords of love" *because* of the chance that "perhaps one might succeed in bringing them to Torah and the service of G-d"!

Who Is a Jew?

This apparent dichotomy in the nature of relations between Jew and Jew also appears in the words of our sages which describe the very definition of Jewishness and a Jew's relationship with G-d.

The Talmud states: "A Jew, although he has transgressed, is a Jew."[3] He may violate, G-d forbid, the entire Torah, yet his intrinsic bond with the Almighty is not affected. In the words of the *Midrash,* "Torah preceded the creation of the world . . . but the thought of Israel preceded all in the mind of G-d."[4]

At the same time, many verses and sayings in Torah imply that a Jew relates to G-d through—and only through—the Torah. In the words of the *Zohar:* "There are three connections that are bound to each other: G-d, the Torah, and Israel. . . . Israel binds itself with Torah, and Torah with G-d."[5]

Both are true. A Jew is a Jew is a Jew, no matter what. He enjoys an unequivocal relationship with the Almighty regardless of the extent to which he actualizes it in his daily behavior. But the *realization* of this relationship, the manner in which his physical being and daily life can be brought to reflect and actualize his quintessential self, is the Torah way of life.

Furthermore, because a Torah life is the ultimate expression of what a Jew is, it cannot, and will not, remain suppressed indefinitely. Sooner or later, his true self will inevitably come to light.

So love him because of what he is, and love him because your love and concern may prove to be the impetus that will bring him to Torah—the two are one and the same.[6]

Endnotes
[1] *Leviticus* 19:18.
[2] *Tanya,* chapter 32.
[3] *Talmud, Sanhedrin* 44a.
[4] *Bereishit Rabba,* 1:4.
[5] *Zohar,* part III, 73 a.
[6] Based on an address by the Rebbe, Nissan 26, 5727.

Rabbi Yanki Tauber, *Beyond the Letter of the Law* (Brooklyn: Meaningful Life Center, 2012), pp. 77–80

Reprinted with permission of the Meaningful Life Center, meaningfullife.com

LOVE AND HATE OF ONE'S FELLOW

BY RABBI ADIN EVEN-ISRAEL (STEINSALTZ)

It has been explained that, for Jews, the love of one's people (Ahavat Yisrael) is not only a commandment concerning the social group, but it is an indication of the way a person stands in relation to G-d. As long as a person identifies himself with his body and concentrates all his attention on a particular "I" in time and space, he can never really love another person; he can only love himself because the "I" is the focus of his whole being. By way of contrast, when the soul is seen as the mainspring of one's being and as the meaning of life, there is no limit to the possibility of love. Because no two bodies can ever become one; at best, they can make good use of each other. Two souls, however, which strive together toward the primal root of things, come closer and closer; and if they continue on an ever higher plane, they can grow into a genuine unity.

Therefore, the concept of Ahavat Yisrael, the love of one's fellow Jew, points to the love of G-d. One does not attain it by remaining in the material body and feeling all sorts of sentiments about one's brethren; it is attained by striving for, and ultimately reaching, that level of being in which one sees oneself as a soul. Consistent with this point of view, a rather extreme notion of Israel as a physical-spiritual collective body has developed over the centuries. It is something so sensitively organic in its unity that any separation of one of its smallest limbs or parts was seen to inflict a serious injury on the whole, which was the Shechinah, the Divine indwelling. A common expression of

RABBI ADIN EVEN-ISRAEL (STEINSALTZ), 1937–

Talmudist, author, and philosopher. Rabbi Even-Israel (Steinsaltz) is considered one of the foremost Jewish thinkers of the 20th century. Praised by *Time* magazine as a "once-in-a-millennium scholar," he has been awarded the Israel Prize for his contributions to Jewish study. He lives in Jerusalem and is the founder of the Israel Institute for Talmudic Publications, a society dedicated to the translation and elucidation of the Talmud.

this is reflected in the words of the blessing: "Bless us all, our Father, as one, with the light of Thy countenance." When we are all one, then we can receive the light of "Thy countenance." When we are not one, the Shechinah is not in its right place, and Israel is in a state of deprivation and suffering.

Consider the talmudic statement that one who sees his friend sinning should hate him; one may add that there are also injunctions against hate in the Scriptures: "Thou shalt not hate thy brother in thy heart." Nevertheless, it is true that, in certain circumstances, it is a mitzvah to hate an evildoer, even to the point of informing on him to his teacher. Again, the dilemma arises: According to the Halachah, any such testimony concerning a person and his sinful actions would be libel or speaking evil. The popular story goes: "Tuvia sinned and Zigud was beaten." Zigud, the moralist, caught Tuvia committing some transgression, and he promptly brought him before the court. There he was told that one witness was not enough to incriminate a fellow Jew; and all he had done, therefore, was to slander the good Tuvia, for which Zigud deserved to be beaten. And he was. Only in exceptional cases is it permissible to publicly assert that someone has trespassed—and that does not mean in a court room—but before the teacher of the one concerned. Indeed, the whole problem of giving testimony against someone is a very delicate matter, and the sages have always had many reservations about it. This does not alter the point being made here, namely, that in exceptional circumstances it is right to hate an evildoer.

Can one hate someone whose way of life is very similar to one's own, someone living according to the same basic principles of Torah and mitzvot? In fact, one should despise such a transgressor even more. The more learned the sinner, the more deserving of our reproach. Whereas, if the sinner is ignorant and unlearned, if he does not know the meaning of his wrong action, and if it is all the same to him, we may be equally repelled by his actions; but it is forbidden to hate him. Like other matters of this nature, the question has been discussed at length by the sages: To what extent should permissiveness be extended towards those who do not know they are transgressing the law? How lenient can one be with someone who uses his ignorance as a general license to do as he likes? And what about those who feel that they have a general authorization to transgress because "they are not religious"? Is it not the same sort of excuse a thief will fall back on: "It's my occupation—I'm a thief—am I not?" The fact that this occupation involves stealing is of secondary importance; the important thing is not to get caught. In such instances, the halachic point of view is quite straightforward and strict. But in human terms, we have a different attitude toward someone who understands the meaning of his actions and still rebels against the Divine as compared to someone who does not know what he is doing.

Someone who is not learned in Torah and mitzvot and does not consider himself a part of the religious framework transgresses in a different way, with another attitude toward the whole concept of sin; thus, it is forbidden to hate him. However, if he is your friend, and especially if he is learned in Torah, you should at least rebuke him. Furthermore, you should not sin against him (by hating him), except if he continues to sin in spite of being rebuked. One's brother—who is anyone of the House of Israel—is not to be hated even in the heart; but one's friend, with whom there is a greater intimacy, is to be severely rebuked and even hated if he persists in sinfulness. The words of the commandment do not specify to love mankind or even Israel, but to love people. This is a very general term, but it is not meant as a subterfuge to avoid relating to specific persons. On the contrary, "people" includes all sorts of individuals, even those whom one would not choose to love of one's own free will. As it is said in the Talmud: "Love peace and pursue peace, love people and bring them close to the Torah." The order of performance is not to bring people close to Torah and then to love them, but the other way around; loving peace and loving people—if you succeed—will help you bring people close to Torah. And if you don't succeed, at least you have kept the precept of love; and that is enough—because this love should not be dependent upon anything else—even coming close to Torah. To love people is a clear, unequivocal commandment with no reservations. This brings us once again to the opposite injunction, that is, to hate those whose actions are not of a certain spiritual level, whose transgressions have continued beyond our love and our rebuke. To be sure, this does not mean there is an end to our duty to love them. The question is: How is it possible to hate and to love at the same time? The answer is: The mitzvah to hate can never be a matter of personal malevolence. Like all mitzvot, it has to be performed out of a sense of awe, a fear of Heaven.

The essential problem, however, is one of relationship. On the one hand, it is forbidden for me to judge my fellow man. It is not for me to decide whether he is innocent or guilty. That may sometimes be the task of a court, within the limits of a specific charge and along the lines drawn by Torah or the law. But as it is written in the Halachah, once a person has received his punishment, he is again a Tzadik, a pure soul, as far as I or any other man of Israel is concerned. Indeed, all these calculations—who is a saint and who is a sinner—all belong to G-d. Only He can make them. As the Rambam said: A person who is bad is inscribed for death; and if we observe that all sorts of people go merrily on their way, it is because we don't know how to make the reckoning. We may calculate according to our reason, but G-d makes His reckoning according to the truth of the Divine attributes. In other words, we cannot possibly ever make any final judgments about anyone. And if, in keeping with the mitzvah to hate the evildoer who has been rebuked and yet persists in his sinfulness, one does repudiate some action, it is not a judgment passed against him, damning him to Hell and purgatory. It is sometimes part of the need to hate and to love at the same time.

The fact is, every person is something of a duality. Every person has two souls, the animal-soul and the Divine Soul; and one cannot hate the Divine Soul of any man, since it is a part of G-d. Because of the complex nature· of the relationships within a family, our feelings are often ambivalent. We harbor all kinds of resentments and display warm affections for the same person. One can entertain a thorough dislike of certain personality traits and, at the same time, be in love with that person's essence. It is not only a simple matter of distinguishing things that are likable or repellent. Nor is it a matter of having to love, in spite of everything else, as in the relationship between parents and children. The truth is that love and hate do not necessarily cancel each other out. They can continue to exist side by side on the same plane. In certain Chabad texts, it is asked: How is it possible to carry out the mitzvah "Thou shalt love thy neighbor as thyself" if the other person is an evildoer and a sinner? How can one bring oneself to love anyone with whom there is no natural affinity? The answer given is connected with the words "as thyself." Just as one knows one's own faults and sins better than one knows those of others, one does not hate oneself; so it is necessary to relate to another. Even when a person hates himself, he continues to love himself also. As it is written: "Love will cover all your transgressions." Of course, love does not really do more to the transgressions than put some sort of veil over them to keep them from being seen. They cannot usually be made to disappear. Nevertheless, one's evaluation of the same facts can be altered. Just as one tends to gloss over one's own transgressions, so one should try to confute the negative reaction to someone else's transgressions, thereby seeing the other as one sees oneself. The double-mindedness here is not a matter of hypocritically closing one's eyes to sin, but rather, seeing it from a different angle—as though it were I who did it and not someone else.

There are many Chasidic stories that are variations on this theme. An interesting one is about Rabbi Levi Yitzchak of Berdichev, who was a great champion of the common people, a lover of Israel. One morning, looking out of his window, he saw a poor Jew, a teamster, driving his horses and wagon through the muddy part of the road. The driver was pulling hard on the reins and, at the same time, with phylacteries on arm and forehead, he was reciting his morning prayers. "L-rd of the Universe," exclaimed Rabbi Levi Yitzchak, "see how devout your people are; even while driving their wagons through the mud of the world, they find it possible to pray to you!" To another onlooker, this irreverent mode of prayer would probably have met with strong disapproval; and Rabbi Levi Yitzchak

himself would scarcely have considered reciting his prayers while doing something else, much less driving horses. He was, nevertheless, able to put himself in the other man's place, to transfer his point of view entirely to that of another person, another way of life.

This may, therefore, be considered a supplement to the commandment: "Thou shalt not hate thy brother in thy heart." Besides personal resentment, there is another more subtle hatred of the heart, and that is the intolerance of another set of standards. One frequently cannot stand the actions of someone who behaves according to a set of values different from one's own. This, too, is forbidden, for a person is to be measured by his own heart and not by another's. All of this comes back to the play of love and hate within the same person. In terms of the Sefirot of the Kabbalah, love is Chesed, hate (and justice) is Gevurah, and the resolution of the two is Tiferet (Harmony and Beauty). Tiferet is also known as Rachamim (Compassion and Mercy). Thus, when one loves someone because of some essential affinity, one can also hate him because of his evil actions and still can have compassion on him because of the desperate straits he is in. The compassion thus destroys hatred and awakens love. It is known that any real feeling of compassion or pity will stir up positive emotions. This becomes the shade of difference between Gevurah and Tiferet, Justice and Mercy. Compassion, or Mercy, accepts the facts of another person's actions without passing judgment. Similarly, what is the difference between Love and Compassion (Chesed and Tiferet)? In love, the shortcomings of the beloved are usually overlooked. What is more, the inner impulse of love, or grace, as it is more precisely called, is a total giving of oneself and of all one has without considering what the loved one needs. It gives out of the very fullness of itself, without stint or measure. The relationship between Compassion and Beauty (Rachamim and Tiferet) is far more complex and necessarily includes right judgment and right measure.

When one has compassion or pity for someone, one is usually aware of his shortcomings as well. It is even maintained that the more one is aware of the faults of the person for whom one has compassion, the more intense the emotion. Thus, instead of causing repulsion, this compassion can augment the attraction and cancel out the hate. In other words, if one has pity, it is almost impossible to hate; and it is very likely that love will be aroused. In this case, one no longer sees the shortcomings that started the whole process, and love can take root and grow.

It is in this sense that it is said that Jacob redeems Abraham. Jacob corresponds to the Sefirah of Tiferet (Mercy) and Abraham is Chesed (Love). When Abraham is held captive, bound by a situation where love cannot be expressed, the attribute of Tiferet can usually stir the emotions; whence, with the aid of this merciful compassion, the door is opened for love to enter. As for those rare individuals whom one cannot love under any circumstances, those whose wickedness is unmitigated, uncompromising, and final, one has to find the point of contact. In almost all human beings there is always, at least, one such point of possible contact, of coexistence with other human beings. If it does not exist, or if it is severed, there is little hope of redemption. To be sure, in an absolute sense, no person can be entirely cut off from such hope so long as he has life in him. Afterwards, after death, it is another matter. Nevertheless, when a person deliberately cuts himself off, he puts himself outside the pale. Moreover, there is a definite relationship between the love of righteousness and the hatred of evil.

Even if, at times, it may appear unjust, the more love a person has for the good, the more clear will be his power to distinguish the good, and he will tend more to be repelled by wickedness; and all that is not good will be regarded with dislike, or more intensely, repugnance amounting to hatred. And of course, the opposite is also true; when one does not hate evil—and not necessarily the evil connected with people, but even the evil that seems to be intrinsic to certain things and situations—when one does not hate this very essence of evil, it is a sign that one is not able to love the good either. There seems to be some common denominator that goes beyond our analytic powers.

The question then is not simply the overtly moral one of being a good person or a bad person, either in action or in thought. Society needs to maintain a network of reliable, impersonal relationships between people, something that is essentially functional. It is like the neutral relation to things for which one does not really care one way or the other. In many aspects of normal social life, it should not make any difference who the other person is; a basic decency is all that is required. Indeed, love becomes an obstacle in formal relations.

The problem becomes acutely apparent when the situation is carried to its extreme, and one's attitude toward people becomes purely and simply functional, an unemotional and even polite correctness. In certain areas of modern life, this has resulted in unspeakable horror precisely because people have ceased to relate to people as persons and think of them as things. The worst acts of brutality were done, not out of cruelty or hatred, but out of a mechanical neutrality. Often, it was more a result of not caring than a profound antipathy.

Hence, when confronted by a living person, it does not matter whether one loves or hates him—the important thing is that it be a living relationship. Total hate is possible only toward someone whose actions are immensely disturbing and distressing, threatening the very essence of one's own life structure. In such a case, one really cannot help oneself. But the inner meaning of it is that when one loves something intensely, one distinguishes the good with a vividness that leaves no room for doubt.

Rabbi Adin Even-Israel (Steinsaltz), *The Long Shorter Way* (Jerusalem: Koren Publishers Jerusalem, 2014), ch. 32

Reprinted with permission of the publisher

INDIVIDUALISM AND LOVE

BY KAREN K. DION, PHD, AND KENNETH L. DION, PHD

At the psychological level, the relation between individualism and love has been debated. There have been competing claims about the relation between individualism and relationship quality. In part, this debate reflects different conceptualizations about the meaning of the term *individualism*. Watchel (1983) pointed out that this term has been used both to stress the uniqueness and dignity of each person and also to describe excessive preoccupation with one's self-interest, such that the needs of the larger community were ignored. Waterman (1981, 1984) proposed that freedom of choice, respect for the integrity of others, and fulfilling one's personal potential are central features of individualism; thus, one might expect a positive relation between individualism and relationship quality. If so, individualism should facilitate the development of love for one's partner.

Paradoxically, when thinking about individualism at both the societal and the personal level, although in societies characterized as individualistic, marriage based on romantic love is a cultural ideal, the presence of some forms of individualism at the personal level can hinder the likelihood of realizing this ideal (K. K. Dion and Dion, 1993). Our research and that of others has found evidence supporting this hypothesis: namely, that psychological individualism can make it more difficult to develop and maintain the desired love-based marriage. Several studies have found that self-contained individualism is negatively related to relationship quality. In this section, the main points will be presented from research that we have conducted examining the relation between psychological

individualism and the affective quality of love for one's partner, as well as one's beliefs about the nature of love and the nature of marriage.

To assess beliefs about the relation between the individual and the group (individualism and collectivism), we have used items developed by Breer and Locke (1965), sampling both domain-specific content and more global items intended to be more general indicators of each construct. Participants in the research to be described were young adults (university students). In our first study (K. K. Dion and Dion, 1991), using a series of simultaneous regression analyses, we examined the contribution of different components of psychological individualism and collectivism, along with age and sex of participants. The most consistent pattern of finding occurred for one component of psychological individualism, which we characterized as reflecting self-contained individualism. The items comprising this component stressed qualities such as the importance of personal freedom and autonomy, personal control over one's life, and valuing self-sufficiency. Greater self-contained individualism was related to lesser likelihood of reporting that one had ever been in love. Individualists also endorsed a more "ludic" view of love as described by Lee's (1973) typology of ideologies of love. The ludic style is characterized by a noncommittal, permissive view of love, as reflected in the idea of love as a type of game.

Of particular interest, among those who did report ever having been in love, self-contained individualism was also negatively related to reported quality of the experience of love and love for one's partner. The experience of love was less likely to be described by qualities such as tender, deep, and rewarding as

KAREN K. DION, PHD

Psychologist. Dr. Dion is a professor of psychology at the University of Toronto. She is primarily interested in examining what factors contribute to the personal importance of cultural/ethnic identity. She also had a long-standing collaboration with her husband, Dr. Kenneth Dion, on the subject of romantic love and close relationships.

KENNETH L. DION, PHD,

Psychologist. Dr. Dion was a professor of psychology at the University of Toronto. His principle area of interest was the study of prejudice and inter-group relations.

self-contained individualism increased. To assess reported love for one's partner, we used Rubin's (1970) measure and analyzed its three subscales (caring, need, and trust) identified by Steck and Colleagues (Steck, Levitan, McLane, and Kelley, 1982), along with Pam, Plutchik, and Conte's (1975) measure of reported physical attraction to one's partner. On all of these measures, we found the predicted negative relation between self-contained individualism and the quality of love for one's partner. This form of psychological individualism was associated with less reported caring, need, and trust of one's partner as well as less reported attraction.

In our second study (K. L. Dion and Dion, 1993b), we once again looked at the relationship quality correlates of psychological individualism and collectivism. In this study, we included some additional measures: attitudes toward marriage and toward divorce. Once again, using the Breer and Locke (1965) items, the "self-contained individualism" component emerged (see K. L. Dion and Dion, 2005, for a description of the self-contained individualism index). Similar to the first study, greater individualism was related to less likelihood of ever having been in love. As predicted, self-contained individualism was related to more negative attitudes toward marriage and a greater wish to marry later.

Other researchers (Agnew and Lee, 1997; Kemmelmeier, Sanchez-Burks, Cytron, and Coon, 1998, study 2) have similarly found evidence for a negative relation between psychological individualism and relationship commitment among samples of university students in the United States. They used scales constructed from the Breer and Locke (1965) items to assess individualism, and a measure developed by Rusbult and her colleagues (see Rusbult, Martz, and Agnew, 1998) to assess commitment in close relationships. There is thus converging evidence from diverse university samples that some aspects of individualism contribute negatively to love and relationship quality. Since these studies involved young adults, specifically, university students, it is relevant to ask about the nature of the relation between individualism and love among a more representative group of adults.

We examined this issue (K. L. Dion and Dion, 2005) by analyzing previous survey data from the General Social Survey (GSS), which were collected in 1993. The General Social Survey, a probability survey of English-speaking adults in the United States, is conducted almost annually (Davis and Smith, 1992). In 1993, five questions were included about individualism. One of these items quite clearly captured the core of self-contained individualism with its strong focus on putting one's own needs and goals before those of other people. Also included in the GSS were questions about satisfaction with different types of relationships, such as marriage and friendship, as well as items about subjective well-being and other items related to the quality of one's life. The pattern of findings across a series of regression analyses found considerable evidence of a negative relation between "self-first" individualism and reported relationship quality, as well as other aspects of subjective well-being.

For example, the greater the individualism, the less reported happiness in romantic relationships, less reported happiness in marriage, and lower satisfaction with family life and with friends. Reported relationship outcomes also emerged as negatively related to individualism; for example, a lower sense of perceived success in one's family life and more likelihood of having been divorced in the past year or the previous five years. (For a more detailed description of these findings, see K. L. Dion and Dion, 2005.) The important point here is that the relationship quality correlates of self-contained individualism for university student samples in Canada and the United States and for a probability sample of adults in the United States were similar. Across these different studies, the pattern of results indicated that psychological individualism negatively contributed to the quality of close relationships and to the experience of love. Our and others' work on individualism and love has focused for the most part on its role in the development, quality, and maintenance of heterosexual relationships in adulthood.

Recent evidence also suggests, however, that the problematic aspects of individualism are evident in other important close relationships and the manifestation of love in those relationships. Although not undertaken to study the psychology of love, research on adult children's attempts to care for their aging parents and their parents' responses to this care, conducted by Pyke and her colleagues, identified several themes consistent with our hypothesis that some forms of psychological individualism have a negative relation to relationship quality. Using a qualitative research methodology based on interviews with members of three generations (aging parents, midlife adult children, and adult grandchildren), Pyke and Bengtson (1996) identified both individualistic and collectivistic systems of beliefs concerning the family. Families whose orientation was largely individualistic stressed the value of personal autonomy of family members, voluntary association, and looser kinship ties among family members. Interestingly, family relations were frequently described in more negative or ambivalent terms.

Pyke and Bengtson (1996) pointed out that among the families whose prevailing ideology was individualism, the adult children were more likely to delegate the physical caregiving to others (nonfamily hired help, nursing homes) and focused on help managing parents' finances and arrangements for eldercare. The underlying motivation when caring for ailing parents seemed to be one of duty rather than affection; hence, caregiving was seen as a burden. From the individualist perspective, aging parents valued their own autonomy and neither expected nor wanted intervention in their lives by their adult daughters and sons. To ask for or need help might threaten the parent's relation with the adult child since autonomy was so highly valued. The following statement poignantly reveals this dilemma. An eighty-nine-year-old mother said of her fifty-three-year-old daughter: "I don't want her to have to be burdened with me. Because I want her to keep on liking me, and if they have to take care of you, you never know if they are going to like you or not" (Pyke and Bengtson, 1996, p. 384).

Older parents thus received relatively little direct help from their children who endorsed a view of the family as supporting the individual autonomy of each member. Pyke (1999) subsequently examined the implications of an individualistic family orientation for eldercare for the power dynamics in a family. By adhering to individualism, older adults could preserve their sense of independence and not yield any of their parental authority to their children. Although this system of beliefs and related behaviors was functional for older adults in good health, with the dependencies related to poor health Pyke (1999) found that endorsing an individualistic view of the family was related to problems for both aging parents and their adult children, who now had to provide a level of care-related behavior that conflicted with these beliefs and often was resented by their parents. Moreover, the previous stress on self-sufficiency meant that adult children would not always be able to provide the most sensitive caregiving since they were unaware of their parents' preferences and wishes, and inexperienced in providing caregiving. In essence, adult children might be least able to be fully emotionally responsive to the needs of aging parents when their parents' needs were the greatest. In some cases, Pyke pointed out, aging parents who were individualists might prefer to forgo closer relationships with their adult children if that meant acknowledging increasing dependency and deferring to their children's wishes, resulting in less companionship and less instrumental assistance from their sons and daughters.

The research conducted by Pyke and her colleagues looked at the relation between individualism and family functioning in a domain different from the one we have been studying. It was independently designed to address other issues than those which have guided our thinking, and used a different research approach. Nonetheless, their results provide striking converging evidence consistent with the pattern of findings in our own program of research on the challenges that individualism poses for the expression of love in close relationships.

References

Agnew, C. R., and Lee, B. (May 1997). Individualism in romantic relationships: Associations with commitment, satisfaction, and self-other inclusion. Paper presented at the annual meeting of the American Psychological Society, Washington, D.C.

Davis, J. A., and Smith, T. W. (1992). *The NORC General Aid Social Survey.* Newbury Park, Calif.: Sage.

Dion, K. K., and Dion, K. L. (1991). Psychological individualism and romantic love. *Journal of Social Behavior and Personality, 6,* 17–33.

——. (1993). Individualistic and collectivistic perspectives on gender and the cultural context of love and intimacy. *Journal of Social Issues, 49,* 53–69.

——. (1993b). Introduction: Toward understanding love. *Personal Relationships, 3,* 1–3.

Dion, K. L., and Dion, K. K. (August 1993 b). Individualism-collectivism and romantic love. Symposium paper presented at the annual convention of the American Psychological Association, Toronto, Canada.

——. (2005). Culture and relationships: The downside of self-contained individualism. In R. M. Sorrentino, D. Cohen, J. M. Olson, and M. Zanna (eds.), *Culture and Social Behavior: The Ontario Symposium,* vol. 10, pp. 77–94. Mahwah, N.J.: Erlbaum.

Kemmelmeier, M., Sanchez-Burks, J., Cytron, A., and Coon, H. M. (August 1988). Individualism and romantic love: A comparison of two hypotheses. Paper presented at the annual convention of the American Psychological Association, San Francisco.

Levine, R., Sato, S., Hashimoto, T., and Verma, J. (1995). Love and marriage in eleven cultures. *Journal of Cross-Cultural Psychology, 26,* 554–571.

Lee, J. A. (1973). *Colours of Love.* Toronto: New Press.

Hofstede, G. (1980). *Culture's Consequences: International Differences in Work-Related Values.* Beverly Hills, Calif.: Sage.

Bellah, R. N., Madsen, R., Sullivan, W. M., Swidler, A., and Tipton, S. M. (1985). *Habits of the Heart: Individualism and Commitment in American Life.* Berkley: University of California Press.

Watchel, P. L. (1983). *The Poverty of Affluence: A Psychological Portrait of the American Way of Life.* New York: Free Press.

Waterman, A. S. (1981). Individualism and interdependence. *American Psychologist, 36,* 762–773.

——. (1984). *The Psychology of Individualism.* New York: Praeger.

Sampson, E. E. (1977). Psychology and the American ideal. *Journal of Personality and Social Psychology, 35,* 767–782.

Breer, P. E., and Locke, E. A. (1965). *Task Experience as a Source of Attitudes.* Homewood, Ill.: Dorsey.

Rubin, Z. (1970). Measurement of romantic love. *Journal of Personality and Social Psychology, 16,* 265–273.

Rusbult, C. E., Martz J. M., and Agnew, C. R. (1998). The investment model scale: Measuring commitment level, satisfaction level, quality of alternatives, and investment size. *Personal Relationships, 5,* 357–391.

Steck, L., Levitan D., McLane, D., and Kelley, H. H. (1982). Care, need, and conceptions of love. *Journal of Personality and Social Psychology, 43,* 481–491.

Pam, A., Plutchik, R., and Conte, H. R. (1975). Love: A psychometric approach. *Psychological Bulletin, 128,* 3–72.

Pyke, K. (1999). The micropolitics of care in relationships between aging parents and adult children: Individualism, collectivism and power. *Journal of Marriage and the Family, 61,* 661–672.

Pyke, K., and Bengtson, V. L. (1996). Caring more or less: Individualistic and collectivistic systems of family eldercare. *Journal of Marriage and the Family, 58,* 379–392.

Karen K. Dion, PhD, and Kenneth L. Dion, PhD, "Individualism and Love," in Robert J. Sternberg (ed.), *The New Psychology of Love* (New Haven, Conn.: Yale University Press, 2006), pp. 299–304

Reprinted with permission of the editor

Acknowledgments

"Tears of sorrow are dangerous—they drown our efforts to serve G-d with joy. Exchange them for tears of joy at union with G-d, and they will prove most beneficial."

—RABBI YISRAEL BAAL SHEM TOV

Some 3300 years ago, G-d presented our ancestors with a precious gift—the Torah. Many view this divine material as a labyrinth of directives detailing the steps G-d expects from us in each area of life. Others recognize that it is simultaneously a brilliant guide to spiritual fulfillment, a ladder to Heaven. What is often overlooked is that the Torah also offers tools to happiness, contentment, and success in our present and material realities. Promoting this third element is a guiding goal of the Rohr Jewish Learning Institute (JLI), which has developed courses on dozens of topics to extract from within the Torah's divine teachings the soundest advice on everyday issues.

We are therefore delighted to launch *Worrier to Warrior*, a six-week course that delivers insights and tools that allow us to overcome, repair, or upgrade key elements of the human experience, such as relationships, suffering, a depreciated self-image, and guilt. Rather than offering quick fixes that rapidly unwind, *Worrier to Warrior* is a guide to transformative and lasting change.

We are grateful to the following individuals for helping shape this innovative course:

Rabbis Mordechai Dinerman and **Naftali Silberberg,** who codirect the JLI Curriculum Department and the Flagship editorial team; **Rabbi Dr. Shmuel Klatzkin,** JLI's senior editor; and **Rabbi Zalman Abraham,** who skillfully provides the vision and strategic planning of JLI course offerings.

Rabbi Naftali Silberberg designed and authored this course. **Rabbis Lazer Gurkow** and **Yaakov Paley** assisted in the development of the curriculum, and **Rabbi Yakov Gershon**—of JLI's Machon Shmuel: The Sami Rohr Research Institute—provided extensive research. **Rabbi Shmuel Gomes** assisted with research and authored the mental health lesson appendices. The course was conceived and developed with guidance and direction from **Casey Skvorc, PhD**. The JLI curriculum team was fortunate to draw on his vast erudition, experience, and expertise in the area of mental health to develop a scholarly and relevant learning experience.

In partnership with the Albert Einstein College of Medicine, we are pleased to be able to offer this course for credits from the American Psychological Association (APA) and the AMA's American Council for Continuing Medical Education (ACCME). We are indebted to **Dr. Casey Skvorc** and **Rabbi Edward Reichman, M.D.** for their dedicated collaboration and patient guidance throughout the process. Special thanks to **Mindy Wallach** for coordinating the accreditation and to **Shulamis Nadler** for her administrative assistance.

We'd like to warmly thank **Avi Webb** for leading the vision for the marketing of this course, and **Mushka Kanner** and **Shifra Tauber** for creating and designing the course marketing materials.

Rabbis Yochonon Goldman, Moshe Gourarie, Avi Richler, Mendy Mangel, and **Aryeh Weinstein,** the Instructors Advisory Committee for this course, spent many hours reviewing the course materials with the JLI team and provided numerous useful suggestions that enhanced the course and ensured its suitability for a wide range of students. **Rabbi Yisroel Altein** reviewed the course materials for accuracy and textual integrity.

Rivki Mockin streamlined and ensured the smoothness and timeliness of the content production, and **Chana Dechter,** JLI Flagship's administrator, capably oversaw the entire project. **Mushka Backman** provided editorial assistance, and **Rakefet Orobona, Mimi Palace, Rabbi Shmuel Super, Shmuel Telsner,** and **Ya'akovah Weber** enhanced the quality and accuracy of the writing with their proofreading. **Rivky Fieldsteel, Shayna Grosh, Rabbi Zalman Korf,** and **Shternie Zaltzman** designed the textbooks with taste and expertise, and the textbook images were researched and selected by **Chany Block. Rabbi Mendel Sirota** directed the book's publication and distribution.

Chany Block, Mushka Druk, and **Baila Goldstein** designed the aesthetically pleasing PowerPoint presentations, and **Moshe Raskin** and **Getzy Raskin** produced the lesson videos. The video scripts were masterfully written by **Rabbi Yaakov Paley.**

We are immensely grateful for the encouragement of JLI's visionary chairman, and vice-chairman of *Merkos L'Inyonei Chinuch*—Lubavitch World Headquarters, **Rabbi Moshe Kotlarsky.** Rabbi Kotlarsky has been highly instrumental in building the infrastructure for the expansion of Chabad's international network and is also the architect of scores of initiatives and services to help Chabad representatives across the globe succeed in their mission. We are blessed to have the unwavering support of JLI's principal benefactor, **Mr. George Rohr,** who is fully invested in our work, continues to be instrumental in JLI's monumental growth and expansion, and

is largely responsible for the Jewish renaissance that is being spearheaded by JLI and its affiliates across the globe.

The commitment and sage direction of JLI's dedicated Executive Board—**Rabbis Chaim Block, Hesh Epstein, Ronnie Fine, Yosef Gansburg, Shmuel Kaplan, Yisrael Rice,** and **Avrohom Sternberg**—and the countless hours they devote to the development of JLI drive the vision, growth, and tremendous success of the organization.

Finally, JLI represents an incredible partnership of more than 1,600 *shluchim* and *shluchot* in more than 1,000 locations across the globe, who contribute their time and talent to further Jewish adult education. We thank them for generously sharing feedback and making suggestions that steer JLI's development and growth. They are our most valuable critics and our most cherished contributors.

Inspired by the call of the **Lubavitcher Rebbe,** of righteous memory, it is the mandate of the Rohr JLI to provide a community of learning for all Jews throughout the world where they can participate in their precious heritage of Torah learning and experience its rewards. May this course succeed in fulfilling this sacred charge!

On behalf of the Rohr Jewish Learning Institute,

RABBI EFRAIM MINTZ
Executive Director

RABBI YISRAEL RICE
Chairman, Editorial Board

20 Av 5779

The Rohr Jewish Learning Institute

JLI INTERNATIONAL

Rabbi Avrohom Sternberg
CHAIRMAN

Rabbi Dubi Rabinowitz
DIRECTOR

Rabbi Berry Piekarski
ADMINISTRATOR

Rabbi Eli Wolf
ADMINISTRATOR, JLI IN THE CIS
IN PARTNERSHIP WITH
THE FEDERATION OF JEWISH
COMMUNITIES OF THE CIS

Rabbi Shevach Zlatopolsky
EDITOR, JLI IN THE CIS

Rabbi Nochum Schapiro
REGIONAL REPRESENTATIVE,
AUSTRALIA

Rabbi Avraham Golovacheov
REGIONAL REPRESENTATIVE,
GERMANY

Rabbi Shmuel Katzman
REGIONAL REPRESENTATIVE,
NETHERLANDS

Rabbi Avrohom Steinmetz
REGIONAL REPRESENTATIVE,
BRAZIL

Rabbi Bentzi Sudak
REGIONAL REPRESENTATIVE,
UNITED KINGDOM

Rabbi Shlomo Cohen
FRENCH COORDINATOR,
REGIONAL REPRESENTITIVE

NATIONAL JEWISH RETREAT

Rabbi Hesh Epstein
CHAIRMAN

Mrs. Shaina B. Mintz
DIRECTOR

Bruce Backman
HOTEL LIAISON

Rabbi Menachem Klein
PROGRAM COORDINATOR

Rabbi Shmuly Karp
SHLUCHIM LIAISON

Rabbi Mendel Rosenfeld
LOGISTICS COORDINATOR

Mrs. Mussi Abelsky
Ms. Rochel Karp
Ms. Zehavah Krafchik
Mrs. Aliza Mayteles
SERVICE AND SUPPORT

JLI LAND & SPIRIT
ISRAEL EXPERIENCE

Rabbi Shmuly Karp
DIRECTOR

Mrs. Shaina B. Mintz
ADMINISTRATOR

Rabbi Yechiel Baitelman
Rabbi Dovid Flinkenstein
Rabbi Chanoch Kaplan
Rabbi Levi Klein
Rabbi Mendel Lifshitz
Rabbi Mendy Mangel
Rabbi Sholom Raichik
Rabbi Ephraim Silverman
STEERING COMMITTEE

SHABBAT IN THE HEIGHTS

Rabbi Shmuly Karp
DIRECTOR

Mrs. Shulamis Nadler
SERVICE AND SUPPORT

Rabbi Chaim Hanoka
CHAIRMAN

Rabbi Mordechai Dinerman
Rabbi Zalman Marcus
STEERING COMMITTEE

MYSHIUR
ADVANCED LEARNING INITIATIVE

Rabbi Shmuel Kaplan
CHAIRMAN

Rabbi Shlomie Tenenbaum
ADMINISTRATOR

TORAHCAFE.COM
ONLINE LEARNING

Rabbi Mendy Elishevitz
WEBSITE DEVELOPMENT

Moshe Levin
CONTENT MANAGER

Avrohom Shimon Ezagui
FILMING

MACHON SHMUEL
THE SAMI ROHR RESEARCH INSTITUTE

Rabbi Zalman Korf
ADMINISTRATOR

Rabbi Gedalya Oberlander
Rabbi Chaim Rapoport
Rabbi Levi Yitzchak Raskin
Rabbi Chaim Schapiro
Rabbi Moshe Miller
RABBINIC ADVISORY BOARD

Rabbi Yakov Gershon
RESEARCH FELLOW

FOUNDING DEPARTMENT HEADS

Rabbi Mendel Bell
Rabbi Zalman Charytan
Rabbi Mendel Druk
Rabbi Menachem Gansburg
Rabbi Meir Hecht
Rabbi Levi Kaplan
Rabbi Yoni Katz
Rabbi Chaim Zalman Levy
Rabbi Benny Rapoport
Dr. Chana Silberstein
Rabbi Elchonon Tenenbaum
Rabbi Mendy Weg

Faculty Directory

ALABAMA

BIRMINGHAM
Rabbi Yossi Friedman 205.970.0100

MOBILE
Rabbi Yosef Goldwasser 251.265.1213

ALASKA

ANCHORAGE
Rabbi Yosef Greenberg
Rabbi Mendy Greenberg 907.357.8770

ARIZONA

CHANDLER
Rabbi Mendy Deitsch 480.855.4333

FLAGSTAFF
Rabbi Dovie Shapiro 928.255.5756

FOUNTAIN HILLS
Rabbi Mendy Lipskier 480.776.4763

ORO VALLEY
Rabbi Ephraim Zimmerman 520.477.8672

PHOENIX
Rabbi Zalman Levertov
Rabbi Yossi Friedman 602.944.2753

SIERRA VISTA
Rabbi Bentzion Shemtov 520.820.6256

SCOTTSDALE
Rabbi Yossi Levertov 480.998.1410

SIERRA VISTA
Rabbi Bentzion Shemtov 520.820.6256

TUCSON
Rabbi Yehuda Ceitlin 520.881.7956

ARKANSAS

LITTLE ROCK
Rabbi Pinchus Ciment 501.217.0053

CALIFORNIA

AGOURA HILLS
Rabbi Moshe Bryski
Rabbi Yisroel Levine 818.991.0991

BAKERSFIELD
Rabbi Shmuli Schlanger
Mrs. Esther Schlanger 661.331.1695

BEL AIR
Rabbi Chaim Mentz 310.475.5311

BURBANK
Rabbi Shmuly Kornfeld 818.954.0070

CARLSBAD
Rabbi Yeruchem Eilfort
Mrs. Nechama Eilfort 760.943.8891

CHATSWORTH
Rabbi Yossi Spritzer 818.718.0777

CONTRA COSTA
Rabbi Dovber Berkowitz 925.937.4101

CORONADO
Rabbi Eli Fradkin 619.365.4728

DANVILLE
Rabbi Shmuli Raitman 213.447.6694

ENCINO
Rabbi Aryeh Herzog 818.784.9986
Chapter founded by Rabbi Joshua Gordon, OBM

FOLSOM
Rabbi Yossi Grossbaum 916.608.9811

FREMONT
Rabbi Moshe Fuss 510.300.4090

GLENDALE
Rabbi Simcha Backman 818.240.2750

HUNTINGTON BEACH
Rabbi Aron David Berkowitz 714.846.2285

LAGUNA BEACH
Rabbi Elimelech Gurevitch 949.499.0770

LAGUNA NIGUEL
Rabbi Mendy Paltiel 949.831.8475

LA JOLLA
Rabbi Baruch Shalom Ezagui 858.455.5433

LOMITA
Rabbi Eli Hecht
Rabbi Sholom Pinson 310.326.8234

LONG BEACH
Rabbi Abba Perelmuter 562.621.9828

LOS ANGELES
Rabbi Leibel Korf 323.660.5177
Rabbi Dovid Liberow 424.261.8770

MALIBU
Rabbi Levi Cunin 310.456.6588

MARINA DEL REY
Rabbi Danny Yiftach-Hashem
Rabbi Dovid Yiftach 310.859.0770

NORTH HOLLYWOOD
Rabbi Nachman Abend 818.989.9539

NORTHRIDGE
Rabbi Eli Rivkin 818.368.3937

OJAI
Rabbi Mordechai Nemtzov 805.613.7181

PACIFIC PALISADES
Rabbi Zushe Cunin 310.454.7783

PALO ALTO
Rabbi Yosef Levin
Rabbi Ber Rosenblatt 650.424.9800

PASADENA
Rabbi Chaim Hanoka
Rabbi Sholom Stiefel 626.539.4578

PLEASANTON
Rabbi Josh Zebberman 925.846.0700

POWAY
Rabbi Mendel Goldstein 858.208.6613

RANCHO MIRAGE
Rabbi Shimon H. Posner 760.770.7785

RANCHO PALOS VERDES
Rabbi Yitzchok Magalnic 310.544.5544

RANCHO S. FE
Rabbi Levi Raskin 858.756.7571

REDONDO BEACH
Rabbi Yossi Mintz
Rabbi Zalman Gordon 310.214.4999

RIVERSIDE
Rabbi Shmuel Fuss 951.329.2747

S. CLEMENTE
Rabbi Menachem M. Slavin 949.489.0723

S. CRUZ
Rabbi Yochanan Friedman 831.454.0101

S. DIEGO
Rabbi Rafi Andrusier 619.387.8770
Rabbi Motte Fradkin 858.547.0076

S. FRANCISCO
Rabbi Gedalia Potash 415.648.8000
Rabbi Shlomo Zarchi 415.752.2866

S. MATEO
Rabbi Yossi Marcus 650.341.4510

S. MONICA
Rabbi Boruch Rabinowitz 310.394.5699

S. RAFAEL
Rabbi Yisrael Rice 415.492.1666

SOUTH LAKE TAHOE
Rabbi Mordechai Richler 530.314.7677

SUNNYVALE
Rabbi Yisroel Hecht 408.720.0553

THOUSAND OAKS
Rabbi Chaim Bryski 805.370.5770

TUSTIN
Rabbi Yehoshua Eliezrie 714.508.2150

UNIVERSITY CITY
Rabbi Yechiel Cagen 832.691.1825

VENTURA
Rabbi Yakov Latowicz 805.658.7441

WEST HOLLYWOOD
Rabbi Mordechai Kirschenbaum 310.275.1215

WEST LOS ANGELES
Rabbi Mordechai Zaetz 424.652.8742

YORBA LINDA
Rabbi Dovid Eliezrie 714.693.0770

COLORADO

ASPEN
Rabbi Mendel Mintz 970.544.3770

DENVER
Rabbi Mendel Popack 720.515.4337
Rabbi Yossi Serebryanski 303.744.9699

FORT COLLINS
Rabbi Yerachmiel Gorelik 970.407.1613

HIGHLANDS RANCH
Rabbi Avraham Mintz 303.694.9119

LONGMONT
Rabbi Yakov Borenstein 303.678.7595

VAIL
Rabbi Dovid Mintz 970.476.7887

WESTMINSTER
Rabbi Benjy Brackman 303.429.5177

CONNECTICUT

FAIRFIELD
Rabbi Shlame Landa 203.373.7551

GLASTONBURY
Rabbi Yosef Wolvovsky 860.659.2422

GREENWICH
Rabbi Yossi Deren
Rabbi Menachem Feldman 203.629.9059

MILFORD
Rabbi Schneur Wilhelm 203.887.7603

NEW LONDON
Rabbi Avrohom Sternberg 860.437.8000

STAMFORD
Rabbi Yisrael Deren
Rabbi Levi Mendelow 203.3.CHABAD

WEST HARTFORD
Rabbi Shaya Gopin 860.232.1116

WESTPORT
Rabbi Yehuda L. Kantor 203.226.8584

DELAWARE

WILMINGTON
Rabbi Chuni Vogel 302.529.9900

DISTRICT OF COLUMBIA

WASHINGTON
Rabbi Levi Shemtov
Rabbi Shua Hecht 202.332.5600

FLORIDA

ALTAMONTE SPRINGS
Rabbi Mendy Bronstein 407.280.0535

BAL HARBOUR
Rabbi Dov Schochet 305.868.1411

BOCA RATON
Rabbi Zalman Bukiet
Rabbi Arele Gopin 561.994.6257
Rabbi Moishe Denburg 561.526.5760
Rabbi Ruvi New 561.394.9770

BONITA SPRINGS
Rabbi Mendy Greenberg 239.949.6900

BOYNTON BEACH
Rabbi Yosef Yitzchok Raichik 561.732.4633

BRADENTON
Rabbi Menachem Bukiet 941.388.9656

CAPE CORAL
Rabbi Yossi Labkowski 239.963.4770

CORAL GABLES
Rabbi Avrohom Stolik 305.490.7572

CORAL SPRINGS
Rabbi Yankie Denburg 954.471.8646

CUTLER BAY
Rabbi Yossi Wolff 305.975.6680

DELRAY BEACH
Rabbi Sholom Ber Korf 561.496.6228

FISHER ISLAND
Rabbi Efraim Brody 347.325.1913

FLEMING ISLAND
Rabbi Shmuly Feldman 904.290.1017

FORT LAUDERDALE
Rabbi Yitzchok Naparstek 954.568.1190

FORT MYERS
Rabbi Yitzchok Minkowicz
Mrs. Nechama Minkowicz 239.433.7708

HALLANDALE BEACH
Rabbi Mordy Feiner 954.458.1877

HOLLYWOOD
Rabbi Leizer Barash 954.965.9933
Rabbi Leibel Kudan 954.801.3367

KENDALL
Rabbi Yossi Harlig 305.234.5654

LAKELAND
Rabbi Moshe Lazaros 863.510.5968

LONGWOOD
Rabbi Yanky Majesky 407.636.5994

MAITLAND
Rabbi Sholom Dubov
Rabbi Levik Dubov 470.644.2500

MIAMI
Rabbi Yakov Fellig 305.445.5444

MIAMI BEACH
Rabbi Yisroel Frankforter 305.534.3895

N. MIAMI BEACH
Rabbi Eli Laufer 305.770.4412

OCALA
Rabbi Yossi Hecht 352.330.4466

ORLANDO
Rabbi Yosef Konikov 407.354.3660

ORMOND BEACH
Rabbi Asher Farkash 386.672.9300

PALM BEACH
Rabbi Zalman Levitin 561.659.3884

PALM BEACH GARDENS
Rabbi Dovid Vigler 561.624.2223

PALM CITY
Rabbi Shlomo Uminer 772.288.0606

PALM HARBOR
Rabbi Pinchas Adler 727.789.0408

PALMETTO BAY
Rabbi Zalman Gansburg 786.282.0413

PARKLAND
Rabbi Mendy Gutnick 954.796.7330

PEMBROKE PINES
Rabbi Mordechai Andrusier 954.874.2280

PLANTATION
Rabbi Pinchas Taylor 954.644.9177

PONTE VEDRA BEACH
Rabbi Nochum Kurinsky 904.543.9301

S. AUGUSTINE
Rabbi Levi Vogel 904.521.8664

S. PETERSBURG
Rabbi Alter Korf 727.344.4900

SARASOTA
Rabbi Chaim Shaul Steinmetz 941.925.0770

SATELLITE BEACH
Rabbi Zvi Konikov 321.777.2770

SOUTH PALM BEACH
Rabbi Leibel Stolik 561.889.3499

SOUTH TAMPA
Rabbi Mendy Dubrowski 813.922.1723

SOUTHWEST BROWARD COUNTY
Rabbi Aryeh Schwartz 954.252.1770

SUNNY ISLES BEACH
Rabbi Alexander Kaller 305.803.5315

VENICE
Rabbi Sholom Ber Schmerling 941.493.2770

WESLEY CHAPEL
Rabbi Mendy Yarmush
Rabbi Mendel Friedman 813.731.2977

WESTON
Rabbi Yisroel Spalter 954.349.6565

WEST PALM BEACH
Rabbi Yoel Gancz 561.659.7770

GEORGIA

ALPHARETTA
Rabbi Hirshy Minkowicz 770.410.9000

ATLANTA
Rabbi Yossi New
Rabbi Isser New 404.843.2464

ATLANTA: INTOWN
Rabbi Eliyahu Schusterman
Rabbi Ari Sollish 404.898.0434

CUMMING
Rabbi Levi Mentz 310.666.2218

GWINNETT
Rabbi Yossi Lerman 678.595.0196

MARIETTA
Rabbi Ephraim Silverman 770.565.4412

IDAHO

BOISE
Rabbi Mendel Lifshitz 208.853.9200

ILLINOIS

CHAMPAIGN
Rabbi Dovid Tiechtel 217.355.8672

CHICAGO
Rabbi Mendy Benhiyoun 312.498.7704
Rabbi Meir Hecht 312.714.4655
Rabbi Dovid Kotlarsky 773.495.7127
Rabbi Yosef Moscowitz 773.772.3770
Rabbi Levi Notik 773.274.5123

DES PLAINES
Rabbi Lazer Hershkovich 224.392.4442

ELGIN
Rabbi Mendel Shemtov 847.440.4486

GLENVIEW
Rabbi Yishaya Benjaminson 847.910.1738

GRAYSLAKE
Rabbi Sholom Tenenbaum 847.782.1800

HIGHLAND PARK
Mrs. Michla Schanowitz 847.266.0770

NAPERVILLE
Rabbi Mendy Goldstein 630.778.9770

NORTHBROOK
Rabbi Meir Moscowitz 847.564.8770

OAK PARK
Rabbi Yitzchok Bergstein 708.524.1530

PEORIA
Rabbi Eli Langsam 309.692.2250

SKOKIE
Rabbi Yochanan Posner 847.677.1770

VERNON HILLS
Rabbi Shimmy Susskind 847.984.2919

WILMETTE
Rabbi Dovid Flinkenstein 847.251.7707

INDIANA

INDIANAPOLIS
Rabbi Avraham Grossbaum
Rabbi Dr. Shmuel Klatzkin 317.251.5573

IOWA

BETTENDORF
Rabbi Shneur Cadaner 563.355.1065

KANSAS

OVERLAND PARK
Rabbi Mendy Wineberg 913.649.4852

KENTUCKY

LOUISVILLE
Rabbi Avrohom Litvin 502.459.1770

LOUISIANA

BATON ROUGE
Rabbi Peretz Kazen 225.267.7047

METAIRIE
Rabbi Yossie Nemes
Rabbi Mendel Ceitlin 504.454.2910

NEW ORLEANS
Rabbi Mendel Rivkin 504.302.1830

MAINE

PORTLAND
Rabbi Levi Wilansky 207.650.1783

MARYLAND

BALTIMORE
Rabbi Velvel Belinsky 410.764.5000
Classes in Russian

BEL AIR
Rabbi Kushi Schusterman 443.353.9718

BETHESDA
Rabbi Sender Geisinsky..................................301.913.9777

CHEVY CHASE
Rabbi Zalman Minkowitz..............................301.260.5000

COLUMBIA
Rabbi Hillel Baron
Rabbi Yosef Chaim Sufrin...........................410.740.2424

FREDERICK
Rabbi Boruch Labkowski..............................301.996.3659

GAITHERSBURG
Rabbi Sholom Raichik...................................301.926.3632

OLNEY
Rabbi Bentzy Stolik......................................301.660.6770

OWINGS MILLS
Rabbi Nochum H. Katsenelenbogen.............410.356.5156

POTOMAC
Rabbi Mendel Bluming..................................301.983.4200
Rabbi Mendel Kaplan....................................301.983.1485

ROCKVILLE
Rabbi Moishe Kavka......................................301.836.1242
Rabbi Levi Raskin...240.444.3345

MASSACHUSETTS

ANDOVER
Rabbi Asher Bronstein...................................978.470.2288

BOSTON
Rabbi Yosef Zaklos.......................................617.297.7282

BRIGHTON
Rabbi Dan Rodkin...617.787.2200

CAPE COD
Rabbi Yekusiel Alperowitz............................508.775.2324

HINGHAM
Rabbi Levi Lezell..617.862.2770

LONGMEADOW
Rabbi Yakov Wolff..413.567.8665

NEWTON
Rabbi Shalom Ber Prus.................................617.244.1200

SUDBURY
Rabbi Yisroel Freeman..................................978.443.0110

MICHIGAN

ANN ARBOR
Rabbi Aharon Goldstein................................734.995.3276

BLOOMFIELD HILLS
Rabbi Levi Dubov..248.949.6210

GRAND RAPIDS
Rabbi Mordechai Haller................................616.957.0770

WEST BLOOMFIELD
Rabbi Elimelech Silberberg..........................248.855.6170

MINNESOTA

MINNETONKA
Rabbi Mordechai Grossbaum
Rabbi Shmuel Silberstein..............................952.929.9922

S. PAUL
Rabbi Shneur Zalman Bendet........................651.998.9298

MISSOURI

S. LOUIS
Rabbi Yosef Landa..314.725.0400

NEVADA

LAS VEGAS
Rabbi Yosef Rivkin.......................................702.217.2170

SUMMERLIN
Rabbi Yisroel Schanowitz
Rabbi Tzvi Bronchtain..................................702.855.0770

NEW JERSEY

BASKING RIDGE
Rabbi Mendy Herson
Rabbi Mendel Shemtov..................................908.604.8844

CHERRY HILL
Rabbi Mendel Mangel...................................856.874.1500

CLINTON
Rabbi Eli Kornfeld..908.623.7000

FAIR LAWN
Rabbi Avrohom Bergstein.............................201.362.2712

FORT LEE
Rabbi Meir Konikov 201.886.1238

FRANKLIN LAKES
Rabbi Chanoch Kaplan 201.848.0449

GREATER MERCER COUNTY
Rabbi Dovid Dubov
Rabbi Yaakov Chaiton 609.213.4136

HASKELL
Rabbi Mendy Gurkov 201.696.7609

HOLMDEL
Rabbi Shmaya Galperin 732.772.1998

MADISON
Rabbi Shalom Lubin 973.377.0707

MANALAPAN
Rabbi Boruch Chazanow
Rabbi Levi Wolosow 732.972.3687

MEDFORD
Rabbi Yitzchok Kahan 609.451.3522

MOUNTAIN LAKES
Rabbi Levi Dubinsky 973.551.1898

MULLICA HILL
Rabbi Avrohom Richler 856.733.0770

OLD TAPPAN
Rabbi Mendy Lewis 201.767.4008

RED BANK
Rabbi Dovid Harrison 718.915.8748

ROCKAWAY
Rabbi Asher Herson
Rabbi Mordechai Baumgarten 973.625.1525

RUTHERFORD
Rabbi Yitzchok Lerman 347.834.7500

SCOTCH PLAINS
Rabbi Avrohom Blesofsky 908.790.0008

SHORT HILLS
Rabbi Mendel Solomon
Rabbi Avrohom Levin 973.725.7008

SOUTH BRUNSWICK
Rabbi Levi Azimov 732.398.9492

TEANECK
Rabbi Ephraim Simon 201.907.0686

TENAFLY
Rabbi Mordechai Shain 201.871.1152

TOMS RIVER
Rabbi Moshe Gourarie 732.349.4199

VENTNOR
Rabbi Avrohom Rapoport 609.822.8500

WAYNE
Rabbi Michel Gurkov 973.694.6274

WEST ORANGE
Rabbi Mendy Kasowitz 973.325.6311

WOODCLIFF LAKE
Rabbi Dov Drizin 201.476.0157

NEW MEXICO

LAS CRUCES
Rabbi Bery Schmukler 575.524.1330

S. FE
Rabbi Berel Levertov 505.983.2000

NEW YORK

BAY SHORE
Rabbi Shimon Stillerman 631.913.8770

BEDFORD
Rabbi Arik Wolf 914.666.6065

BINGHAMTON
Mrs. Rivkah Slonim 607.797.0015

BRIGHTON BEACH
Rabbi Moshe Winner 718.946.9833

BROOKLYN
Rabbi Nissi Eber 347.677.2276

BROOKVILLE
Rabbi Mendy Heber 516.626.0600

CEDARHURST
Rabbi Zalman Wolowik 516.295.2478

CHESTNUT RIDGE
Rabbi Chaim Zvi Ehrenreich 845.356.6686

COMMACK
Rabbi Mendel Teldon 631.543.3343

DIX HILLS
Rabbi Yaakov Saacks 631.351.8672

DOBBS FERRY
Rabbi Benjy Silverman 914.693.6100